INDUSTRIAL POLICY IN TURKEY

INDUSTRIAL POLICY IN TURKEY

Rise, Retreat and Return

Mina Toksöz, Mustafa Kutlay and William Hale

EDINBURGH
University Press

Edinburgh University Press is one of the leading university presses in the UK. We publish academic books and journals in our selected subject areas across the humanities and social sciences, combining cutting-edge scholarship with high editorial and production values to produce academic works of lasting importance. For more information visit our website: edinburghuniversitypress.com

Cover image: Industrial-scale tanker with fisherman looking at it. The image represents the challenge of economic development by late industrialiser, middle-income economies like Turkey. Photographer: Uğur Can.
Cover design: www.paulsmithdesign.com

Edinburgh University Press Ltd
The Tun – Holyrood Road
12 (2f) Jackson's Entry
Edinburgh EH8 8PJ

Typeset in 11/15 EB Garamond by
IDSUK (DataConnection) Ltd, and
printed and bound in Great Britain

A CIP record for this book is available from the British Library

ISBN 978 1 3995 1014 1 (hardback)
ISBN 978 1 3995 1017 2 (webready PDF)
ISBN 978 1 3995 1016 5 (epub)

CONTENTS

ILLUSTRATIONS

Figures

Boxes

Tables

ACKNOWLEDGEMENTS

Our collective focus on Industrial Policy in Turkey began at a workshop at City, University of London: 'Different Paths to Development: The Politics of New Developmentalism in Emerging Markets' in May 2019 (funded by an GCRF Institutional Block Grant, 48240AY). The workshop included presentations by an international group of colleagues, including Mina Toksöz who with Mustafa Kutlay, the convenor of the workshop, later came together to work on the present book.

The year 2019 also corresponded to the publication of Turkey's Eleventh Five-Year Development Plan with an accompanying industrial policy, the 'Tech-driven Industry Initiative'. This topic constituted a return to a previous interest for Mina Toksöz who had completed a Masters in 'Economic Theory and Planning' at Sussex University in the 1970s. However, 'the theory' has since undergone many changes, with the role of the state in industrialisation demoted from the 1980s onwards until a renewed interest since the global financial crisis. Meanwhile, the publication of this book coincides with industrial policy becoming almost mainstream, as adopted by advanced economies as well as late industrialisers. Mustafa Kutlay has provided the conceptual framework with which to analyse these shifts in approach towards industrial policies. This allowed Mina Toksöz to concentrate on the macroeconomic trends. With his long dedication to covering Turkey, William Hale contributed the historical chapter, thus giving the project the depth of a longer-term perspective. All chapters were extensively discussed among the authors and revised several times accordingly.

We would like to give a special thanks to Brian Beeley for his encouragement and the unique contribution of his memoirs at the State Planning Organisation in Ankara in its initial years, as a young OECD intern. We are grateful to Judit Ricz at the Institute of World Economics, Hungarian Academy of Sciences, for her excellent overview of Industrial Policy in Brazil. The authors would also like to thank the series editors of the Edinburgh Studies on Modern Turkey, Alpaslan Özerdem and Ahmet Erdi Öztürk, for their interest in our project and their support along the way. We extend our thanks to the Edinburgh University Press production team – Eddie Clark, Emma House, Isobel Birks and Louise Hutton – for their guidance during the production process. We also thank Ziya Öniş, H. Emrah Karaoğuz, Şevket Pamuk and Paola Subacchi for their support in different forms. Finally, we would like to thank our families for their support and patience.

Mina Toksöz, Mustafa Kutlay, William Hale

INTRODUCTION
THE ROAD (NOT) TAKEN

The fifteenth of May 1961 was an important day for the short but eventful history of the Republic of Turkey. On that day, General Cemal Gürsel, who had come to power with the 27 May 1960 military *coup*, delivered a speech at a conference on the automobile industry. In the early 1960s, the country's economy was mainly based on agricultural production and export, and most of its population lived in rural areas. Although the Turkish governments in the early years of the Republic had pushed for industrialisation, the country lacked a strong industrial base.[1] Gürsel pointed to the problem and proposed a solution: Turkey needed to industrialise; the country 'can barely purchase 7–8 buses by selling a shipload of cotton'.[2] He pointed out that Turkey would produce its own indigenous car. He claimed that the statement that '[an indigenous] car cannot be produced in Turkey is the product of a dark thought'.[3]

The president asked for the country's first indigenous automobile to be revealed on 29 October 1961, Republic Day. Several actors, including high-level bureaucrats, journalists and certain economic interest groups, raised their eyebrows when they heard about the project. They suggested that it was not compatible with the country's comparative advantages and, as a result, not feasible. In fact, for the opponents, Turkey was not even capable of producing simple industrial goods, and the country's comparative advantage lay somewhere else. However, a group of Turkish engineers shouldered the responsibility of the Devrim arabaları ('cars of the Revolution' or 'Devrim cars') project. Despite poor infrastructure and inadequate resources, they produced four prototypes to display at the Republic Day ceremony in Ankara.

President Gürsel wanted to take a short trip in one of the 'Devrim cars' in front of hundreds of people, including journalists, bureaucrats, politicians and engineers. Unfortunately, after moving a few hundred metres, the car suddenly stopped; this was followed by an awkward conversation between the president and the engineer in the driver's seat, Rıfat Serdaroğlu. 'What happened?' asked Gürsel. Serdaroğlu, who together with his team had spent night and day on the project over the past few months, uttered one of the perhaps saddest sentences of his life: 'We probably ran out of fuel, Paşam'.[4] Apparently, whilst transferring the cars to the display area in Ankara from Eskişehir where they had been assembled, the fuel tank was emptied to avoid potential safety risks, but not refilled before the ceremony. The baffled Turkish president moved on to the next 'Devrim car' and took a tour around the city. However, the unfortunate incident shadowed the entire ceremony. It was reported that the president expressed his disappointment in one sentence, also subtly reflecting the Turkish elites' decades-long quest for modernisation and Westernisation as two sides of the same coin: 'We managed to produce a car with a Western mindset but forgot to fill it with gas with an Eastern mindset'.[5] As expected, for various reasons the project was discontinued, and plans to mass-produce domestic cars were postponed. Even so, the following years featured intense industrialisation in a series of five-year development plans, lasting until the late 1970s.

The story of the 'Devrim cars' project is inspiring, as it encapsulates the combined pursuit of industrialisation and economic transformation in a country trying to catch up with its comparably more advanced counterparts on multiple fronts. It shows that effective industrialisation takes careful planning, a strong commitment of state and business actors, as well as collective patience. It also gives a clear idea about the nearly insurmountable domestic and external challenges in the bureaucratic, financial and human resources aspects of industrialisation in late developers. It is striking that half a century later, in 2011, the Turkish prime minister was still looking for 'brave' business entrepreneurs to produce fully domestic cars in Turkey (see Chapter 5).[6]

In a way, the history of global capitalism is a story of continuous struggle for economic 'catch-up'. Since capitalism emerged and became consolidated in Western Europe, the late-developing countries in the non-Western world have constantly tried to catch up. In mostly well-intended attempts to hit a distant and moving target, the quest for industrialisation constitutes one of the key forces driving modernisation in the global South. However, as explained in Chapter 1, development is a complex, multifaceted and (often) messy process. It is also so unpredictable that it requires a certain degree of pragmatism. On the one hand, some late developers have achieved significant convergence with advanced economies; on the other hand, most of the ambitious industrialisation initiatives have failed.[7] The Turkish case is illustrative on both counts.

This book offers an in-depth historical-empirical analysis of Turkey's long-term industrial policy performance, characterised by striking continuities, repeated failures and a certain degree of achievement. The rest of this short introduction is organised as follows: the next section places Turkey in the global economy, by providing a brief overview of its long-term development. Section three covers the main arguments of the book. The final section summarises the organisation of following chapters and sketches what lies ahead.

Turkey in the Global Economy

Industrial policy has been an integral part of Turkey's long-term economic development, but its impact has been both contested and controversial. The Turkish governments implemented different sets of industrial policy to facilitate structural transformation and economic convergence with the advanced countries. There are two fundamental ways to analyse Turkey's long-term industrialisation performance: we can take either an inward-looking or an outward-looking approach.

If we interpret overall economic development by looking at how far Turkey has come since the foundation of the Republic (*the inward-looking approach*), the results seem encouraging. When the Republic of Turkey was established in 1923, following an exhausting period of wars, the country was significantly undeveloped, with limited capital accumulation, insufficient human capital and a very low level of industrialisation (see Chapter 2). For instance, in 1929, the share of the rural population was 76 percent, and the share of agriculture in the total labour force was 85 percent.[8] Over the next century, economic diversification increased, and the country's production capacity expanded significantly. The share of the rural population over the total population decreased to 24 percent in 2019.[9] Significant economic diversification towards industry and services also took place. Employment in agriculture declined to 18 percent of total employment in 2019; the share of agricultural value-added in Turkey's overall GDP also decreased to 6.4 percent, compared to almost 55 percent in 1960.[10] Turkey is now well integrated with the global economy through trade and foreign investments, and it has become an 'upper middle-income country', according to the World Bank classification. Turkey has an industrialised economy with a relatively young and dynamic population, is situated close to the centres of high-value-added supply chains and shows considerable entrepreneurial dynamism with several successful start-ups.

If we take an *outward-looking approach*, however, we interpret the road that Turkey has (not) taken by looking at the country's position globally. It is true that Turkey has achieved significant transformation over the past century, but this can be at least partly explained by globalisation processes and technological advancements in the global political economy, which have lifted several countries to a higher level of economic prosperity.[11] As a result, Turkey's place in the global economy (especially *vis-à-vis* advanced economies) is not so much a success story as one of continuity. For instance, Turkey's GDP within the global economy remained mostly stable, fluctuating between 0.6 percent and 1.3 percent of the world's GDP over the last six decades.[12] The average wealth of Turkish citizens, whilst increasing significantly in absolute terms, has remained stagnant in comparison to advanced countries. For instance, in 1950, the average wealth of a Turkish citizen was 13.6 percent that of an American citizen; it increased to almost 35 percent in 2018. This sounds promising – that is, until we look at comparative figures, for instance, of South Korea. The average wealth of a Korean citizen was 6.6 percent that of an American in 1950 and almost 70 percent in 2018 (Figure I.1).[13] Furthermore, the economic situation was further undermined in Turkey since 2018, due to the unconventional economic policies and significant institutional deterioration following the transition to a presidential system without proper checks-and-balance mechanisms (Chapter 5). Turkey's technological production capacity also remained insufficient.[14] Although policy-makers constantly reiterated the importance of improving national technology production and innovation capacity as a key geopolitical and economic goal, the share of high technology exports over total manufactured exports has hovered around just 3 percent – significantly lower than the world average of around 20 percent (Figure I.2).

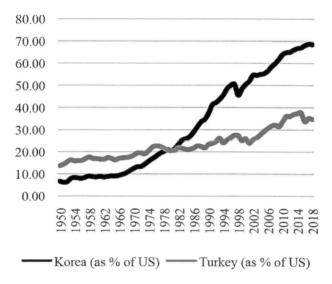

Figure I.1 Real GDP per capita: Turkey and South Korea

Source: Jutta Bolt and Jan Luiten van Zanden, 'Maddison Style Estimates of the Evolution of the World Economy: A New 2020 Update', Maddison Project Database (2020), in 2011 USD.

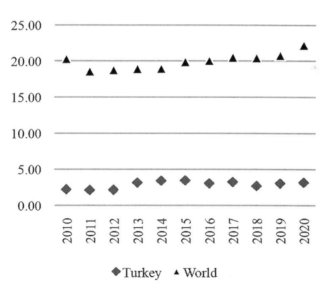

Figure I.2 High-tech exports as a share of total manufactured exports

Source: World Bank, World Development Indicators database.

Taken together, this all suggests that Turkey has demonstrated a moderate industrialisation and growth performance, following global economic trends. As Altuğ, Filiztekin and Pamuk have pointed out in their insightful article, 'Turkey has not been able to close during the twentieth century the large gap that opened up between it and the developed countries during the nineteenth century'.[15] The *continuity* of Turkey's long-term comparative industrialisation performance notwithstanding, the scope and content of industrial policy measures implemented – and the governments' economic policies – have demonstrated significant *changes*. This book documents Turkey's industrial policies over the past century to analyse the causes and consequences of what can be called as 'continuity in change'.

The Scope of the Book and its Main Arguments

In his well-known book *The Road to Serfdom*, first published in 1944, Friedrich August von Hayek severely criticised economic planning and suggested that 'the tendency towards monopoly and planning is not the result of any "objective facts" beyond our control, but the product of opinions fostered and propagated for half a century till they have come to dominate all our policy'.[16] Hayek's book was reprinted in 1976, just as neoliberalism, fostering completely opposite ideas to central economic planning, was about to gain ascendancy around the world. Ironically, this time, neoliberal ideas, 'fostered and propagated' by advanced countries and international financial institutions, began to dominate policy-making in developing countries since the 1980s. 'Monoeconomics', as Albert O. Hirschman has coined the term, progressively established its dominance, whereas development economics gradually lost its 'old liveliness'.[17] As a result, the role of the state in the economy was reduced, public enterprises were privatised, and unrestricted capital flows became the norm. Industrial policy also fell from favour, becoming synonymous with 'corruption', 'inefficiency' and 'waste of public resources'.

In retrospect, the nature of structural change in several economies was significant. The share of manufacturing in total GDP declined in many countries, and de-industrialisation became a dominant trend in the developing world. Brazil, for example, constitutes one of the most striking cases, as manufacturing value-added in total GDP declined from 34 to 10 percent between 1984 and 2019. Turkey was no exception (Figure I.3). The scale of de-industrialisation in the Turkish case was not as dramatic as it was in Brazil; furthermore,

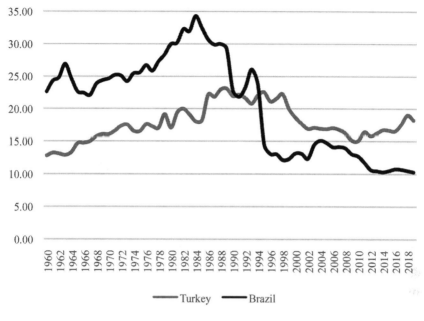

Figure I.3 Manufacturing, value added (% of GDP)
Source: World Bank, World Development Indicators.

manufacturing value-added as percent of GDP started to improve in Turkey in the mid-2010s. Yet, as Şenses and Taymaz have pointed out, 'industrialisation as a social purpose' was also downgraded in the priority list of Turkish policy-makers in the same period.[18]

Since the 2008 global financial crisis, however, industrial policy has become fashionable again. Realising market-oriented policies did not yield the expected growth and prosperity, several countries have started to experiment with different shapes and forms of industrial policy. In a sense, the ideologically loaded debate about the role of the 'state' and the 'market' has become much more balanced and pragmatic over time, as the limits of both state-led and market-led development are better grasped by researchers and policy-makers (see Chapter 1). As a result, industrial policy is no longer a 'forbidden word'. *The Economist*, for instance, has recently published a special report disconcertingly heralding the 'new era of interventionism'.[19] As the US–China rivalry intensifies and the market-driven logic of efficiency is increasingly giving way to the geoeconomics-driven logic of national resilience, several countries are adopting more active industrial policies to reduce their reliance on other states and trying to increase their autonomy in strategic sectors in the face of 'weaponised interdependence'.[20] In addition to geopolitical imperatives, climate change, the growing income and wealth inequality in both developed and developing countries – as well as the uncertainty and anxiety exacerbated by the COVID-19 pandemic – has brought back the idea of a more interventionist state.

In the US, the Obama, Trump and Biden administrations adopted industrial policy measures under different names – such as 'Buy American', 'America first' and 'Build Back Better'. This was followed in 2022 with the Inflation Reduction Act (IRA) and the CHIPS and Science Act, both of which were in line with the principles set out by the Biden administration's National Economic Council Director Brian Deese; accordingly, the new US industrial strategy 'is built on five core pillars: supply chain resilience, targeted public investment, public procurement, climate resilience, and equity'.[21] European countries have similarly announced industrial policy measures to boost domestic production and 'bring jobs back home'. The European Commission declared the start of a 'European Industrial Renaissance' in 2014, a vision promoting smart specialisation strategies for twenty-first-century Europe.[22]

The adoption of industrial policies by major powers with their protectionist implications also adds a dangerous element to the current rise in geostrategic rivalries and narrows the policy space for developing countries. Nevertheless, many late developers have adopted industrial policies in a bid to maintain their development trajectory with R&D policies, selective industrial policy measures, education and skill formation policies, and public–private partnerships. Since the early 2010s, the Turkish government has also introduced a new industrial policy strategy and incentive packages along with R&D support schemes to private firms.

Given this renewed interest, this book focuses on the historical evolution of industrial policy in Turkey to develop three interrelated arguments.[23] First, as several different cases testify, industrial policy is not a choice but a *necessity* for late developers to achieve structural transformation and facilitate economic catch-up. The market fundamentalist approach, which limits industrial policy to horizontal measures addressing 'market failures', has failed to produce inclusive economic growth in most countries in the global South (see Chapter 1). In this book, we place the Turkish case within global discussions on the political economy of industrial development. As discussed above, in recent years the discussion of the 'return' of industrial policy has attracted critical attention around the world, gaining prominence among policy-makers. We join this endeavour by analysing how the nature, scope and practice of industrial policy has changed in Turkey since the 1920s and place the attempts of the Justice and Development Party (*Adalet ve Kalkınma Partisi*, or AKP) government into their historical and global contexts.[24]

Second, designing and implementing effective industrial policy is hard. The literature documents several cases when even well-intended attempts failed. The example of 'Devrim cars' mentioned at the outset is one of many efforts to end in failure. This may well be the case for different approaches to industrial policy. As this book documents in the relevant chapters, in the Turkish case, the outcomes of economic liberalisation pursued in the early 1950s and post-1980s provide ample evidence that market-oriented policies did not result in expected developmental outcomes. Even though an unassailable trust in the capacity of the markets to allocate resources in the most effective way proves to be flawed, this, however, does not mean state-directed industrialisation is necessarily superior to market-oriented policies. As we will demonstrate with reference to the 1960–80 and post-2011 periods in the Turkish political economy, this might also end in a *cul-de-sac*, wasting public resources and delaying competitiveness-enhancing reforms. This suggests that industrial policy debates in Turkey should go beyond a simplistic understanding of 'state versus market' or of the state 'picking winners'. Instead, as we argue, 'state capture' – a situation where private interests capture state bureaucracy to serve their narrow interests – and 'market capture' – a situation where powerful governments decide who-gets-what in the marketplace based on the political loyalty of private firms – are equally corrosive for effective industrialisation in late developers. The latter is likely to hamper the potential of a country to enhance its comparative advantages, while the former is likely to create serious rent-seeking and corruption problems. The following chapters cover ample evidence of both.

This brings us to the third point, which suggests that three key factors have conditioned the nature, scope and effectiveness of industrial policy in the Turkish context: (1) global trends, (2) macroeconomic instability, and (3) domestic institutional context. As we will demonstrate, Turkey has adopted 'vertical' (active) or 'horizontal' (passive) industrial policies in line with dominant global economic trends. Each time, however, ambitious initiatives gradually waned, and macroeconomic instability followed, rendering long-term planning a blurred objective for political and economic actors. Macroeconomic instability has diverted the attention of policy-makers, as well as business actors, and hindered the practical implementation of ambitious industrial policy goals. The key puzzle in Turkey's lacklustre industrial policy, as we put it, is the country's *half-committed approach* to industrialisation; unsurprisingly, this inhibited the consolidation of developmental institutions fostering successful long-term economic catch-up. We suggest that it was not the degree of state intervention that directly informed the outcome of Turkey's industrial policies, but the domestic institutional context and how state intervention worked. In this context, state capacity (or the lack thereof) constitutes a salient factor in avoiding 'market capture' or 'state capture' in the Turkish political economy.[25]

On a broader scale, states can play certain critical roles that improve comparative advantages, but this depends on the institutional capacity of a state in steering market actors towards a high-technology frontier, overcoming information asymmetries and designing long-term performance-based incentive schemes to support domestic firms in their internationalisation attempts. States can also create a conducive environment for domestic firms by promoting innovation ecosystems and facilitating state-business coordination.[26] The empirical chapters demonstrate that the main challenge in the Turkish context has been sub-optimal domestic institutional context within which industrial policies were designed and implemented – both 'vertical' and 'horizontal.'

A caveat is in order at this point: this book does not focus on the origins of state capacity or developmental institutions in Turkey. Nor does it develop a theory of state capacity that applies to the Turkish case. Instead, we focus on the transformation and phases of industrial policy in Turkey, through an in-depth historical-empirical analysis to document the half-committed approach to industrial policy that has persisted despite significant policy variation – that is, what we call 'continuity in change.' We show how the specific form of industrial policy has been shaped over time by the waves following economic crises, the dearth of long-term financing for industrialisation and, more recently, the need to address issues such as a low-tech industrial structure and premature de-industrialisation. This book, in short, examines the evolution of Turkey's industrial policies in a global context to explore the 'rise' (the early Republic until 1980),[27] 'retreat' (1980–2008) and 'return' of industrial policy since the 2008 global financial crisis.[28]

Organisation of the Chapters

The chapters are organised with a view to substantiate the main points developed in the preceding sections. Chapter 1 reviews the theory and practice of industrial policy in the global political economy. This conceptual chapter starts with a brief analysis of the 'rise', 'retreat' and 'return' of industrial policy, by focusing on key political and economic junctures leading to its transformation across a range of late-developing countries, including Turkey. It then delineates key determinants of industrial policy in Turkey to assess the key factors that explain policy-makers' half-committed approach to industrial policy in the long run. Rather than interpreting economic development in dichotomic terms, painting a zero-sum picture between 'state' and 'market', the chapter underlines the central role of state capacity to steer market actors towards higher value-added production in the industrialisation process.

Chapter 2 offers an in-depth historical account of the 'rise' of industrial policy in Turkey from the establishment of the Republic until the transition to a neoliberal export-oriented paradigm in the early 1980s. The chapter is organised into six sub-periods. (1) During the 1920s, economic policies concentrated on overcoming the severe losses caused by the Great War and its aftermath, with the overly optimistic assumption that this could be achieved by a state-supported private sector. (2) Under the impact of the Great Depression of the 1930s, an étatist programme of industrial development by state-owned industries was begun under the First Five-Year Industrialisation Plan (1934–38). (3) A second plan was launched in 1939, but implementation was abruptly curtailed by the beginning of World War II. Although Turkey remained neutral, the war years saw a sharp cutback in industrial development, with increased state control over the economy. (4) After 1945, both domestic and American pressure developed for more liberal economic policies. During the 1950s, the Democrat Party government under Adnan Menderes was officially committed to economic liberalisation. There was some development of private industry and state aid for agriculture, which expanded impressively during the first half of the decade. There was almost no privatisation of the state sector, however, and the development of the State

Economic Enterprises (SEEs) in industry continued apace, albeit in a haphazard manner, undermining state capacity and mainly expressing political patronage. (5) By the period of 1958–60, the short-sighted policies had led to lower economic growth, combined with rising inflation and a severe balance of payments crisis. (6) Following the *coup d'état* on 27 May 1960, which overthrew the Menderes government, attempts to redirect the economy centred on the establishment of a State Planning Organisation and the adoption of import-substituting industrialisation (ISI) strategy. This produced a series of Five-Year Development Plans aimed at directing the pattern of investment in agriculture and services, as well as industry, and concentrating on import replacement industrialisation in both the private and public sectors. As the chapter argues, this led to impressive industrial growth in consumer goods and intermediate industries, but there were few attempts to develop high-value-added exports. Compounded by serious political instability, rising urban terrorism and the effects of the oil price explosion of the 1970s, this brought about a further deterioration of the domestic institutional context, an acute balance of payments crisis, soaring inflation and a general economic collapse, resulting in a third military takeover in 1980.

Chapter 3 examines the paradigmatic shift in the Turkish political economy and the 'retreat' of active industrial policy after 1980. The ISI-led protectionist policies were replaced by an export-oriented free market paradigm that saw Turkey joining the WTO and the Customs Union with the EU by the mid-1990s. Major tenets of industrial policy included export incentives and other 'horizontal' measures in this period. Turkey's neo-liberal transition did not pave the way for a more enhanced state capacity. However, the state remained a central actor in the domestic economy, through state enterprises, export incentives, new forms of political patronage and extra-budgetary funds. Problematically, its role turned out to be market-distorting, as state–business relations lacked proper institutional co-operation and information exchange mechanisms. This chapter traces Turgut Özal's attempts to restructure the state bureaucracy; these mostly consisted of *ad hoc* measures often implemented with prime-ministerial decrees that increased the centralisation of authority and discretionary policy-making. A major victim of this weakening institutional quality and the reduced capacity for transformative industrial policies was the State Planning Organisation, the role of which declined precipitously. The abrupt financial liberalisation in the 1980s also failed to make a significant change in the structure of the financial sector; it continued to be dominated by the funding needs of the public sector, thus undermining the basis for longer-term investments in industry by the private sector. Moreover, the liberalisation of finance before the requisite regulatory institutions were established encouraged speculative activity, further weakening the capacity of the state to guide the private sector towards high-value-added production. As the chapter argues, this trend, accompanied by the growing dynamics of 'state capture' in the 1990s, culminated in the 2001 financial crisis.

Chapter 4 discusses the 2001 economic crisis and attendant economic reforms, designed in line with the post-Washington Consensus and its emphasis on institutions, curbing the state's role in the economy and re-positioning it into a regulatory role. The reforms improved the Turkish state's regulatory capacity, but industrial upgrading was not on the agenda post-2001. Whilst the restructuring of the banking sector was a significant achievement, the commercialisation of state banks perpetuated the problem of the scarcity of long-term credit for industrial investments. Attempts to increase savings by establishing a private pension scheme and developing capital markets failed to attract sufficient funds. The privatisation of key state assets, such as energy and telecommunications, mostly aiming to raise budget revenues and meet multilateral funding requirements, was rife with irregularities. Industrial policy was hemmed in by fiscal constraints and 'horizontal' policies that reinforced the existing structure of industry, based on low- and medium-technology production. The growth of high-tech exports slowed, as an opportunity was missed to develop nascent Information and Communications Technology (ICT) industries in the early 2000s. The key weakness of the dominant growth model at the time was exposed by the 2008 global financial crisis. As the AKP became increasingly defensive and focused on consolidating its political power, the independence of the autonomous regulatory institutions was whittled away, and economic policies shifted towards more centralisation, political interference and authoritarianism.

Chapter 5 examines the 'return' of industrial policy in the 2010s, when the state's role in the economy increased considerably. Turkey almost acquired 'high-income status' and reported significant achievements in infrastructure over the past few decades. But the favourable global and regional conditions that had prevailed before the 2008 global financial crisis are now in reverse, and the AKP regime has become increasingly authoritarian to stay in power. The country is facing several challenges, including growth driven mainly by the low-productivity sectors of construction and services as well as credit-supported consumption. Income, regional and gender inequalities persist, and environmental issues have been neglected. There is also a problem of possible premature de-industrialisation. This chapter reviews the efforts to reconstruct an industrial policy framework in this context. A series of initiatives introduced since 2009 have brought back sectoral selectivity: a 2011 Ministry of Science, Industry, and Technology (MSIT) strategy document, a 2012 investment incentives law focused on 'strategic investments' and the 2016 Super Incentive Scheme provided investment incentives to help small and medium-sized enterprises grow. These initiatives were codified in the Eleventh Five-Year Plan (2019–23), which also included a central focus on the Tech Driven Industry Initiative. The plan calls for a re-emphasis on industry, arguing for the use of trade policy to support strategic industries, the need to attract foreign direct investment, the importance of exports and the benefits of increased integration with global supply chains. 'New' industrial policy instruments include incentives for high-tech investments, public–private partnerships and the creation of a Sovereign Wealth Fund. Yet, the effectiveness of these policies is counterbalanced by the decreasing institutional capacity of the state and increasing discretionary interventions. Also, there has been a rapid increase in the use of 'old' industrial policy instruments, such as revolving funds, extra-budgetary funds, treasury guarantees, investment incentives and access to state bank credit. The chapter concludes that, in the 2010s, the growing dynamics of 'market capture', along with more interventionist tones, narrowed the potential transformative capacity of industrial policy to a few sectors, such as the indigenous defence industry, whilst undermining policy effectiveness in overall terms that set a new crisis dynamic in motion towards the end of the 2010s.

Notes

1. For a succinct overview of this period in Turkish economy, see Fikret Şenses, *İktisada (Farklı Bir) Giriş* (İstanbul: İletişim Yayınları, 2021), pp. 240–44.

2. Süleyman Aşık, *Devrim Arabaları* (İstanbul: Kopernik Kitap, 2020), p. 51. The extraordinary story of 'Devrim cars', which also features an excerpt of Cemal Gürsel's speech, is told in a movie, *Cars of the Revolution* (*Devrim Arabaları*), produced in 2008.

3. See Vatan, 16 May 1961, as quoted in Süleyman Aşık, *Devrim Arabaları* (İstanbul: Kopernik Kitap, 2020), p. 52. Aşık provides an in-depth review of the process in his book, through an analysis of the news, archives and interviews with key figures who participated in the project.

4. *Devrim Arabaları Belgeseli*, Anadolu Üniversitesi İletişim Fakültesi Belgeseli (Eskişehir, 1997), as quoted in Süleyman Aşık, *Devrim Arabaları* (İstanbul: Kopernik Kitap, 2020), p. 107.

5. Müge Akgün, 'Cemal Paşa Bile Devrim'e Sırtını Döndü', *Hürriyet*, 25 October 2008. This news article is based on an interview with Kemalettin Vardar, one of the engineers of the 'Devrim cars' project. In another interview, Vardar said that it was not clear why the car had stopped. It could have been a problem with the fuel gauge or something else. This was not revealed because nobody investigated the incident. See https://www.youtube.com/watch?v=hmYAkcLJ7hs (in Turkish).

6. Gazete Vatan, 'Babayiğit Arıyorum', 26 September 2011.

7. For a critical account of why several ambitious state-led planning and development projects failed, see James C. Scott, *Seeing Like a State: How Certain Schemes to Improve the Human Condition Have Failed* (New Haven: Yale University Press, 1998).

8. Sumru Altuğ, Alpay Filiztekin and Şevket Pamuk, 'Sources of Long-Term Economic Growth for Turkey, 1880–2005', *European Review of Economic History*, Vol. 12, No. 3 (2008), p. 399, table 2.

9. Data from the World Bank, World Development Indicators database.

10. Data from the World Bank, World Development Indicators database. Agricultural value added also includes forestry and fishing.

11. Şevket Pamuk provides an extensive comparative account of Turkey's long-term development performance over the past two centuries in his book *Uneven Centuries: Economic Development of Turkey Since 1820* (Princeton: Princeton University Press, 2018). Ziya Öniş has also underlined that 'Turkey is a case of moderate growth' in comparative terms in the post-1945 era. See Ziya Öniş, 'Crises and Transformations in Turkish Political Economy', *Turkish Policy Quarterly*, Vol. 9, No. 3 (2010), pp. 45–61.

12. Based on the World Bank data measured in constant 2015 USD between 1960 and 2021. The current GDP per capita figures are also from the World Bank database.

13. Based on data from the Maddison Project Database, version 2020. See Jutta Bolt and Jan Luiten van Zanden, 'Maddison Style Estimates of the Evolution of the World Economy: A New 2020 Update', Maddison-Project Working Paper No. WP-15, October 2020.

14. For an in-depth study of Turkey's R&D policies, see Hüseyin Emrah Karaoğuz, 'The Political Dynamics of R&D Policy in Turkey: Party Differences and Executive

Interference during the AKP Period', *Journal of Balkan and Near Eastern Studies*, Vol. 20, No. 4 (2018), pp. 388–404.

15. Sumru Altuğ, Alpay Filiztekin and Şevket Pamuk, 'Sources of Long-Term Economic Growth for Turkey, 1880–2005', *European Review of Economic History*, Vol. 12, No. 3 (2008), pp. 400–1. In this comprehensive study, Altuğ, Filiztekin and Pamuk assess Turkey's long-term growth record in absolute and relative terms.

16. F. A. Hayek, *The Road to Serfdom* (London and Henley: Routledge and Kegan Paul, 1976 [1944]), p. 32.

17. Albert O. Hirschman, 'The Rise and Decline of Development Economics', in *Essays in Trespassing: Economics to Politics and Beyond* (Cambridge: Cambridge University Press, 1981), pp. 1, 3–5. The story of the 'decline' of development economics is, of course, a complicated one with several factors at work. See Hirschman's work above for a nuanced analysis of this.

18. Fikret Şenses and Erol Taymaz, 'Unutulan Bir Toplumsal Amaç: Sanayileşme Ne Oluyor? Ne Olmalı?' ERC Working Papers in Economics No. 03/01, February 2003.

19. The Economist, 'Beware of the Bossy State', 15–21 January 2022.

20. For the revival of industrial policy in the face of the US–China rivalry, see *The Economist*. On 'weaponised interdependence', see Henry Farrell and Abraham L. Newman, 'Weaponized Interdependence: How Global Economic Networks Shape State Coercion', *International Security*, Vol. 44, No. 1 (2019), pp. 42–79.

21. Brian Deese, 'The Biden White House Plan for a New US Industrial Policy', speech delivered at the Atlantic Council, 23 June 2021, https://www.atlantic-council.org/commentary/transcript/the-biden-white-house-plan-for-a-new-us-industrial-policy/

22. European Commission, 'For a European Industrial Renaissance', Brussels, 22 January 2014, COM(2014) 14 final.

23. Several studies have examined various aspects of Turkey's economic history. We do not intend to replicate them in the following pages. Instead, we specifically focus on industrial policy in Turkey. For some of the well-known works, see Korkut Boratav, *Türkiye İktisat Tarihi 1908–2015* (Ankara: İmge Yayınevi, 2019); Yakup Kepenek, *Türkiye Ekonomisi* (Ankara: Remzi Kitabevi, 2019); Gülten Kazgan, *Tanzimattan 21. Yüzyıla Türkiye Ekonomisi* (İstanbul: Bilgi Üniversitesi Yayınevi, 2021); Şevket Pamuk, *Uneven Centuries: Economic Development of Turkey Since 1820* (Princeton: Princeton University Press, 2018). For a detailed economic analysis of the early era in the modern Turkish Republic, see Bilsay Kuruç, *Mustafa Kemal Döneminde Ekonomi: Büyük Devletler ve Türkiye*, 3rd

ed. (İstanbul: Bilgi Üniversitesi Yayınları, 2018). For the political economy of neoliberal transformation in Turkey in the 1980s, see Galip Yalman, *Transition to Neoliberalism: The Case of Turkey in the 1980s* (İstanbul: Bilgi Üniversitesi Yayınları, 2009).

24. Several important studies also cover different periods of industrial policy and industrialisation in Turkey. For Turkey's industrialisation policies in the 1980s, see Fikret Şenses, ed., *Recent Industrialization Experience of Turkey in a Global Context* (Westport: Greenwood Press, 1994). For a comparative analysis of the planning era in Turkey and France, see Vedat Milor, *Devleti Geri Getirmek: Türkiye ve Fransa'da Planlama ve Ekonomik Kalkınma Üzerine Karşılaştırmalı bir Çalışma* (İstanbul: İletişim Yayınları, 2022). For a rich collection of essays on different aspects of industrial production in Turkey, see Murad Tiryakioğlu, *Türkiye'nin Yerli Üretimi ve Politik Ekonomisi* (İstanbul: Bilgi Üniversitesi Yayınları, 2021).

25. As such, this book adds to the extensive list of works examining the role of state capacity in different aspects of the Turkish economy. For a general framework on the role of state capacity in Turkey's long-term economic development, see Ziya Öniş and Fikret Şenses, 'Global Dynamics, Domestic Coalitions and Reactive State', *METU Studies in Development,* Vol. 34, No. 2 (2007), pp. 255–56. On state–business relations, see Ayşe Buğra, *State and Business in Modern Turkey: A Comparative Study* (Albany: SUNY Press, 1994). For a recent edited volume on the political economy of the state's role in Turkey's development performance, see Murad Tiryakioğlu, ed., *Devletle Kalkınma* (İstanbul: İletişim Yayınları, 2020). On state–society relations and political patronage, see Metin Heper and E. Fuat Keyman, 'Double-Faced State: Political Patronage and the Consolidation of Democracy in Turkey', *Middle Eastern Studies,* Vol. 34, No. 4 (1998), pp. 259–77.

26. See Chapter 1 for a more extensive conceptual discussion.

27. The period between the early Republic and 1980 does not constitute a monolithic bloc. The 1920s and the early 1950s should be noted in terms of a series of liberalisation attempts. For an in-depth discussion of this era with reference to its six sub-periods, see Chapter 2.

28. This book was submitted before the May 2023 election, but the post-election U-turn in policy is very much in line with the inconsistent policy trends and unexpected changes that heighten macro-instability and increase uncertainty for investors as highlighted in the book.

1

THE POLITICAL ECONOMY OF
INDUSTRIAL POLICY

Introduction

Development is a much desired but hardly achieved goal. The World Bank reports that out of 101 middle-income economies in 1960, only thirteen had managed to reach high-income status by 2008.[1] All others either stagnated at middle-income levels or saw a decrease in per capita wealth over time. While it is true that most countries increased their per capita income over the past two centuries and the world is richer now than at any other period in human history,[2] in relative terms, apart from certain countries in Asia – such as Japan, South Korea, Taiwan, or more recently China – success stories of rapid economic catch-up with the advanced world are rare among late developers. In fact, only a handful of developing countries have achieved significant convergence with the advanced economies since 1945, largely because development is a path-dependent, complex and often messy process.

It is well-documented that certain institutional configurations emerging at a particular time in history are likely to have path-dependent effects on future political and economic development trajectories.[3] Path dependence means that, 'once a country or region has started down a track, the costs of reversal are very high. There will be other choice points, but the entrenchments of certain institutional arrangements obstruct an easy reversal of the initial choice'.[4] More often than not, it proves difficult for countries to reform dysfunctional institutions, overcome resistance of rent-seeking interest groups and reverse existing paradigms so as to upgrade economic structures towards high-value-added production. Furthermore, path dependence is not *only* reinforced by domestic ideas, interests or institutions. It is also conditioned by the uneven nature of capitalist development, global power constellations and predominant economic paradigms advocated by international financial institutions, all of which may constrain alternative policy options for developing countries.[5]

Development is also a complex process. It takes a cohesive collective effort, with state and non-state actors co-operating through multiple streams, not to mention underlying institutional complementarities to foster technological improvement, capital accumulation, property rights, mass education, training and skill formation, rule of law and much more. Furthermore, development is about more than material improvement in the human condition. In his conceptualisation of 'development as freedom', Amartya Sen has suggested that development cannot be limited to the 'culmination outcomes' which do not take 'any note of the process of getting there, including the exercise of freedom'; rather, development is also about 'comprehensive outcomes' that focus on the process itself – that is, whether it enhances human capabilities and individual freedoms along the way.[6]

This book constrains itself to a specific, albeit fundamental, aspect of industrialisation and development processes: industrial policy. As we will show throughout, industrial policy aims to upgrade the economic production and export structures of a country during the quest for sustainable development. Long-term development requires technological innovation, high-quality education, economic dynamism and competition, as well as the involvement of successful entrepreneurs as drivers of the 'perennial gale of creative destruction', to quote Schumpeter.[7] Hence, our take-off point is that successful economic catch-up can only be achieved by empowering market players. At the same time, however, structural economic transformation demands more than harnessing the entrepreneurial spirit of private actors; it requires active state involvement and well-designed industrial policy in developing countries.

There are multiple paths to development, and states play a key role in the process, with varying developmental outcomes. This suggests that 'the issue is not one of state intervention in the economy [. . .] all states intervene in their economies for various reasons [. . .] the question is how the government intervenes and for what purpose'.[8] As government intervention takes different forms and leads to different outcomes, industrial policy should be analysed beyond reductionist dichotomies describing it as a curse or blessing for developing economies. Effective industrial policy is an outcome of institutional design, and appropriate policy targets cross-cutting multiple streams (such as firm-, cluster- and national-level).[9] It is also shaped by past experiences, lessons drawn from earlier mistakes and the ability of governments to adjust the policy mix when change dictates that they do so.[10]

This book examines the political economy of the rise, retreat and return of industrial policy among late developers, by referring to the Turkish case. In the Turkish context, the key argument is that industrial policy is a necessity, not a choice, to achieve sustainable and inclusive economic growth. This chapter provides a conceptual overview to inform the historical-empirical analysis in the following chapters. The rest of the chapter proceeds as follows: the next section covers terminological issues. The third section reviews the transformation of industrial policy post-1945 to contextualise its historical evolution in Turkey. The fourth section takes stock of the decades-long debate on industrial policy and goes beyond four specific dichotomies that have restricted the scope of the debate on industrial policy. The fifth section examines the determinants of industrial policy in Turkey to provide a framework for analysis in the following chapters. The final section concludes the chapter.

The Many Colours of Industrial Policy

Industrial policy is defined in different ways, with no consensus on precisely what it entails.[11] Pack suggests: 'Industrial policies comprise a variety of actions designed to target specific sectors to increase their productivity and their relative importance within the manufacturing sector'.[12] Industrial policy is mainly about upgrading the production structure of national economies to climb the ladder of economic development. We draw on Wade's definition, whereby a set of policies implemented by governments is 'targeted at changing the structure of the economy, partly through the development of new export industries and partly through the development of industries substituting for imports'.[13] Conventional industrial policies generally focus on the manufacturing industry to achieve structural transformation, promote export sectors and reduce dependence on imports. As Naudé has aptly pointed out, in addition to the 'old issues', 'new' themes recently emerged in the industrial policy debates among scholars and policy-makers.[14] Industrial policy, in the current context, primarily targets R&D sectors, technological innovation, knowledge production and 'green growth' – areas where global challenges are transnationalised and state involvement is considered paramount. Evans, for instance, has highlighted the rejuvenated role of the state in the 'bit-driven' global economy;[15] Greenwald and Stiglitz have conceptualised the 'production and dissemination of knowledge (learning)' as a public good;[16] and Mazzucato has emphasised the 'mission-oriented innovation policies' targeting today's complicated problems, notably 'environmental threats like climate change, demographic, health and well-being concerns, and the difficulties of generating sustainable and inclusive growth'.[17]

Beyond the content of policy, different types of industrial policy can take different forms. Schneider has distinguished between *passive* and *active* industrial policy: 'passive policies seek to change the public sector [. . .] to reduce costs for business on the assumption that these changes will improve business performance'. On the other hand, 'active policies [. . .] target deeper changes in the private sector, in firm behaviour [. . .] and rely on direct subsidies from the state'.[18] This distinction overlaps with the 'horizontal' versus 'vertical' industrial policy debate. Although it is not easy to demarcate the two in practice, horizontal policies 'are the equivalent of general business environment policies'[19] and are considered 'neutral', as they do not 'target specific industries'.[20] In contrast, vertical policies are selective in that they target certain sectors and 'support specific industries'.[21] Stated differently, vertical industrial policy aims to go beyond correcting market failures to assist private actors by targeting a set of comparative advantage-defying measures.

State intervention in the economy remains a contentious topic among experts and policy-makers. For industrial policy sceptics, active industrial policy measures do more harm than good, because governments often prioritise their narrow political interests to construct winning coalitions with a view to gaining short-term advantages, over concerns for the long-term welfare of society. This short-sighted view leads to corruption, rent-seeking and the waste of precious resources.[22] Furthermore, when associated with information problems – that is, the argument that central governments are incapable of possessing the required information to make optimal decisions – industrial policies distort market dynamics and undermine economic activity. A modified version of neoclassical economic theory accepts that market mechanisms might fail under certain conditions, and some degree of state intervention may be required to correct those failures.[23] However, the 'market failure' argument assigns a temporary and restricted role to the state when it intervenes to mitigate economic imperfections – for example, by allowing market actors to operate more effectively by providing infrastructure support, investing in health and education, protecting property rights and upholding contracts through the rule of law. In this view, the state is not considered a strategic actor who shapes markets through active industrial policy to guide structural transformation and economic catch-up. Instead, the state is conceived as a facilitator, clearing the path for otherwise 'self-regulating markets' by correcting market failures and exploiting national comparative advantages.[24]

Scepticism about industrial policy does not rest on strong fundamentals, however.[25] From a conceptual viewpoint, state economic involvement has solid foundations. The institutionalist political economy tradition has extensively documented how states have played – and continue to play – a fundamental role, creating, shaping and remaking the institutional context within which market actors operate.[26] Long-term development necessitates industrial upgrading to reorient the domestic economic structure from low-value-added sectors (such as agriculture) towards high-value-added ones (such as information technology). This requires not only correcting market imperfections through active state involvement to exploit existing comparative advantages in labour-intensive industries, but also generating new comparative advantages in capital-intensive sectors. A range of active state policies – mostly changing, based on the development level of the country and the international context – is used to achieve this transformation: steering private actors towards changing their preference functions, providing financial assistance, mitigating information asymmetries in the marketplace, adjusting the value of domestic currency, protecting domestic firms against foreign competition in the early stages of their lifecycle, and absorbing risks by directly assuming an investor role in new high-technology industries considered too risky by private firms.[27]

The theoretical underpinnings of industrial policy were developed by Alexander Hamilton (ca 1755–1804) and Friedrich List (1789–1846) in their 'infant industry argument'.[28] The infant industry argument rests on the idea that protecting national industries in their early stages will help them survive in a competitive international environment. The infant industry protection, so the argument goes, will give firms in developing countries the time and space they need to develop 'advanced technologies' and 'effective organizations'.[29] The manufacturing industry plays a central role in this process by creating extensive backward and forward linkages. As Andreoni and Chang have pointed out, manufacturing constitutes the motor of 'technology-driven productivity growth'; it promotes significant learning with spillover effects to other sectors through forward and backward chains, drives 'organisational innovation', generates demand for other sectors and 'has higher tradability' than the agriculture and services sectors.[30]

From a conceptual point of view, the cases for and against industrial policy are well-established in the literature. This suggests the importance of empirical evidence, if we want to assess whether and under what circumstances industrial policy works. Several cases of state intervention have led to successful industrial transformation. The Asian developmental states – Japan, South Korea, Taiwan and Singapore – are well-documented cases.[31] For example, in the 1960s, South Korea was a poor country, dependent on agricultural production and foreign aid. However, thanks to effective government intervention and selective industrial strategy, South Korea became a wealthy country in only a few decades.[32] More recently, China has emerged as a success story through export-oriented state-led development. China grew at almost 10 percent annually after 1978. The country has never experienced negative growth over the past four decades, including the COVID-19 years, and the share of exports in GDP has increased significantly (Figure 1.1). In relative terms, over time, China has increased its GDP *vis-à-vis* the United States (Figure 1.2). In nominal terms, China's GDP was 70 percent of the US GDP in 2020. In purchasing power parity (PPP) terms, China has already overtaken the US in economic size, even though it was less than 20 percent of the US in 1990. China's remarkable growth spurt was supported by selective liberalisation and its integration into the global economy, and its extraordinary development has triggered significant discussions in the political economy literature, with state-led development gaining prominence once again. The important point for the purposes of our argument is that China did not adopt wholesale neoliberal policies and managed to escape 'shock therapy',[33] thus running counter the experiences of several

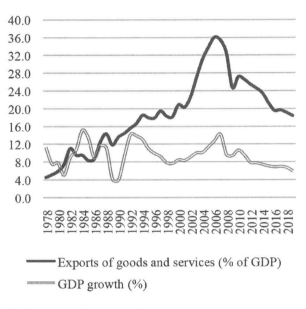

Figure 1.1 China's export and GDP growth
Source: World Bank, World Development Indicators.

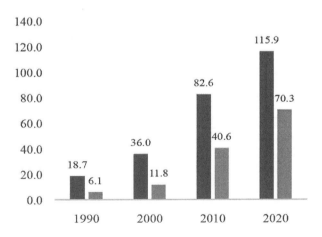

Figure 1.2 China's GDP compared to the US (percent)

transitioning and developing countries during the 1990s and early 2000s – the period when free-market-oriented Washington Consensus policies were strongly promoted in the global economy and active industrial policies were downgraded.[34]

A common criticism of the 'case-study-based' success stories is that they suffer from 'selection bias'.[35] For each case in favour of industrial policy, there is a counter-case, where state intervention failed to produce meaningful economic transformation and welfare improvement. State intervention may even make things worse, leading to rampant corruption, misallocation of resources, rent-seeking and the failure of bureaucracy to 'pick winners' due to information issues. In the heyday of free-market policies, in the 1990s, a piece in *The New York Times* summed up this popular sentiment: 'Trying to pick winners as an industrial strategy is no easier than it is at the racetrack. It may even be harder. A mounting body of evidence suggests that governments that bet good money on their favorite industries usually lose their shirts'.[36] Pack has also suggested that industrial policy seldom solves the challenges of development, and that it is not 'the secret of success'.[37]

This is an important point and should not be ignored. However, as we highlighted in the introduction, development is a rare commodity, difficult to achieve because of its complex nature. It is not hard to find cases attesting to the failure of state-led development, yet there is almost no case where long-term development has occurred without considerable state intervention. It is, in fact, hard to find any major case of climbing the ladder of development without active state involvement. Stated differently, although state intervention is likely to fail in certain cases, historically informed analysis suggests that almost all of today's developed countries benefitted from state-led policies in their path to economic development and prosperity. In *Kicking Away the Ladder*, Ha-Joon Chang has explored how the state played a transformative role in the economic take-off stages of today's developed countries. A variety of industrial policies were used by the leading proponents of free-market policies today, such as the United Kingdom and the USA.[38]

More recent experiences in both advanced and developing countries underline the central role of the state in economic development and the continued relevance of industrial policy – although its scope and nature have changed over time (see below).[39] As both historical and recent examples suggest, sustainable growth takes more than fixing market imperfections and clearing the ground for market actors.

This book joins other efforts suggesting that the most intriguing questions about successful industrial policy revolve around *the conditions under which state intervention works*, rather than *whether* the state should intervene in the economy. The *how* question brings the importance of institutional design and state capacity to the fore and is covered in the final section of this chapter. Then, in the book's empirical chapters, we will assess how Turkey's industrial policy has evolved since the 1920s, setting it against the changing scope and context of industrial policy in the international political economy. To put the Turkish case into historical-empirical context, however, we should first cover the key episodes when industrial policy and the state's role in the economy were transformed over the last century.

The Rise, Retreat and Return of Industrial Policy

Since 1945, the predominant discourse on industrial policy has broadly followed the patterns of international economic paradigms that shaped state–market relations. The post-war manifestations of industrial policy can be analysed under the headings of 'rise', 'retreat' and 'return'. First, following World War II, industrial policy constituted a central aspect of economic policy-making in many developed and developing countries. In this period, states were actively involved in the economy to create state-owned national monopolies in key sectors – such as energy, telecommunications and manufacturing – to facilitate economic recovery and mitigate unemployment. Second, with the free-market-oriented Washington Consensus paradigm gaining prominence in the 1980s, conventional industrial policy was relegated to the backseat. In this period, developing countries increasingly adopted mass privatisation, free trade policies and financial liberalisation, and these altered the role of the state in the economy. The scope for implementing active industrial policies for those countries shrank considerably in this period. Third, following the 2008 global financial crisis, the market fundamentalist approach to a certain extent lost its appeal around the world, opening new space for neo-developmentalist ideas and renewing interest in industrial policy. As dominant policy paradigms were transformed in the global economy, so too were the debates on the nature and scope of industrial policy. This section briefly reviews these episodes as they are closely related to the long-term determinants of industrial policy in Turkey.

Active Industrial Policy (1945–70s)

Following World War II, the Keynesian paradigm dominated economic policy-making in different parts of the world. Two aspects of this era were directly related to industrial policy. First, in terms of state–market relations, the balance decisively shifted in favour of the former. Ruggie has called the post-1945 settlement 'embedded liberalism', the core traits of which were the domestic interventionism of the state and managed internationalism within a multilateral framework: 'unlike the economic nationalism of the thirties, [the embedded liberalism compromise] would be multilateral in character; unlike the liberalism of the gold standard and free trade, its multilateralism would be predicated upon domestic interventionism'.[40] In the West, states assumed a market-making role by being directly involved in economic production and industrial transformation through large state-owned enterprises in key sectors. Governments built critical infrastructure, formed public monopolies in important sectors (electricity, railways, telecommunications and so on) and supported private firms through a set of generous subsidies. In late developers, state-led development gained more substantial ground during the 1960s and 1970s. With the onset of anti-colonial nationalist movements, several post-colonial states adopted ambitious industrialisation policies.[41] For example, in Latin America, dependency scholars advocated a set of ambitious *comparative advantage-defying policies* through extensive public investment in heavy industries, as well as import substitution industrialisation (ISI) to promote trade protectionism and reduce dependence on the global North, by reversing the unequal exchange mechanisms in the global capitalist system. To support technological innovation and industrial upgrading as well as to 'foster domestic knowledge accumulation', governments invested in state-owned enterprises and public research institutions, with 'national research councils' and 'national development banks' an essential part of their comprehensive development plans.[42] ISI-led planning became popular in many late-developing countries, including Turkey.

Second, in terms of inter-sectoral balance, the manufacturing sector was seen as driving economic development and structural transformation. The

Bretton Woods system based on a fixed exchange rate provided a certain degree of stability in foreign trade relations, and international financial transactions were controlled.[43] The financial sector was seen as a complement to industrial production, and economic security was the main legitimate objective.[44] Finally, the organisational power of labour in industrial sectors *vis-à-vis* capital peaked in the post-war context, with labour unions accumulating considerable power and influence in terms of political representation and the distribution of economic resources.[45]

State-led development and active industrial policy fell from grace in the late 1970s, due to the confluence of economic stagnation, increasing consumer prices, unemployment and massive economic problems associated with state-owned monopolies. Despite the ambitious start of several late developers, it became clear at later stages that heavily subsidised public enterprises could not survive without constant state support and protection. Apart from highly successful East Asian cases, most late developers could not transition to a competitive export-oriented industrialisation model; they proved unable to 'discipline' market actors, made poor policy decisions and inefficiently allocated scarce resources.[46] As we go on to show in the Turkish case, an essential problem was weak state capacity, and this, in turn, led to inefficient state interventions. In the Turkish case, for instance, the first five-year development plan (adopted in 1963) was sophisticated in terms of economic fundamentals and sectoral analysis.[47] The Turkish state, however, suffered from weak capacity, hindering the effective implementation and governance of state–business relations and incentivising business actors to pursue export-oriented industrial upgrading (see Chapter 3). Not unlike Turkey, the outcome of export-pessimism in many developing countries was economic stagnation and balance of payments crises. Consequently, with the massive turbulence in the global economy of the 1970s, caused by the collapse of the Bretton Woods system and the subsequent oil shocks, the perceptions of vertical industrial policies underwent a paradigm shift.

The Neoliberal Turn and Passive Industrial Policy (1980s–2008)

The 1980s represented a turning point in state-market relations. The state was relegated to a more residual role in the economy, in line with the rise of the neoliberal Washington Consensus paradigm advocated by the US and international financial institutions.[48] Industrial policy took a back seat in economic policy-making, and privatisation of state-owned enterprises and financial liberalisation became the 'new orthodoxy'. The late developers in the global South adopted free-market policies in the early 1980s, when the IMF conditionality and structural adjustment programmes forced them to abandon vertical (or active) industrial policy.[49] After two decades of relentless marketisation with the pendulum swinging towards finance capital *vis-à-vis* the manufacturing industry and organised labour, the Washington Consensus policies led to more frequent economic crises and exacerbated macroeconomic instability in the developing world. As a result, in the early 2000s, what was later known as the 'post-Washington Consensus' brought about an edited version of neoliberal policies, with a more explicit emphasis on governance institutions, tackling corruption, improving the rule of law and correcting market failures.[50]

In this period, horizontal industrial policy measures became more common, covering all firms and entire sectors, such as R&D support and infrastructure investments, rather than vertical industrial policy, with governments targeting specific sectors or firms by 'picking winners' and awarding them exclusive subsidies, tax breaks and import protection. This does not mean that industrial policy or the state's role in the economy disappeared after the 1980s, however. Even in advanced countries, which are supposed to have stronger private sector firms well-positioned to compete in global markets, states continued to play a critical role, albeit in subtler ways. For instance, as Bulfone has pointed out, 'behind the rhetoric of free markets, even the most liberally minded member states [of the EU] continued to engage sotto voce in interventionist policies'.[51] Several advanced members of the EU – including Germany, Italy and Spain – supported the internationalisation of their previously subsidised 'national champions' in banking, telecommunications, electricity and steel, through mergers, acquisitions, R&D assistance and economic diplomacy – a disguised form of industrial policy which is also called 'open-market industrial policy'.[52] Yet, the developmental outcomes of free-market policies generally failed to meet expectations in the developing world. This process was accompanied by premature de-industrialisation,[53] along with structural adjustment reforms and growing financial instability in several low- and middle-income countries in the global South (see box in Chapter 5 on industrial policy in Brazil).[54]

The Post-2008 Era and Renewed Interest in Industrial Policy

The 2008 global financial crisis changed the nature of the debate because it undermined the strong belief in the self-correcting capabilities of markets. At a time when the limits of market-led growth came under close scrutiny, industrial policy made an unexpected comeback.[55] Admittedly, IMF and World Bank circles remain somewhat resistant to industrial policy. And what is understood by effective industrial policy and the proper role of the state in the process can be difficult to reconcile. That being said, even the international financial institutions seem to have gradually revised their approach to industrial policy in the 2010s. The World Bank, for instance, appointed Justin Yifu Lin as senior vice president and chief economist (2008–12). Lin is well known for his endorsement of active state intervention in industrial upgrading.[56] Moreover, in their 2019 working paper, Reda Cherif and Fuad Hasanov, senior economists at the IMF, have emphasised 'the preeminent role of industrial policy' in the development of successful Asian economies and endorse its relevance for other economies trying to reach high income status.[57]

There are two reasons for this renewed interest. First, the 2008 global financial crisis triggered growing criticism against a market fundamentalist approach. The crisis set off shockwaves in the advanced Western countries and simultaneously put American and European economies to a severe test. Second, 'the China factor' brought state-directed development back into fashion, especially in the wake of the global financial turmoil. China adopted a set of heterodox policies that 'fundamentally challenges the established Western-led neoliberal governance paradigm' through 'the active role of the state in promoting industrial transformation and shaping market dynamics along with geopolitical autonomy from the West'.[58]

At a time when 'democratic capitalism' experienced major challenges,[59] developed countries, which for a long time had advocated the neoliberal policy compact in the developing world, became more attuned to interventionist economic policies. Hence, state interventionism has become more common over the last decade, including in the USA. As Wade, for example, has pointed out, . . .

> The Obama administration has engaged in sectorally targeted measures of the kind the American government has long denied – to raise bank lending, defend the auto sector, and boost innovation in selected sectors (such as energy, medical, pharmaceuticals, IT), using overt and covert 'buy American' clauses.[60]

The COVID-19 pandemic further tilted the balance in favour of state interventionism, as economic stagnation, interruptions in supply chains and rising protectionism in global trade made governments more sceptical of the virtues of unfettered markets. Revitalising domestic industries, 'bringing jobs back home' and promoting 'green growth' were increasingly central items on governments' agendas. For instance, in 2021, the Biden administration launched a USD 2-trillion 'Build Back Better' initiative. The UK government designed a 'levelling up' agenda, and French President Emmanuel Macron introduced the 'France 2030' investment plan, which targets USD 35 billion at 'reducing carbon emissions while also revitalising the industrial sector'.[61] On a broader scale, in 2022, a comprehensive study found that 'international industrial policies doubled throughout the 2010s'.[62] In the midst of escalating trade and technology wars between China and the US, industrial policy is once again seen as an instrument able to boost domestic production and increase national resilience.

Industrial Policy Redux: Beyond Dichotomies

So far, the global economy in the twenty-first century has produced growing interdependence among developed and developing countries. The complex nature of global supply chains, the internationalisation of national firms in goods and services sectors, the emergence of disruptive technologies and mega cities, systemic crises such as climate change and new forms of economic statecraft – all these necessitate significant revisions of conventional approaches and understandings of industrial policy. In the current political and economic landscape, the scope of industrial policy extends beyond 'industrial production' to include 'all elements of contemporary production dynamics', as industry and other sectors become ever more intertwined due to the increasing complexity of economic networks.[63] While industrial policy retains its central importance in economic development and sustainable growth, its nature has significantly transformed. The evolution of industrial policies has had to accommodate a number of dichotomies that, at times, have undermined their effectiveness. This book suggests that, instead of falling back on traditional hierarchical and dichotomic approaches, a flexible and inclusive perspective is needed to advance the debate on industrial transformation in developing countries.[64] Although somewhat eased in recent years, the debate over industrial policies has polarised around the following four dichotomies.[65]

Import substitution industrialisation vs export-oriented industrialisation: A major historical divide has been centred on the contest between import substitution and export-oriented industrialisation. ISI draws on one of the major pillars of industrial policies: the infant industry argument. As discussed above, this thesis argues that the manufacturing sector is the key driver of development, and strategic comparative advantage-defying sectors need protection from imports and state support as they emerge. These policies have been associated with the successful industrialisation of the US and Germany in the nineteenth century and Japan and South Korea in the twentieth century. ISI was a central tenet of development policies after World War II in most Latin American economies (see box on Brazil in Chapter 5), as well as in Turkey. However, by the early 1970s, mounting evidence suggested ISI was not delivering on its objectives. One problem was that, instead of selectively protecting strategic sectors, governments were resorting to *ad hoc* widespread protectionism in response to short-term foreign payments constraints. In addition, import protection applied at the discretion of state authorities became a source of unproductive rents for favoured special interests, bringing with it increased corruption. As summarised in the preceding paragraphs, this debate intensified in the late 1970s, as the state-led import substitution model was replaced by the market-led export-oriented industrialisation policies codified in the Washington Consensus. Wholesale reforms aiming at export-led growth and the liberalisation of finance, trade and capital were promoted, along with plans for the privatisation of state enterprises. Any remaining industrial policy was framed by the neoclassical critique of state intervention: the costs of government failure outweigh the costs of market failure.

It is now widely accepted that the success of the Asian development programme rested on the combined use of import substitution and export promotion measures. Industrialisation policies adopted since the 2008 global financial crisis have tacitly accepted that late industrialisers, as well as advanced economies positioning themselves for the new industrial revolution, or Industry 4.0, should take a pragmatic approach and adopt 'a blend of measures that mix import substitution with export promotion'.[66] This 'modern' industrial policy framework even seems to accept a moderate relaxation of restrictions on policy space embodied in international commitments in order to accommodate COVID-19-related health and environmental measures. However, steps by advanced economies away from open international investment and trade regimes may be risky in the current global environment, possibly leading to the 'securitisation' of industrial policies. The acceptance of elements of protectionism – such as 're-shoring' or 'friend-shoring' of global supply chains and restrictions on sharing technology internationally – deepen the fragmentation of the global economy. This fragmentation has accelerated since the Russian invasion of Ukraine in February 2022, especially with the extensive economic sanctions imposed on Russia.[67]

Horizontal vs vertical industrial policy: The major departure in global economic thinking away from import substitution industrialisation that demoted industrial policies came with a critique of vertical policies that prioritised specific sectors and had a transformative objective. These were discouraged because of the inability of the state to pick winners (see above). Horizontal or neutral measures were promoted, as these allowed market forces and comparative advantage to determine sector choice. For many developing countries which in the 1990s joined the WTO, and in the case of Turkey also the EU Customs Union, vertical policies were further restricted by World Trade Organization rules and EU state-aid regulations. This framework sought to encourage private-sector growth with 'business environment reforms [. . . as] the new industrial policy'.[68]

However, with the global shift away from the small-state paradigm of the neoliberal framework after the global financial crisis and given the urgency of addressing climate change and the COVID-19 pandemic, the polarised distinctions of horizontal versus vertical measures have receded. An increasingly pragmatic approach has been adopted by advanced and developing countries, typified by the new 'Cornwall Consensus' that suggests a revitalised economic role for the state, with government policies moving from '*reactively fixing* market failures to *proactively shaping* and making the kinds of markets we need'.[69] In line with this, new industrial policies include vertical sector-targeting strategies, as well as wider horizontal measures, such as skills development and environmental sustainability. This also recognises that, in Industry 4.0, government policy can no longer be limited to providing a business environment for comparatively advantaged sectors to thrive. Instead, governments need to implement industrial policies directly supporting the new disruptive technologies and managing the structural changes that they bring.[70] Hence, horizontal or vertical industrial policy measures are being superseded by policies that merge the two and target 'technical processes' and 'digital technologies'.

Macroeconomic stability or industrial policy: The third dichotomy in industrial policy debates centres on whether sound macroeconomic policies or industrial policies were responsible for the transformation of Asian economies. This debate arose in the 1990s, when a World Bank report argued that *sound economic policies* were the main drivers of growth in East Asian economies, thus challenging earlier work by Chalmers Johnson in which he argued that government support for specific industries was responsible for Japan's post-war economic growth.[71] As we go on to demonstrate in the following chapters, the example of Turkish industrial policies suggests that both are needed. Indeed, history is full of industrial policies that were overwhelmed by macroeconomic instability, most notably in Latin America during the debt crises in the 1980s. Since the 1990s, industrial and macro-policy management has also had to deal with the policy dilemma arising from capital account liberalisation, the negative impact on export-oriented industries of exchange rate appreciation from high capital inflows, and, conversely, the inflationary consequences of maintaining a depreciating currency to boost competitiveness. This dilemma, combined with the impact of the commodity price boom and the competition from Chinese manufactures, derailed the tech-upgrade industrial policies adopted in the early 2000s in Latin America, including those under the Lula administration in Brazil (see box in Chapter 5). Meanwhile, in the Turkish economy, the dilemma was exacerbated by an inappropriate macro-policy mix and populist political cycles, with the effect of undermining industrial policy objectives. Macro-stability is important to encourage high-tech industries, as they are extremely sensitive to market uncertainty and volatility.

This dilemma was largely avoided by countries such as South Korea and Taiwan. They retained an effective mix of state controls over capital flows and finance, providing macro-stability and assisting the development of globally competitive export industries in the 1960s and 1970s. However, the Turkish economy did not opt for this type of policy sequencing; industry had to shift from its domestic market orientation towards exports, at the same time as the capital account and finance were liberalised in the 1980s. The liberalisation of the Turkish economy before a competitive industrial base had emerged, combined with its high-energy import needs and low domestic savings, created an economy with a high dependence on volatile foreign capital inflows to close the foreign payments gap and the instability that comes with it. However, chronic macroeconomic instability is more than a reflection of a mistaken policy-mix or the wrong sequencing of policy. It is also a sign of deeper institutional issues, notably weak state capacity.

State capacity matters, not state size: As explained in the previous sections, the debate on the size of the state and the extent of state economic intervention has been fundamental in shaping industrial policies. However, this focus on the *more-or-less-state role* ignores the main issue of *state capacity* and the *effectiveness of government institutions* in managing what are often a complex mix of measures in industrial policies. It is no coincidence that Germany – the country with proven institutional coherence and a strong state capacity in implementing industrial policies – coined the term Industry 4.0 in 2011.[72] Yet, other advanced economies that have recently half-heartedly revived industrial policies, such as the UK, have revealed the problem of weakened state capacity after decades of paring back the state role in the economy.[73] The importance of state capacity is starkly evident in the case of Turkey. The country has been able to pursue industrialisation in the past (see below). For example, in the 1960s and 1970s, favourable global conditions and a coherent industrialisation strategy directed by the State Planning Organisation and its five-year development plans led to the emergence of a diverse industrial base. More recently, Turkey's technology and manufacturing value-added indicators improved after the adoption of industrial policies in 2011. However, progress remained uneven, partly reflecting the difficulty of managing a tech upgrade involving complex technical processes and requiring higher education and skill levels – things were easier in the 1960s. A deeper problem of the tech upgrade in Turkey has been the deterioration of industrial policy management and institutions, especially since the establishment of the authoritarian presidential system. The resulting centralisation and personalisation of economic policy, along with de-institutionalisation, has further undermined state capacity in Turkey (see Chapter 5). Combined with high levels of uncertainty, this has discouraged longer-term investment in tech upgrades and the spread of productivity improvements across economic sectors.

Determinants of Industrial Policy in Turkey

What are the key determinants of industrial policy in Turkey? In the subsequent empirical chapters, we will offer a more systematic documentation and analysis of specific industrial policies implemented by Turkish governments and take a closer look at the four dichotomies specified above. Before doing so, however, we will first develop a framework to explore the long-term political economy dynamics that shaped the preferences of Turkish governments to use different industrial policy instruments (or not) since the 1920s. More precisely, we identify three fundamental factors that interactively structured Turkey's industrial policies and shaped the country's long-term performance: global trends in development paradigm, domestic institutional context and macroeconomic (in)stability.

Global Trends in the Development Paradigm

Global trends in the development paradigm constitute the first, and arguably most important, factor informing the extent to which Turkish policy-makers have used industrial policy and ascribed importance to it in Turkey's economic transformation. Turkey is a late developer that closely followed global trends and tried to align with them. In this sense, the rise, retreat and return of industrial policy in the global political economy reflects the trajectory of industrial policy in Turkey. With the establishment of the Turkish Republic, barring brief experimentation with liberal market-oriented policies in the early 1950s, state-led industrialisation was the driving force of economic development until the early 1980s. Parallel to the statist turn in the global political economy, between 1960 and 1980, Turkey established the State Planning Organisation to coordinate national economic production through comprehensive five-year development plans. Turkish governments invested heavily in key manufacturing industries, hoping to transform the country from an agricultural into an industrial economy. Today's large private conglomerates, for instance, were established and expanded their activities thanks to ample state support and across-the-board protection during this period.

The import substitution industrialisation strategy led to substantial economic transformation in Turkey. The share of agriculture in the total labour force, for instance, decreased from 84 percent in 1950 to 51 percent in 1980, whereas the share of industry rose to 21 percent, from 13 percent three decades previously.[74] However, the 1970s were also crisis years in the Turkish political economy – again reflecting the main global trends. The causes of stagnation in Turkey's import substitution model are explained in Chapter 2, but at the heart of the issue was the failure to transition to export-led economic growth, marking a significant divergence from the trajectory of South Korea and other successful late developers. In Turkey, the state-owned enterprises experienced acute competitiveness problems, and key private sector actors opposed export-led integration with the world economy in the 1970s, because they feared that they would not be able to compete with foreign firms.[75] As a result of the accumulation of structural problems and the failure of the government to address economic stagnation in line with a renewed vision of industrial policy, the Turkish economy plunged into a major economic crisis amidst political turmoil in the late 1970s.

The early 1980s brought paradigmatic shifts in state–market relations. The 'neoliberal turn' in the global political economy and the declining appeal of vertical industrial policy measures had major ramifications for the Turkish economy. With the 24 January 1980 Decisions, the Turkish economy transitioned to a completely new economic paradigm, advocating liberalisation of trade and the gradual dismantling of state-owned enterprises as well as culminating in capital account liberalisation in 1989.[76] Although most of those policies did not result in a retreat of the economic role of the state as anticipated, many industrial policy measures were dismantled and replaced with indirect support mechanisms, such as export incentive schemes.[77] Turkish liberalisation, however, was mostly a reaction to the problems associated with state-led economic planning in the 1970s. There were no institutional checks-and-balance mechanisms to regulate market activity and manage financial flows. Hence, Turkey's transition to neoliberalism reflected some of the major flaws of the Washington Consensus during the 1990s and triggered a series of economic shocks.

It is important to note that, reflecting the neoliberal reforms in the early 1980s, Turkey became one of the countries in the developing world to adopt the post-Washington Consensus policies. Following the 2001 economic crisis, the Turkish government approved an ambitious reform package strongly supported by the IMF, the World Bank and the EU. The reform package endorsed a set of institutional adjustments reflecting a 'good governance' agenda, as well fiscal discipline and financial regulation measures.[78] This period also coincided with a horizontal industrial policy strategy, as Turkish governments did not formulate a specific industrial policy approach targeting certain sectors or firms. Instead, creating a favourable institutional environment for private sector firms and providing diplomatic support to Turkish corporations operating abroad shaped the parameters of industrial policy measures.

Table 1.1 The global market share of selected countries in advanced industries

	GDP (current US $, billion)	Share in global GDP (percent)	Global market share in advanced industries (percent of total)
United States	20,530	23.73	22.51
China	13,890	16.06	21.54
Japan	5,040	5.83	8.37
Germany	3,970	4.59	8.03
South Korea	1,720	1.99	4.11
India	2,700	3.12	3.55
Taiwan	609	0.70	1.54
Mexico	1,220	1.41	1.36
Switzerland	726	0.84	1.35
Brazil	1,920	2.22	1.26
Russia	1,660	1.92	0.88
Indonesia	1,040	1.20	0.65
Israel	377	0.44	0.58
Turkey	778	0.90	0.57
Poland	589	0.68	0.55
South Africa	404	0.47	0.21

Sources: GDP data are retrieved from the World Bank, World Development Indicators database. 'Global market share in advanced industries' data retrieved from the Hamilton Index of Advanced-Industry Performance. The index is published by the Hamilton Centre on Industrial Strategy, part of the Information Technology & Innovation Foundation. The 'advanced industries' included in the index include pharmaceuticals; electrical equipment; machinery and equipment; motor vehicles and other transport; computer, electronic, and optical; and IT and other information services. All figures belong to 2018.

The 2008 global financial crisis constituted yet another turning point for industrial policy in Turkey. Following global trends, once again, industrial policy made a comeback in the Turkish political economy of the early 2010s. For the first time since the 1980s, Turkey adopted a set of active industrial policy measures that prioritised certain sectors and allocated incentive schemes for those priority fields. The industrial strategy document, adopted in 2011, stated its goal as transforming Turkey into 'the production base of Eurasia in medium and high-tech products'.[79] As Atiyas and Bakış have pointed out, 'with the introduction of sectoral orientation, identification of priority investments, and strategic investments, the new direction of the incentive scheme has competitive-advantage-defying characteristics and leapfrogging aspirations'.[80] These policies yielded some project-based gains, a competitive defence industry and the emergence of science and technology clusters around Techno-parks.[81] However, in terms of an economy-wide industrial and technological upgrading, the results of the industrial policies of the 2010s have not matched expectations. For instance, the share of high-tech exports remained significantly below successful cases of late development and the world average. Relative to world averages, an index of global market share of 'advanced industries' showed Turkey with 0.57 percent (see Table 1.1) by 2018 which was several multiples below 4.11 percent for South Korea – with double the size of Turkish GDP of USD 778 billion at that time – but also below comparable sized industrial economies such as Switzerland (USD 726 billion GDP) or Taiwan (USD 609 billion GDP) with 1.35 percent and 1.54 percent respectively. Furthermore, as the autonomy of regulatory institutions was revoked and de-institutionalisation accelerated in the 2010s, the Turkish economy once again ran out of steam (see Chapter 5).

The Domestic Institutional Context

Global development paradigms and the way in which state–market relations are reconfigured at the international level have had major effects in structuring the scope and nature of industrial policy in Turkey. However, global drivers alone are not enough to explain Turkey's industrial transformation performance. The main puzzle is what explains Turkish governments' *half-committed approach* to industrial upgrading. That is, recurrently, policy-makers aim for economic development as a long-cherished idea that motivates them to make an ambitious start each time, but the effort dwindles into rent-seeking, policy uncertainty and economic stagnation, often ending in a major crisis.

An answer to this puzzle lies in the fact that industrial policy, first and foremost, is a 'political economy issue that is shaped by a set of institutions and underlying interests'.[82] Political economy is primarily concerned with 'who gets what?' questions, or as Susan Strange has put it: 'Who benefits (cui bono)?'[83] Industrial policy, at its core, aims at reconfiguring production from labour-intensive to more capital-intensive and high-value-added industries. It is therefore a typical 'who gets what' question in that it requires designing specific institutional structures and aligning preferences of social coalitions towards this purpose. Industrial upgrading, seen this way, creates a set of losers and winners.

This brings the three-pronged role of the state to the forefront. The literature suggests that the state can play a central role in industrial upgrading by assuming 'entrepreneurial',[84] 'transformative'[85] and 'conflict resolution' roles.[86] As covered above, the state's direct involvement in transforming the overall economic structure of a national economy is well-known. In addition to performing 'entrepreneurial' and 'transformative' functions to help create internationally competitive firms and sectors, the state can regulate industry standards and financial markets, co-ordinate development-oriented policy coalitions in their attempts to integrate with global supply chains and strengthen links between the financial system and the manufacturing industry through a set of regulatory instruments. Finally, the state can assume a critical 'conflict resolution function',[87] by designing policies to consolidate welfare state practices for those left behind, investing in education to improve the skill set of the labour force and creating other distributive mechanisms to manage societal tensions.

Is it too much to ask the state to implement, coordinate and manage the distributive outcomes of industrial policies, all at the same time, and in cooperation with non-state actors? This is clearly not an easy task, and it highlights the central role of the domestic institutional context and state capacity in designing and administering effective industrial policy. A large volume of work has shown that a 'strong state' is needed to take advantage of globalisation processes and to upgrade domestic economic structures by steering private actors, penetrating society, ensuring high-quality information flows between state and business organisations, and administering industrial policy through a meritocratic bureaucratic corps.[88] Thus, effective industrial policy relies on a solid domestic institutional context that facilitates co-operation and information exchanges between state and business actors. As Rodrik has stated:

The institutional framework must be designed carefully to ensure that there is a productive dialog between the private sector and the government, information flows adequately in both directions, needs are well identified, policy instruments are appropriately targeted, and self-correction mechanisms are in place.[89]

In terms of state capacity, the Turkish case seems mysterious, as Turkey is variously depicted in the literature as a 'strong' and a 'weak' state. Political scientists claim that the state tradition in Turkey diverges from that of several other post-colonial countries in the global South, as the state historically enjoyed significant autonomy *vis-à-vis* key social groups. Migdal has shown that the phenomenon of 'weak states' confronting 'strong societies' became a major challenge when countries could not control their territories, especially if non-state groups rejected the authority of the state and people placed their loyalty in those actors.[90] As colonial powers followed a 'cost-effective ruling strategy' in most cases, they did not invest in state institutions and impeded industrial development by supporting local power-brokers, prioritising their narrow interests at the expense of the professionalisation of the state bureaucracy.[91] As such, 'decentralised despots' reigned supreme, even in the post-colonial period, hampering autonomously functioning state institutions.[92]

This has never been the case for Turkey. Even though Turkey's relatively late integration into global capitalism reflected key patterns of 'peripheralisation', Turkey was not colonised by Western powers.[93] Despite ups and downs and recurring tugs-of-war between central administrations and various non-state power groups during the political-economic modernisation over the past two centuries, the path towards the centralisation of political authority triumphed. In this sense, the state holds an almost 'transcendental' position in the eyes of most Turkish citizens; as such, the state is capable of projecting significant power and can enfeeble the development of an autonomous civil society.[94] Heper has suggested, for instance, that 'the state in the Ottoman-Turkish polity has been far too strong' compared to the Prussian-German case, even though both represent 'polities with strong states'.[95] In any event, Turkey is a 'strong state' in that it is 'isolated from and autonomous vis-à-vis civil society'.[96]

In contrast, political economists have highlighted Turkey's historically conditioned weak capacity to foster industrialisation. Karaman and Pamuk have demonstrated that the state capacity of the Ottoman Empire, measured in terms of 'per capita tax revenues in days of unskilled workers' wages', stagnated between 1500 and 1800, when 'there was a strong pattern of gains in state capacity across Europe'.[97] Following a series of modernisation reforms in the nineteenth century, the Ottoman Empire increased central revenues considerably, but it was not enough to reduce the gap with the major European powers.[98] Öniş and Şenses have gone beyond a conventional state-capacity-as-resource-extraction approach and examined the modern Turkish state by focusing on its capacity to discipline market actors. Their examination has led them to conclude that Turkey is predominantly a 'reactive state' with weak capacity. Its limited success in steering industrial upgrading compares unfavourably to the experience of successful East Asian developmental states characterised by high state capacity and transformative power.[99]

This disconnection mostly stems from diverging interpretations of what 'state capacity' means in the Turkish context. The main problem of the 'Turkey-as-strong-state' thesis is that it conceives power distribution in dichotomic terms, implying a zero-sum game between state and civil society.[100] To address this puzzle, we might refer to Mann's terminology, distinguishing between the 'despotic' or 'coercive power' and the 'infrastructural power' of a state. Mann has defined the former as the 'the range of actions which the elite is empowered to undertake without routine, institutionalised negotiation with civil society groups',[101] while the latter refers to a state's capacity to 'penetrate civil society, and to implement logistically political decisions throughout the realm'.[102] Seen this way, thanks to an established state tradition and bureaucratic infrastructure, Turkey has been a 'strong state' in terms of controlling borders and civil society, but has some typical characteristics of a 'weak state' in terms of co-operating with society (economic actors, for the purposes of this book), or steering the process of changing the behaviour of private firms toward capital-intensive production through a set of incentives and disciplinary tools. Stated differently, public institutions in Turkey have not been set in a way to empower social coalitions that construct new comparative advantages for the country and contribute to its high-value-added production capabilities.

Within the context of industrial policy debates, state capacity involves two dimensions, which interact with and reinforce each other.[103] The first concerns the bureaucratic capabilities of a state. Evans has demonstrated that 'embedded autonomy' is a fundamental aspect of successful state interventions.[104] It is critical for state bureaucracy – composed of skilled technical staff recruited through meritocratic procedures – to be insulated, to a certain extent, from the political elite and organised business actors. This enables it to develop rational economic policies supporting long-term developmental goals, monitoring implementation via clearly stated performance-based criteria to avoid bureaucratic fragmentation and resisting politically motivated discretionary policy changes.

The second dimension of state capacity is the governance of state–society relations. Bureaucratic 'autonomy' needs to be 'embedded': bureaucratic elites should develop institutionalised co-operation mechanisms with non-state economic actors to facilitate high-quality information flows, ensure credible commitments and build reciprocity. Designing and implementing effective industrial policy necessitates the close institutional co-operation of state and business actors. Although institutional design in state–business relations takes various shapes depending on the idiosyncratic aspects of different cases, as Schneider has aptly suggested, '[f]eatures of institutional design can foster effective business-government collaboration to the extent that they promote three mutually reinforcing functions – meaningful information exchange, authoritative allocation, and minimal rent seeking'.[105] The state needs to have a certain capacity to 'discipline' private firms, in Amsden's words,[106] steering them toward capital-intensive production. But it is also crucial for governments to follow market signals and regularly communicate with the private sector to provide credible incentive structures (such as subsidies and market regulations) in exchange for commitment to clearly stated industrial policy objectives. Otherwise, the problems associated with weak bureaucratic 'autonomy' might lead to 'state capture' by rent-seeking private interests. Alternatively, the problems associated with weak 'embeddedness' might lead to 'market capture' by power-hungry political actors, both ending in rampant corruption, competitiveness problems and economic stagnation.

Both dynamics have appeared throughout Turkey's long experience with industrialisation. The Turkish state fits into the weak state category in terms of infrastructural power (on industrial upgrading), as its capacity remains limited when it comes to penetrating society, disciplining private business actors and cohesively implementing well-defined industrial objectives. This was the case even in the heyday of central planning, when industrialisation was a priority target. With the transition to import-substitution industrialisation in the early 1960s, as part of the 'Planning Law', the planners also proposed forming an 'Economic Council' to represent 'all interests and pressure groups'.[107] This may have improved the 'embeddedness' of state bureaucracy and may also have helped to discipline the private sector, but the proposal was rejected. At the same time, frequent state interventions, mostly 'market-repressing' in nature, sent uncertain signals to market actors.[108] As we demonstrate in the later chapters, the Turkish governments, capitalising on the deeply entrenched state tradition, have frequently used coercive instruments to keep civil society and the business community under control. For their part, dominant business groups have used various instruments and policies to protect their deeply entrenched interests, thus locking the country in a low-level institutional equilibrium in terms of economic upgrading and industrial transformation. As a result, Turkey has closely followed global development patterns, without becoming an outlier, in either a positive direction (the developmental state) or a negative one (the predatory state).[109]

Macroeconomic (In)Stability and Uncertainty

The third pillar shaping the trajectory of industrial policies in Turkey has been the state's macroeconomic performance. We suggest that ensuring macroeconomic stability is a *necessary* condition, albeit not sufficient, to implement effective industrial policies, and this has often been underestimated by policy-makers in Turkey. Although stable macro-policy is not enough to achieve sustainable long-term economic growth, and even might become a constraining factor, its absence hampers purposeful, focused economic transformation. In the case of Turkey, frequent macroeconomic crises, both big and small, created uncertainty in economic activity, hampered purposeful industrial policy and jeopardised long-term development plans. The Turkish economy has been marked by a chronic macroeconomic instability that transformed into periodic financial and foreign payments crises after the late 1970s. The crises have invariably corresponded to deteriorating global conditions that exposed domestic vulnerabilities. In more recent times, for example, regional geopolitical conflicts, such as the Russian invasion of Ukraine in February 2022, have added to the volatility and destabilised export markets. On the one hand, the historical legacy of weak state capacity has resulted in frequent policy changes, shortening the horizons of economic actors and making state-dependent business elite hesitant to invest in competitive capital-intensive sectors. On the other hand, the macro-instability and foreign payments crises have a number of recurring economic drivers. In the empirical chapters, we will focus on the high import dependence of the economy and the dearth of long-term funding due to low domestic savings and the slow development of capital markets.

The high import dependence reflects institutional weakness in policy effectiveness – that is, the *half-committed approach* to transformative industrial policies, as described in this book. Turkey's industrialisation policies have achieved a diversified industrial base producing low-medium technology consumer goods and heavy industries. But they have yet to reduce dependence on imported intermediate goods, or to produce an economy-wide technological upgrade into capital goods and high-tech sectors. Efforts to increase domestic savings with the introduction of private pensions in the early 2000s and the development of a capital market have not reached levels sufficient to meet the long-term funding requirements for transformative investments. As a strong technological upgrading towards high-value-added production and exports has not taken place (unlike in South Korea), current account deficits remain a major problem in the Turkish economy, making the country dependent on foreign capital flows to sustain economic growth (see Figures 1.3 and 1.4 for a comparison). Inflation has also remained a major concern since the

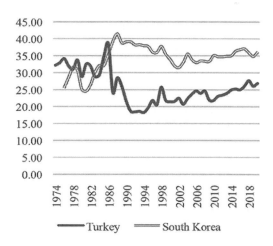

Figure 1.3 Gross savings (% of GDP)
Source: World Bank, World Development Indicators.

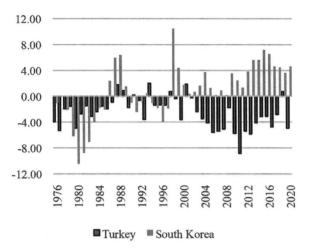

Figure 1.4 Current account balance (% of GDP)
Source: World Bank, World Development Indicators.

mid-1970s – except for a sharp decline in the early 2000s. The continued macro-instability associated with a dependence on volatile foreign capital inflows to fund investment has created high market uncertainty for producers, with respect to demand and the cost of funds and inputs.

Chronic macroeconomic instability also leads to the persistent need for state support to mitigate the shocks. In the midst of weakly institutionalised governance mechanisms and rent-seeking, Turkish governments have resorted to *ad hoc* administrative measures and increased executive control to tackle economic challenges. This reactive policy-making, with frequently changing and discretionary interventions by governments, only serves to increase uncertainty. The combination of macro-instability and uncertainty, in turn, undermines long-term savings and investments, creating a vicious cycle that encourages short-term gains in rent-rich sectors. Periods when a semblance of macroeconomic stability was established can be explained by an increase in external funding, such as the rise in inward foreign direct investment associated with the privatisation programme and the prospect of EU membership in the first decade of the 2000s.

Industrial policies adopted since 2011 have aimed to reduce the Turkish economy's import dependence and to overcome the periodic currency and foreign payments crises. Technological upgrades and the more recently introduced 'green agenda' to raise the share of renewables in Turkey's energy consumption would reduce its import dependence – but only if effectively pursued. Some progress has been made, such as increased domestic content in the defence sector. Yet, the tech upgrade has yet to translate into an economy-wide productivity increase and a higher share of tech exports. Investment incentives associated with industrial policies have expanded into a complex web of measures that are difficult for business to navigate and show signs of increased patronage, with incentives not reaching their targeted aims (see Chapter 5). Contributing to the problem of policy management was the deterioration of transparency and accountability, with the AKP government increasingly centralising policy-making and undermining central bank independence since the establishment of the presidential system in 2017.

The general trajectory of the Turkish economy has been mostly negative since then, culminating in 2021–22 with the sharpest slump in the Lira since the 2001 crisis, with inflation levels last seen in the 1990s, and with the growing dollarisation of the economy. The policy mix of maintaining negative real interest rates despite a sharp depreciation of the currency and accelerating inflation has been driven by the AKP's electoral strategy to maintain growth wrapped in a moral objection to interest-derived earnings. Industrial policies were subsumed by the AKP's efforts to stay in power. This hurried attempt to reduce Turkey's external vulnerabilities was also a response to geopolitical crises, growing protectionist trends and extensive international sanctions in the region.[110] It thus seemed that there was a return to a version of the import substituting industrialisation paradigm, but with monetary policy 'shock-therapy' replacing import tariffs.[111]

Hence, despite the centralisation of power and an established loyal business circle, the AKP's management of the economy generated more instability and uncertainty for business, and these continue to undermine long-term investments.[112] Moreover, those policies run counter Turkey's long-term developmental goal of a tech upgrade to overcome the middle-income trap. Export growth relying on a weak currency tends to increase exports of the *existing* technological base as seen with the stagnation of the share of high tech exports, even though the Turkish Lira real exchange rate has been declining for a decade. More recently, Turkey has benefited from a shift in supply chains away from Asia. However, predictably, these are in low-to-medium technology sectors, such as textiles and clothing, where low wages drive investment decisions – no microchip plants are yet to relocate to Turkey. Overall, the policy mix of the late AKP government undermined its industrial policies and contributed little to the development objective of raising technological and income levels.

Conclusion

This chapter has sketched a framework for an historical-empirical analysis of Turkey's industrial policies as part of the country's quest for modernisation and long-term economic development. Industrial policy is a loaded concept, surrounded by ideological priors, conceptual misrepresentations and empirical ambiguity. One point seems clear, however: given that market failures are quite common and successful economic transformation requires some sort of state activism, the idea and practice of industrial policy has become more acceptable in a knowledge-based global economy. However, critics and proponents alike say that it is hard to implement effective industrial policy, as state intervention might result in wasting national resources. Effective policy implementation calls for solid institutional fundamentals, patience, perseverance and pragmatism, because development is a path-dependent, complex and messy process.

This chapter maintains that developing countries need clearly formulated industrial policy supported by a suitable combination of institutional and macroeconomic pillars to catch up with the developed world, in line with their priorities and capabilities. Industrial policy and state-led development were commonly used by today's industrialised countries during their take-off phases, but late developers, like Turkey, experience both challenges and advantages when it comes to industrial upgrading and economic catch-up. On the one hand, it is easier for them to absorb existing technologies in the goods and services sectors, and this is likely to support economic growth and accelerate development. On the other hand, institutional factors and political constraints – both external and internal – are likely to generate significant impediments, leading to implementation failures if state capacity is inadequate. Accordingly, state capacity acts as a safety valve in state–market relations and is instrumental in striking a delicate balance between government and private firms. Most developing countries, including Turkey, experience 'state capture' or 'market capture', depending on how the balance is shifted in favour of one (government) or the other (private firms). In what follows, we examine the Turkish case in detail to explore how economic and political factors have interacted, leading to a half-committed approach in industrial policy and moderate performance in the long run.

Notes

1. The World Bank reports these countries as follows: 'Equatorial Guinea; Greece; Hong Kong SAR, China; Ireland; Israel; Japan; Mauritius; Portugal; Puerto Rico; Republic of Korea; Singapore; Spain; and Taiwan, China'. See World Bank, *China 2030: Building a Modern, Harmonious, and Creative High-income Society* (Washington DC: World Bank, 2013), p. 12.

2. For an extensive study substantiating this point, see Mark Koyama and Jared Rubin, *How the World Became Rich: The Historical Origins of Economic Growth* (Cambridge: Polity Press, 2022).

3. For an in-depth survey on the 'stickiness' of institutions, the path-dependent nature of political-economic development and the role of 'critical junctures' in breaking path-dependence, see Orfeo Fioretos, Tulia G. Falleti and Adam Sheingate, eds, *The Oxford Handbook of Historical Institutionalism* (Oxford: Oxford University Press, 2016). For the fundamental role of institutions on economic development, see Daron Acemoglu and James A. Robinson, *Why Nations Fail* (London: Profile Books, 2013).

4. Margaret Levi, 'A Model, a Method, and a Map: Rational Choice in Comparative and Historical Analysis', in Mark I. Lichbach and Alan S. Zuckerman, eds, *Comparative Politics: Rationality, Culture, and Structure* (Cambridge: Cambridge University Press, 1997), p. 28. Quoted in Paul Pierson, 'Increasing Returns, Path Dependence, and the Study of Politics', *American Political Science Review*, Vol. 94, No. 2 (2000), p. 252. On the role of path-dependence in economic development, see W. Brian Arthur, *Increasing Returns and Path Dependence in the Economy* (Ann Arbor: University of Michigan Press, 1994).

5. Different theoretical accounts highlight non-domestic sources of development problems in the developing world. For example, the uneven nature of capitalist development and how it perpetuates 'underdevelopment' in the global South is extensively analysed by Dependency Theory and World-Systems Analysis. See Fernando Henrique Cardoso and Enzo Faletto, *Dependency and Development in Latin America*, transl. Marjory Mattingly Urquidi (Berkeley: University of California Press, 1979); Immanuel Wallerstein, *World-Systems Analysis: An Introduction* (Durham, NC and London: Duke University Press, 2004). For more on the adverse effects of international financial institutions (the IMF and the World

Bank) on developing countries during neoliberal globalisation, see Joseph Stiglitz, *Globalisation and Its Discontents* (New York: W. W. Norton, 2002).

6. Amartya Sen, *Development as Freedom* (New York: Anchor Books, 2000), p. 27.

7. Joseph A. Schumpeter, *Capitalism, Socialism, and Democracy* (London and New York: Routledge, [1942] 2010), p. 73.

8. Chalmers Johnson, *MITI and the Japanese Miracle: The Growth of Industrial Policy, 1925-1975* (Palo Alto: Stanford University Press, 1982), p. 17. Quoted in Arkebe Oqubay, 'The Theory and Practice of Industrial Policy', in Arkebe Oqubay, Christopher Cramer, Ha-Joon Chang and Richard Kozul-Wright, eds, *The Oxford Handbook of Industrial Policy* (Oxford: Oxford University Press, 2020), p. 40.

9. Robert Wade frames this as micro-, meso- and macro-levels of industrial policy. For details, see Robert Wade, 'Return of Industrial Policy?' *International Review of Applied Economics*, Vol. 26, No. 2 (2012), p. 229–30. The transnationalisation of the production processes and a growing sophistication of the global value chains brought about new complexities in terms of the design and implementation of industrial policy in the twenty-first century. For a comprehensive review of the relevant literature, see Laurids S. Lauridsen, 'New Economic Globalization, New Industrial Policy and Late Development in the 21st Century: A Critical Analytical Review', *Development Policy Review*, Vol. 36, No. 3 (2018), pp. 329–46.

10. For a comprehensive analysis of the 'varieties of industrial policy' in the developed and developing countries, see Antonio Andreoni, 'Varieties of Industrial Policy: Models, Packages, and Transformation Cycles', in Akbar Noman and Joseph E. Stiglitz, eds, *Efficiency, Finance, and Varieties of Industrial Policy* (New York: Columbia University Press, 2016), pp. 245–305.

11. Antonio Andreoni and Ha-Joon Chang, 'Industrial Policy and the Future of Manufacturing', *Economia e Politica Industriale*, Vol. 43 (2016), p. 493.

12. Howard Pack, 'Industrial Policy: Growth Elixir or Poison?' *The World Bank Research Observer*, Vol. 15, No. 1 (2000), p. 48.

13. Robert Wade, 'Return of Industrial Policy?' *International Review of Applied Economics*, Vol. 26, No. 2 (2012), p. 227.

14. Wim Naudé, 'Industrial Policy: Old and New Issues', UNU-WIDER Working Paper No. 2010/106, 2010. Naudé, in this working paper, offers a comprehensive review and nuanced analysis of the traditional and recent themes in the industrial policy debates.

15. Peter Evans, 'In Search of the 21st Century Developmental State', University of Sussex, The Center for Global Political Economy, Working Paper No. 4, 2008.

16. Bruce Greenwald and Joseph E. Stiglitz, 'Industrial Policies, the Creation of a Learning Society, and Economic Development', in Joseph E. Stiglitz and Justin Yifu Lin, eds, *The Industrial Policy Revolution I* (London: Palgrave Macmillan, 2013), pp. 43–71.

17. Mariana Mazzucato, 'Mission-oriented Innovation Policies: Challenges and Opportunities', *Industrial and Corporate Change*, Vol. 27, No. 5 (2018), p. 803. For more on the role of industrial policy in tackling climate change and the growing challenges in food and energy sectors, see Wim Naudé, 'New Challenges for Industrial Policy', UNU-WIDER Working Paper No. 2010/107, 2010.

18. Ben R. Schneider, *Designing Industrial Policy in Latin America* (Basingstoke: Palgrave Macmillan, 2015), p. 4.

19. Ken Warwick, 'Beyond Industrial Policy: Emerging Issues and New Trends', OECD Science, Technology and Industry Policy Papers No. 2, 2013, p. 28.

20. Joseph E. Stiglitz, Justin Yifu Lin and Celestin Monga, 'Introduction: The Rejuvenation of Industrial Policy', in Joseph E. Stiglitz and Justin Yifu Lin, eds, *The Industrial Policy Revolution I* (London: Palgrave Macmillan, 2013), p. 6.

21. Ibid.

22. For critical reviews and analysis, see Howard Pack, 'Industrial Policy: Growth Elixir or Poison?' *The World Bank Research Observer*, Vol. 15, No. 1 (2000), pp. 47–67; Howard Pack and Kamal Saggi, 'Is There a Case for Industrial Policy? A Critical Survey', *The World Bank Research Observer*, Vol. 21, No. 2 (2006), pp. 267–97.

23. For more on the 'negative' and 'positive' externalities and the state's role in knowledge production and economic development, see Bruce Greenwald and Joseph E. Stiglitz, 'Industrial Policies, the Creation of a Learning Society, and Economic Development', in Joseph E. Stiglitz and Justin Yifu Lin, eds, *The Industrial Policy Revolution I* (London: Palgrave Macmillan, 2013), pp. 43–71.

24. Christopher Cramer and Fiona Tregenna, 'Heterodox Approaches to Industrial Policy and the Implications for Industrial Hubs', in Arkebe Qqubay and Justin Yifu Lin, eds, *The Oxford Handbook of Industrial Hubs and Economic Development* (Oxford: Oxford University Press, 2020), p. 45.

25. On the theoretical and empirical justification of industrial policy, see Dani Rodrik, 'Normalizing Industrial Policy', Commission on Growth and Development, Working Paper No. 3, 2008. Rodrik suggests 'normalising' industrial policy and recommends focusing on *how* industrial policy should be designed and implemented in the twenty-first century, rather than *whether* industrial policy should be on the agenda of governments.

26. Among many others, Polanyi, for instance, demonstrated how active state policies created the modern 'market economy'; Karl Polanyi, *The Great Transformation: The Political and Economic Origins of Our Time*, 2nd ed. (Boston: Beacon Press, 2001). For a classical account of the institutional pillars of economic growth, see Douglas C. North, *Institutions, Institutional Change and Economic Performance* (Cambridge: Cambridge University Press, 1990). For an institutionalist interpretation of state–market relations, see Ha-Joon Chang, 'Breaking the Mould: An Institutionalist Political Economy Alternative to the Neo-Liberal Theory of the Market and the State', *Cambridge Journal of Economics*, Vol. 26, No. 5 (2002), pp. 539–59.

27. For a succinct analysis, see Dani Rodrik, 'Normalizing Industrial Policy', Commission on Growth and Development, Working Paper No. 3, 2008, pp. 3–7; for more on multiple instruments of industrial policy, also see Wim Naudé, 'Industrial Policy: Old and New Issues', UNU-WIDER Working Paper No. 2010/106, 2010, table 2. For the history of industrial policies – and varying instruments – see, Michele Di Maio, 'Industrial Policies in Developing Countries: History and Perspectives', in Mario Cimoli, Giovanni Dosi and Joseph E. Stiglitz, eds, *Industrial Policy and Development: The Political Economy of Capabilities Accumulation* (Oxford: Oxford University Press, 2009), pp. 107–43.

28. For an in-depth intellectual history of F. List and A. Hamilton, see Eric Helleiner, *The Neomercantilists* (Ithaca: Cornell University Press, 2021), chapters 1 and 2.

29. Ha-Joon Chang, *Bad Samaritans: The Guilty Secrets of Rich Nations and the Threat to Global Prosperity* (London: Random House Business Books, 2007), p. 66.

30. Antonio Andreoni and Ha-Joon Chang, 'Industrial Policy and the Future of Manufacturing', *Economia e Politica Industriale*, Vol. 43 (2016), pp. 494–95.

31. For a comprehensive review, see Hüseyin Emrah Karaoğuz, 'The Developmental State in the 21st Century: A Critical Analysis and a Suggested Way Forward', *Panoeconomicus*, Vol. 69, No. 1 (2022), pp. 55–72.

32. The case of South Korea is extensively covered in the political economy literature. For instance, see Alice Amsden, *Asia's Next Giant: South Korea and Late Industrialization* (New York and Oxford: Oxford University Press, 1989); Ha-Joon Chang, 'The Political Economy of Industrial Policy in Korea', *Cambridge Journal of Economics*, Vol. 17, No. 2 (1993), pp. 131–57. For a comparative edited volume on state economic intervention, industrial policy and developmental states, see Meredith Woo-Cumings, ed., *The Developmental State* (Ithaca and London: Cornell University Press, 1999).

33. Isabella M. Weber, *How China Escaped Shock Therapy: The Market Reform Debate* (London: Routledge, 2021).

34. The successful state intervention in Taiwan and the MITI experience in Japan are also well-documented in the literature. Apart from the 'Asian tigers', researchers have also studied several other cases on the political economy of industrial policy in Latin America, Europe and Africa. For a review, see Dani Rodrik, 'Industrial Policy for the Twenty-First Century', Harvard University, 2004, https://drodrik.scholar.harvard.edu/files/dani-rodrik/files/industrial-policy-twenty-first-century.pdf.

35. For details, see Dani Rodrik, 'Normalizing Industrial Policy', Commission on Growth and Development, Working Paper No. 3, 2008, pp. 8–11.

36. Reginald Dale, 'Governments Fail at Picking Winners', *The New York Times*, 22 April 1994.

37. Howard Pack, 'Industrial Policy: Growth Elixir or Poison?' *The World Bank Research Observer*, Vol. 15, No. 1 (2000), p. 64.

38. Ha-joon Chang, *Kicking Away the Ladder: Development Strategy in Historical Perspective* (London: Anthem Press, 2002).

39. For instance, see Atul Kohli, *State-Directed Development: Political Power and Industrialization in the Global Periphery* (Cambridge: Cambridge University Press, 2004).

40. John Gerard Ruggie, 'International Regimes, Transactions, and Change: Embedded Liberalism in the Postwar Economic Order', *International Organization*, Vol. 36, No. 2 (1982), p. 393.

41. Atul Kohli, *State-Directed Development: Political Power and Industrialization in the Global Periphery* (Cambridge: Cambridge University Press, 2004), chapter 1.

42. Michele Di Maio, 'Industrial Policies in Developing Countries: History and Perspectives', in Mario Cimoli, Giovanni Dosi and Joseph E. Stiglitz, eds, *Industrial Policy and Development: The Political Economy of Capabilities Accumulation* (Oxford: Oxford University Press, 2009), p. 110.

43. For more on the Bretton Woods system and later developments in the global monetary system, see Paola Subacchi, 'From Bretton Woods onwards: The Birth and Rebirth of the World's Hegemon', *Cambridge Review of International Affairs*, Vol. 21, No. 3 (2008), pp. 347–65.

44. For more on the role and re-emergence of global finance in the post-1945 period, see Eric Helleiner, *States and the Reemergence of Global Finance: From Bretton Woods to the 1990s* (Ithaca and London: Cornell University Press, 1994).

45. The post-1945 era until the mid-1970s is called the 'golden age' of capitalist development, due to several reasons including rapid economic development, low

unemployment and strong domestic demand guided by active state interventions. For details, see Angus Maddison, *Dynamic Forces in Capitalist Development* (Oxford: Oxford University Press, 1991), pp. 167–94.

46. Ziya Öniş, 'The Logic of the Developmental State', *Comparative Politics*, Vol. 24, No. 1 (1991), pp. 109–26.

47. For an extensive analysis, see Vedat Milor, *Devleti Geri Getirmek: Türkiye ve Fransa'da Planlama ve Ekonomik Kalkınma Üzerine Karşılaştırmalı bir Çalışma* (İstanbul: İletişim Yayınları, 2022). See also Sadık Ünay, *Neoliberal Globalization and Institutional Reform: The Political Economy of Development Planning in Turkey* (New York: Nova Science Publishers, 2006).

48. Babb has suggested that 'the Washington Consensus was a transnational policy paradigm produced by both intellectual and political forces'. For more on the origins and evolution of the Washington Consensus paradigm, see Sarah Babb, 'The Washington Consensus as Transnational Policy Paradigm: Its Origins, Trajectory and likely Successor', *Review of International Political Economy*, Vol. 20, No. 2 (2013), pp. 268–97.

49. For a critical assessment of the Washington Consensus and international financial institutions, see Joseph Stiglitz, *Globalization and Its Discontents* (New York: W. W. Norton, 2002).

50. For an early critical analysis of the post-Washington Consensus policies, see Ziya Öniş and Fikret Şenses, 'Rethinking the Emerging Post-Washington Consensus', *Development and Change*, Vol. 36, No. 2 (2005), pp. 263–90.

51. Fabio Bulfone, 'Industrial Policy and Comparative Political Economy: A Literature Review and Research Agenda', *Competition & Change*, Vol. 27, No. 1 (2023), p. 8.

52. Ibid.

53. Brazil is arguably one of the most striking cases. According to *The Economist*, 'in the 1980s manufacturing peaked at 34% of Brazil's GDP. In 2020 it was just 11%'. See The Economist, 'Why Industrial Decline Has Been So Stark in Brazil', 5 March 2022.

54. In the Turkish context, even though neoliberal policies have gained prominence since the early 1980s, mass privatisations were realised especially following the 2001 economic crisis and the associated reform package designed in line with the post-Washington Consensus paradigm. For details on this issue within the context of industrial policy in Turkey, see Chapter 4.

55. Ha-Joon Chang and Antonio Andreoni, 'Industrial Policy in the 21st Century', *Development and Change*, Vol. 51, No. 2 (2020), p. 324.

56. For instance, see Justin Yifu Lin, 'New Structural Economics: A Framework for Rethinking Development', *The World Bank Research Observer*, Vol. 26, No. 2 (2011), pp. 193–221.

57. Reda Cherif and Fuad Hasanov, 'The Return of the Policy That Shall Not Be Named: Principles of Industrial Policy', IMF Working Paper, WP 19/74, 2019.

58. Ziya Öniş and Mustafa Kutlay, 'The New Age of Hybridity and Clash of Norms: China, BRICS, and Challenges of Global Governance in a Postliberal International Order', *Alternatives: Global, Local, Political*, Vol. 45, No. 3 (2020), p. 125.

59. For more on the 'crisis of democratic capitalism', see Martin Wolf, 'The "Elites" against the "People": The Crisis of Democratic Capitalism', in Luís Catão and Maurice Obstfeld, eds, *Meeting Globalization's Challenges: Policies to Make Trade Work for All* (Princeton and Oxford: Princeton University Press, 2019), pp. 237–60.

60. Robert Wade, 'Return of Industrial Policy?' *International Review of Applied Economics,* Vol. 26, No. 2 (2012), p. 228.

61. DW, 'Macron Unveils Massive "France 2030" Green Investment Plan', 12 October 2021, https://www.dw.com/en/macron-unveils-massive-france-2030-green-investment-plan/a-59478618

62. Réka Juhász, Nathan Lane, Emily Oehlsen and Verónica C. Pérez, 'The Who, What, When, and How of Industrial Policy: A Text-Based Approach', *SocArXiv*, https://doi.org/10.31235/osf.io/uyxh9, 2022, p. 3.

63. Andrea Ferrannini, Elisa Barbieri, Mario Biggeri and Marco R. Di Tommaso, 'Industrial Policy for Sustainable Human Development in the Post-Covid19 Era', *World Development*, Vol. 137 (2021), p. 3.

64. This is broadly in line with what Ha-Joon Chang has long advocated: a 'heterodox framework' for industrial policy, arguing that the historical experience of advanced industrial countries shows that the old dichotomies must be overcome to create transformative opportunities for middle-income economies. See also Ha-Joon Chang and Antonio Andreoni, 'Industrial Policy in a Changing World: Basic Principles, Neglected Issues and New Challenges', *Cambridge Journal of Economics: 40th Year Conference*, https://cpes.org.uk/wp-content/uploads/2016/06/Chang_Andreoni_2016_Industrial-Policy.pdf, 2016; Ha-Joon Chang, *Kicking Away the Ladder: Development Strategy in Historical Perspective* (London: Anthem Press, 2002).

65. This section draws on the following work where these dichtotomies have already been summarised: Mina Toksöz, 'The Return of Industrial Policy in Turkey', in Judit Ricz and Tamás Gerőcs, eds, *The Political Economy of Emerging Markets and Alternative Development Paths* (London: Palgrave Macmillan, 2023), pp. 203–28. Chapter 5 is also an extensively revised and extended version of this work.

66. UNCTAD, *World Investment Report: Investment and New Industrial Policies* (Geneva: United Nations Publication, 2018), p. 144.

67. Creon Butler, 'Today's Sanctions Change Everything', *World Today*, Chatham House, June/July 2022.

68. John Weiss, 'Neoclassical Economic Perspectives on Industrial Policy', in Arkebe Oqubay, Christopher Cramer, Ha-Joon Chang and Richard Kosul-Wright, eds, *The Oxford Handbook of Industrial Policy* (Oxford: Oxford University Press, 2020), p. 130.

69. See G7, 'Panel on Economic Resilience', Cornwall, October 2021, and Mariana Mazzucato, 'A New Global Economic Consensus', *Project Syndicate*, 13 October 2021.

70. Patrizio Bianchi and Sandrine Labory, 'European Industrial Policy, a Comparative Perspective', in Arkebe Oqubay, Christopher Cramer, Ha-Joon Chang and Richard Kozul-Wright, eds, *The Oxford Handbook of Industrial Policy* (Oxford: Oxford University Press, 2020), p. 611.

71. World Bank, *East Asian Miracle: Economic Growth and Public Policy* (Oxford: Oxford University Press, published for the World Bank, 1993); Chalmers Johnson, *MITI and the Japanese Miracle: The Growth of Industrial Policy, 1925–1975* (Palo Alto: Stanford University Press, 1982). For a summary of the debate, see Gary Hufbauer and Euijin Jung, 'Scoring 50 Years of US Industrial Policy', PIIE Briefing 21-5, November 2021.

72. Patrizio Bianchi and Sandrine Labory, 'European Industrial Policy, a Comparative Perspective', in Arkebe Oqubay, Christopher Cramer, Ha-Joon Chang and Richard Kozul-Wright, eds, *The Oxford Handbook of Industrial Policy* (Oxford: Oxford University Press, 2020), p. 605.

73. Craig Berry, Julie Froud and Tom Baker, eds, *The Political Economy of Industrial Strategy in the UK* (London: Agenda Publishing, 2021). The authors suggest several problems with the 2016 UK industrial policy adopted by the May government (but which had been prepared under the previous coalition government), including too many objectives (ten sector deals for aerospace, AI, automotive, construction, creative industries, life sciences, nuclear, offshore wind, rail and tourism; as well as four 'Grand Challenges' of post-industrial economies: AI and data, the ageing society, clean growth and the future of mobility) and a frequent changing of responsible ministries and entities ('institutional churn'), as well as varying commitment by different governments.

74. Sumru Altuğ, Alpay Filiztekin and Şevket Pamuk, 'Sources of Long-Term Economic Growth for Turkey, 1880–2005', *European Review of Economic History*, Vol. 12, No. 3 (2008), p. 399.

75. For an assessment of the early 1970s from this perspective, see Ali Tekin, 'Turkey's Aborted Attempt at Export-Led Growth Strategy: Anatomy of the 1970 Economic Reform', *Middle Eastern Studies*, Vol. 42, No. 1 (2006), pp. 133–63.

76. For an analysis of this period, see Fikret Şenses, *1980 Sonrası Ekonomi Politikaları Işığında Türkiye'de Sanayileşme: Bugün ve Yarın* (Ankara: V Yayınları, 1989).

77. For further analysis of the 1980s in the Turkish economy, see Ziya Öniş, 'Political Economy of Turkey in the 1980s: Anatomy of Unorthodox Liberalism', in Metin Heper, ed., *Strong State and Economic Interest Groups: The Post-1980 Turkish Experience* (Berlin: De Gruyter, 1991), pp. 27–39.

78. Ziya Öniş and Fikret Şenses, eds, *Turkey and the Global Economy: Neoliberal Restructuring and Integration in the Post-Crisis Era* (London: Routledge, 2009).

79. See Ministry of Science, Industry and Technology, *Turkish Industrial Strategy Document*, 2011. See also Mustafa Kutlay, 'The Politics of State Capitalism in a Post-liberal International Order: The Case of Turkey', *Third World Quarterly*, Vol. 41, No. 4 (2020), p. 691.

80. İzak Atiyas and Ozan Bakış, 'Structural Change and Industrial Policy in Turkey', *Emerging Markets Finance and Trade*, Vol. 51, No. 6 (2015), p. 1223.

81. The 2021 Global Innovation Index report has cited Istanbul, along with Delhi and Mumbai, as seeing significant growth in science and technology clusters. Turkey had also moved up the ranking into the top fifty. However, its overall rank of 41 was dragged down by a very weak Institutional score, where it ranked 93 among the 132 countries in the index.

82. For more on industrial policy as 'an institutional political economy process', see Antonio Andreoni and Ha-Joon Chang, 'The Political Economy of Industrial Policy: Structural Interdependencies, Policy Alignment and Conflict Management', *Structural Change and Economic Dynamics*, Vol. 48 (2019), pp. 145–46.

83. For more on Susan Strange's approach to the international political economy, see *States and Markets* (London: Pinter Publishers, 1988).

84. Mariano Mazzucato, *The Entrepreneurial State: Debunking Public vs. Private Sector Myths* (London: Anthem Press, 2013).

85. Linda Weiss, *The Myth of the Powerless State* (Ithaca: Cornell University Press, 1998).

86. On the state's 'conflict resolution' role as part of an effective industrial policy, see Antonio Andreoni and Ha-Joon Chang, 'The Political Economy of Industrial Policy: Structural Interdependencies, Policy Alignment and Conflict Management', *Structural Change and Economic Dynamics*, Vol. 48 (2019), pp. 145–46.

87. Ibid., p. 146. For more extensive analysis, see also Ha-Joon Chang and Antonio Andreoni, 'Industrial Policy in the 21st Century', *Development and Change*, Vol. 51, No. 2 (2020), pp. 324–51.

88. There exists voluminous literature on the importance of state capacity in economic development. See, for instance, Linda Weiss, *The Myth of the Powerless State* (Ithaca: Cornell University Press, 1998); Peter Evans, *Embedded Autonomy: States and Industrial Transformation* (Princeton: Princeton University Press, 1995); Peter Evans, 'The Eclipse of the State? Reflections on Stateness in an Era of Globalization', *World Politics*, Vol. 50, No. 1 (1997), pp. 62–87.

89. Dani Rodrik, 'Normalizing Industrial Policy', Commission on Growth and Development, Working Paper No. 3, 2008, p. 25.

90. Joel S. Migdal, *Strong Societies, Weak States: State–Society Relations and State Capabilities in the Third World* (Princeton: Princeton University Press, 1989).

91. For an analysis of how a 'cost-effective ruling strategy' of Britain in Nigeria (as well as in other cases) led to 'a dysfunctional state' and underdevelopment, see Atul Kohli, *Greed and Guns: Imperial Origins of the Developing World* (Cambridge: Cambridge University Press), pp. 50–51.

92. Ibid., p. 51.

93. For a comprehensive analysis of Turkey's 'peripheralisation' within the global capitalist system during the nineteenth and early twentieth centuries, see Şevket Pamuk, *Osmanlı Ekonomisinde Bağımlılık ve Büyüme (1820–1913)* (İstanbul: İş Bankası Kültür Yayınları, 2017).

94. Metin Heper, *The State Tradition in Turkey* (North Humberside: Eothen Press, 1985).

95. Metin Heper, 'The Strong State as a Problem for the Consolidation of Democracy: Turkey and Germany Compared', *Comparative Political Studies*, Vol. 25, No. 2 (1992), p. 170.

96. Ibid, p. 187.

97. K. Kıvanç Karaman and Şevket Pamuk, 'Different Paths to the Modern State in Europe: The Integration Between Warfare, Economic Structure, and Political Regime', *American Political Science Review*, Vol. 107, No. 3 (2013), p. 606.

98. K. Kıvanç Karaman and Şevket Pamuk, 'Ottoman State Finances in European Perspective, 1500–1914', *The Journal of Economic History*, Vol. 70, No. 3 (2010), pp. 593–629.

99. Ziya Öniş and Fikret Şenses, 'Global Dynamics, Domestic Coalitions and Reactive State', *METU Studies in Development*, Vol. 34, No. 2 (2007), pp. 255–56. See also Vedat Milor, 'The Genesis of Planning in Turkey', *New Perspectives on Turkey*, Vol. 4, No. 2 (1990), pp. 1–30.

100. On the flawed logic of the 'zero-sum game' between state and non-state actors, see also Atul Kohli, *State-Directed Development: Political Power and Industrialization in the Global Periphery* (Cambridge: Cambridge University Press, 2004), p. 20.

101. Michael Mann, 'The Autonomous Power of the State: Its Origins, Mechanisms and Results', *European Journal of Sociology*, Vol. 25, No. 2 (1984), p. 188.

102. Ibid., p. 189.

103. For a more extensive discussion of different aspects of state capacity and how they operate in the Turkish context, see Mustafa Kutlay and Emrah Karaoğuz, 'Neo-Developmentalist Turn in the Global Political Economy? The Turkish Case', *Turkish Studies*, Vol. 19, No. 2 (2018), pp. 289–316.

104. Peter Evans, *Embedded Autonomy: States and Industrial Transformation* (Princeton: Princeton University Press, 1995).

105. Ben R. Schneider, *Designing Industrial Policy in Latin America* (Basingstoke: Palgrave Macmillan, 2015), pp. 13–14.

106. Alice H. Amsden, *Asia's Next Giant: South Korea and Late Industrialization* (Oxford: Oxford University Press, 1989), p. 14.

107 Vedat Milor, 'The Genesis of Planning in Turkey', *New Perspectives in Turkey*, Vol. 4, No. 2 (1990), p. 16. In this article, Milor has demonstrated that planners (bureaucrats at the State Planning Organisation) tried to rationalise state intervention in the economy, to reform state-owned enterprises and to increase transparency of state support provided to the market actors (p. 23) – most of the planners' proposals received strong reactions from businesspeople, political elites and other branches of the state bureaucracy (pp. 17–19). The process culminated in the resignation of four high-level SPO bureaucrats in October 1962 (p. 25). For a book-length and comparative analysis of Turkey's planning experience, see also Vedat Milor, *Devleti Geri Getirmek: Türkiye ve Fransa'da Planlama ve Ekonomik Kalkınma Üzerine Karşılaştırmalı Bir Çalışma* (İstanbul: İletişim Yayınları, 2022).

108. Ayşe Buğra, 'Political Sources of Uncertainty in Business Life', in Metin Heper, ed., *Strong State and Economic Interest Groups: The Post-1980 Turkish Experience* (Berlin: De Gruyter, 1991), pp. 152, 159.

109. For different state types based on their capacity, see Peter B. Evans, 'Predatory, Developmental, and Other Apparatuses: A Comparative Political Economy Perspective on the Third World State', *Sociological Forum*, Vol. 4, No. 4 (1989), pp. 561–87.

110. This difficult balancing act is also taking place in Turkey's foreign relations. See Mustafa Kutlay and Ziya Öniş, 'Turkish Foreign Policy in a Post-Western Order: Strategic Autonomy or New Forms of Dependence?' *International Affairs*, Vol. 97, No. 4 (2021), pp. 1085–1104.

111. 'Kavcıoğlu: Current Account Surplus Would Mean Price Stability', *Bloomberg*, 28 October 2021. Following the May 2023 elections, there was a U-turn in policies by a new economic team led by the former Minister of Finance Mehmet Simsek. Policy reverted to orthodox monetary policy by raising interest rates. But great uncertainty remains as to how long this policy stance will be sustained.

112. Even Müsiad, the business association loyal to the AKP, has reluctantly admitted that the currency volatility is negatively affecting its members. 'Müsiad Başkanı Asmalı: Kurdan Etkilenmiyorum Diyen Sanayici Doğru Söylemiyor' [Müsiad Chairman Asmalı: Industrialists Who Say They Are Not Affected by the Currency Are Not Being Honest), *Dünya*, 8 December 2021.

2

TURKEY'S INDUSTRIALISATION: THE HISTORICAL EXPERIENCE, 1923–80

Any analysis of Turkey's economic development is likely to be highly eclec-
tic and a poor fit for any of the classic models, Marxian or liberal.[1] Its
historical evolution over the past century is discontinuous and erratic, with
repeated changes of direction, in accordance with fluctuating international
and domestic conditions, political and economic. Nevertheless, in the context
of this study, a number of recurring dominant drivers of Turkey's industrialisation experience are identifiable. As highlighted in Chapter 1, they include a
high sensitivity to global conditions and the adoption of global development
paradigms. Second is the tendency to rent-seeking and patronage in state-
business relations, which has been the legacy of the establishment of a post-
Ottoman private sector under the wing of the state in the early years of the
Republic. And third is the persistent macro-instability and uncertainty that
has undermined the transformative objectives of industrial policies.

This chapter presents a brief overview of the first fifty years of industrial
development of the Turkish Republic. These years include the two planning
periods in the 1930s and the 1960s –with the latter coinciding with the hey-
day of industrial policies globally, which were based on import-substituting
industrialisation (ISI) strategies. These policies established Turkey's diverse,
but inward-looking, industrial base of state-owned heavy industry and private-
sector consumer goods industries. The chapter also covers the 1950s when
there was a failed attempt at liberalisation and in the early 1970s when, for a

brief period, policies were introduced to encourage export orientation to prepare industry to compete in global markets.

To schematise, this complicated story can be broken down into the following phases: (1) reconstruction and early industrialisation in a market system, 1923–30; (2) etatism and the first planning period, 1930–39; (3) wartime travails and retrenchment, 1939–45; (4) post-war debate and transition, 1945–50; (5) liberalisation and its failure, 1950–60; and (6) the second planning period, including progress, adaptation and collapse, 1960–80. In what follows, each of these phases is discussed in turn, leaving the post-1980 story to the following chapter.

Early Approaches, 1923–30

After the defeat of its armies in World War I, the Ottoman Empire was shorn of all its former territories in the Arab Middle East, being reduced to the Turkish heartland of Anatolia, in addition to eastern Thrace – the small triangle of territory on the south-eastern tip of Europe. In 1919, a resurgent Greece landed troops in İzmir and began an advance which took them to within 50 miles of Ankara, before suffering a devastating defeat by Turkish nationalist forces led by Mustafa Kemal (later Atatürk) in 1922. Following the deposition of the last sultan and the abolition of the Ottoman Sultanate in November 1922, a peace treaty was finally signed in July 1923 in the Swiss resort of Lausanne, between Turkey and its former enemies of World War I. In the following October, a Republic was proclaimed with Atatürk as its President. Under the Republican People's Party (*Cumhuriyet Halk Partisi*, or CHP) Turkey remained effectively a single-party state from 1924 until 1945.

For Atatürk and his colleagues, the main objective was to rebuild the Turkish state on modern lines, basing its authority on the idea of popular sovereignty rather than attachment to Islam, and to modernise its structures so as to avoid the decline and external dependency of the late Ottoman Empire. In February 1923, they organised an Economic Congress in İzmir, at which Atatürk emphasised the need for 'economic victories', now that the war against the Greeks had been won.[2] However, the leaders of the new state had no clear idea on how to achieve this and faced a range of daunting obstacles. During the late nineteenth century, a few modern factories had been established, producing textiles, cement and food products, and the beginnings of a railway system constructed by foreign concessionaires. However, it is estimated that non-agricultural production only accounted for about 10 percent of national income, and a large part of this was still carried out in small unmechanised workshops.[3] Much of what little modern infrastructure there was (such as railways) had been destroyed by ten years of warfare.[4] The massacres and deportations of the Ottoman Armenians in 1915, battlefield losses, disease and high infant mortality, combined with the population exchanges with Greece and other countries, meant that the population of what became Turkey in 1923 suffered a net loss of around 3–4 million between 1914 and 1924 (from just under 16 million to around 12–13 million).[5] By 1924, around 2.4 million Greeks had left Turkey, in exchange for 360,000 Muslims who left Greece for Turkey, while the Armenian population in Anatolia had been almost wiped out by enforced emigration or massacres in 1915, leaving only small clusters in major cities.[6]

These changes had seriously damaging effects on Turkey's economy, since non-Muslim entrepreneurs had accounted for 80 percent of the 172 industrial enterprises surveyed in a census of 1915.[7] The result was that post-war the country was left with a severe shortage of experienced businessmen and skilled artisans, representing a major brake on potential industrial growth. Prospects for industrial development were further restricted by the fact that, under a Commercial Convention attached to the Treaty of Lausanne, the government was obliged to maintain the Ottoman customs tariff of 1916.[8] This was a specific tariff, fixing import duties for different goods by volume, but has been estimated as providing for an *ad valorem* rate of 13 percent.[9] Turkey was thus left with limited ability to protect potential 'infant industries' behind import tariff barriers.

The Kemalists' main objective was to strengthen and modernise their country by developing a 'national bourgeoisie', to be allied with the CHP, and to improve government finances so as to avoid the chronic foreign indebtedness of the late Ottoman years. However, they had no pet economic theories to experiment with. During the 1920s, the global capitalist economy was generally flourishing, and they evidently saw no good reason to challenge its assumptions. Their main aim was to produce a new Muslim-Turkish technocratic and entrepreneurial bourgeoisie, to fill the gap caused by the loss of most of the non-Muslim minorities.[10] The result was a patchwork of state-financed enterprises, and legislation aimed at encouraging private industrial development without breaking the Lausanne rules. The state's main instrument for industrial development was the quasi-private Business Bank (*Türkiye İş Bankası*) set up in 1924. This was nominally in the private sector, but with the initial capital paid up by Atatürk himself. Celal Bayar, a prominent member of the regime and the only one with a business background, was its General Manager.[11] A second state bank, the Bank for Industry and Mining (*Türkiye Sanayi ve Maadin Bankası*) took over four factories for the manufacture of cotton and woollen cloth (primarily for the army), which it inherited from the Ottoman government, besides investing in private firms producing textiles, ceramics, food products and electric power.[12] From 1925 on, the state tobacco monopoly administration took over the four cigarette factories previously run by the foreign-controlled *Régie des Tabacs* of the Ottoman era, but state monopolies in matches, petroleum products and explosives were farmed out to foreign concessionaires.[13]

In 1913, the Ottoman government had passed a Provisional Law for the Encouragement of Industry, providing tax and other concessions to newly established industrial firms. This was continued under the Republic until 1927, when it was succeeded by a new Industrial Encouragement Law. Firms benefitting from the law were exempted from land and property taxes, as well as import taxes on machinery, with government bodies and other beneficiary firms obliged to purchase their products. In this way, the government sought to provide protection for import-substituting industries by circumventing the provisions of the Lausanne Treaty.[14]

Summing up the effects of these policies, estimates for national income during the 1920s suggest that the Gross National Product (GNP) rose by almost 90 percent between 1923 and 1930, or at an average rate of 9.6 percent per annum. This looks like a healthy rate of growth, but most of it is likely to be accounted for by natural post-war recovery, as peasants returned to cultivate their fields and rebuild their stock of cattle and sheep. Thus, agricultural output rose by an estimated 86 percent between 1923 and 1926, but it would appear that this merely took it back to pre-war levels, with subsequent growth (1927–30) much slower. Thanks to the measures outlined above, there was some increase in the production of textiles and sugar as domestic production began to replace imports, but overall, the share of industry in GNP remained virtually static, at around 12 percent.[15] The conclusion is that government efforts had some effect on industrial output, but that most production still came from small artisanal workshops. Without effective tariff protection, and a more direct and effective intervention by the state, it would be hard to effect a lasting structural change in the Turkish economy.

Etatism and the First Planning Period, 1929–39: Import-substituting Industrialisation Begins

With the expiry of the Lausanne tariff restrictions in 1929, it became possible to change direction through the imposition of a protective import tariff. However, it was not initially envisaged that the state itself would take over the ownership and management of the new factories, leaving this function to private initiative and capital. In October 1929, the government immediately seized the opportunity to increase import duties by rates varying from 13 to 46 percent *ad valorem* on all imports except those granted exemptions under the Encouragement of Industry Law of 1927. Duties on foodstuffs and imported consumer goods saw the highest increases, with those on machinery and industrial raw materials kept relatively low.[16] Apparently, it was initially expected that private entrepreneurs would exploit protection and identify those industries for which there was a secure home market. In fact, in 1929 a group of officials working for the Minister of Economy, Şakir Kesebir, had prepared an economic development plan, putting substantial emphasis on private sector development.[17]

Expectations then changed dramatically, as the global depression shattered confidence in the free-market system's ability to even out periodic downturns in economic activity. In the wake of the depression, agricultural prices collapsed by around 50–60 percent between 1928/9 and 1932/3,[18] with the prospect of overseas capital as the basis of industrialisation virtually eliminated. Like other countries, Turkey moved to a system of managed exchange rates, with the value of the Turkish Lira pegged first to the Pound Sterling (1930–31), then to the French Franc (until 1936) and finally its gold parity as of 1936 (until 1946). Foreign trade was also officially managed by a series of clearing agreements with Germany and Turkey's other main trading partners.[19] Managed or planned economies were meanwhile being promoted in Russia, Germany and Italy, and by 1933 even the United States was experimenting with Roosevelt's 'New Deal' programme. In 1931, the Republican People's Party officially committed itself to an interventionist strategy, by proclaiming etatism (*devletçilik*) as the basis of its economic policy.

In general, the regime was reluctant to define etatism too closely. Diplomatically, it continued the cooperative relationship with the USSR, which had been established during the post-war years, and in 1934 received a Soviet loan worth USD 8 million to finance industrial development. However, Atatürk and his colleagues were careful to distinguish etatism from socialism. Instead, they presented it as a unique and home-grown plant. In the president's words, 'Turkish étatism is not a system translated from the socialist theories developed since the nineteenth century – instead, it is a system that emerges from the specific needs of Turkey – a system peculiar to her'.[20] As a corollary, the Kemalist state promoted the principle of '*halkçılık*' (normally translated as 'populism', but best defined as 'social solidarism') – the idea that Turkey did not have a class-divided society, but one united around national ideals.[21]

What all this meant in practice was spelled out in 1933, when Turkey's first Five-Year Industrialisation Plan was drawn up, to be put into operation in 1934–38.[22] In adopting this programme, no attempt was made to develop an overall plan of economic development, embracing non-industrial sectors, national income, fiscal policy and the like. Instead, the plan limited itself to defining investment and output targets for a range of consumer and intermediate products industries, embracing cotton and wool textiles, paper, ceramics, glass, cement, semicoke and some chemical products. To finance and control the new industries, the state established a development bank, known as Sümerbank ('Sumerian Bank'), which also invested part of its funds in private firms manufacturing textiles, sugar, power generation, ceramics and sulphur. In 1935, it was joined by a second state bank, the Etibank ('Hittite Bank'), which took over the operation of the Zonguldak coalfield from the previous French concessionaires. It later acquired monopoly rights in the mining of iron ore and copper, besides competing with private mining firms in the production of lignite and chromite.

In principle, Etibank and Sümerbank were expected to operate as normal retail banks, opening branches and accepting deposits from the public. In practice, their banking functions were limited, since their initial capital was subscribed by the government, or inherited as the value of previously established factories (in the case of Etibank, mines) which they took over at the start of operations. Later investment capital was derived from reinvested profits,[23] from further direct allocations from the government budget, or from government loans in the form of Treasury-guaranteed bills at the Central Bank.[24] In effect they served as state-owned holding companies with only minor banking functions. The firms they controlled were known as State Economic Enterprises (SEEs), and the administrative arrangements were defined by a special law (No. 3460) passed in 1938. Under this legislation, a General Economic Commission was established under the prime minister and including relevant ministers, members of parliamentary committees and the directors of state banks. The commission undertook an annual review of the finances and operational performance of all enterprises in which the state owned more than 50 percent of the capital. Etibank, Sümerbank and the state Agricultural Bank each had a board of directors appointed by the cabinet, with a general director, who oversaw the managers of individual plants. Article 2 of Law No. 3460 emphasised the legal and financial independence of the SEEs, while Article 3 freed them from certain routine government procedures which were regarded as obstacles to their efficient management. All their employees were paid according to the '*barem*' scale applied to all state bureaucrats. On the positive side, they were independent of the general budget and were supposed to operate independently, much like normal firms aiming to make a profit. In practice, however, their management was top-heavy, subject to frequent political interference and overly bureaucratic.[25]

It is hard to make an exact assessment of the results of the etatist programme, since national income statistics for the period are uncertain and inconsistent. According to estimates by Tuncer Bulutay, Nuri Yıldırım and Yahya S. Tezel,[26] manufacturing output grew by over 11 percent per annum between 1930 and 1939. Against this, recalculations by Şevket Pamuk reduce this figure to 5.2 percent for 1930–39, although, as he admits, the lower rate 'is still remarkable for the decade of the Great Depression'.[27] On the positive side, however, it is also clear that the state-led industrialisation had a significant import-replacement effect in some sectors such as in cotton products, where imports fell from TL 28.5 million in 1930 to TL 17.3 million in 1938, while imports of iron and steel rose from TL 20.2 million to TL 28.2 million, and of machinery from TL 11.7 to 23 million over the same period.[28]

More strikingly, it seems to be generally agreed that, while etatism gave the state a leading role in industrial development, it did not stifle the growth of the private sector, as its critics claimed. Admittedly, among its original proponents, a radical group within the CHP, known as the Cadre (*Kadro*) movement, urged the adoption of etatism as a permanent and preferable alternative to capitalism. Against this, however, government leaders stressed that they did not oppose development of the private sector, and Law No. 3460 included a provision for transferring state-owned enterprises to private capital.[29] Apart from the survival of small, artisanal workshops, which may have accounted for as much as 75–80 percent of manufacturing employment, of the larger industrial firms, which were covered by the Law for the Encouragement of Industry, output by value increased by a multiplier of about 2.4 between 1932 and 1939, with private-sector investment still accounting for around 5 percent of GNP, or about the same as that of the state.[30] In 1939, private firms accounted for 65 percent of cotton products output, 40 percent of wool products, 38 percent of leather and 45 percent of cement production. Sugar production was a *de facto* monopoly of the Turkish Sugar Factories company, set up in 1935 and jointly owned by the para-statal İş-Bank, Sümerbank and private interests, with only paper, artificial silk – and later iron and steel – being entirely produced by state enterprises.[31]

Other evidence suggests that in the pre-war period successful private entrepreneurs often worked closely with the state rather than independently, or against it. Thus, of the eight biographies of leading businessmen surveyed by Ayşe Buğra, the three who were important actors in the 1930s were also active members or supporters of the CHP, and all were quite heavily dependent on contracts from the government or armed services. These included, most notably, Vehbi Koç, founder of what is now one of Turkey's biggest industrial and financial conglomerates.[32] In this way, regardless of ideology, the state connection was vital to the development of the private sector. Although their immediate macroeconomic effects may have been limited, the industries established under etatism played a vital role in future industrial development, by nurturing a new class of technocrats and entrepreneurs and thus providing the human material for Turkey's later industrial revolution.

Wartime Travails, 1939–45

When Atatürk died in November 1938, there was a smooth transfer of the presidency to İsmet İnönü, his former comrade-in-arms and principal lieutenant since 1922, as Turkey remained a single-party state under the CHP. By 1939, nearly all the projects included in the first five-year industrialisation plan had been completed. A notable exception was Turkey's first iron and steel works constructed at Karabük, near the Black Sea, with the help of a GBP 2.5-million loan from Britain, which did not begin production until September 1939.[33] However, further progress was immediately curtailed by the outbreak of war. A second five-year industrialisation plan had been prepared in 1936, to be put into operation in 1939–43,[34] but this remained a dead letter. In October 1939, Turkey signed a tripartite alliance treaty with Britain and France, but in June 1940, following the collapse of France, announced that it would effectively remain neutral.[35] It maintained this stance until February 1945, when it formally declared war on Germany and Japan, so as to qualify for founder-membership of the United Nations.

Thanks to its strategic location, close to the zone of conflict, neutrality could not save Turkey's economy from serious damage. The most immediate effect of the war was on foreign trade. During the 1930s, through clearing agreements offering a ready market for Turkey's exports, but payable only in non-convertible Reichsmarks, Germany came to occupy a dominant role in Turkey's foreign trade, accounting for just over half its total imports, and almost one third of its exports, by 1939. The alliance with Britain and France then forced it to change direction, so that the respective proportions changed to 8.1 percent and 9.2 percent in 1940.[36] With the defeat of France and with Britain fighting alone at the far end of Europe, the western allies were unable to make good the deficit, so that the total volume of foreign trade fell from just under USD 234 million in 1938 to just under USD 131 million in 1940 and USD 146 million in 1941. In October 1941, a new trade agreement (the 'Clodius agreement') was negotiated with Germany, so that the value of imports from Germany recovered, from USD 50 million in 1940 to USD 155 million in 1943, before falling back in 1944–45, thanks to the disruption of trade routes during the war.[37]

The effect was that Turkey was unable to import the machinery and other inputs that it would have needed for further industrial expansion, and that it was forced to concentrate what resources it had on defence. Given the danger of invasion, the army was mobilised, with around one million men conscripted for military service, putting a severe strain on the supply of labour as well as government finances. Due also to the population losses of 1912–23, as well as the demands of an unmechanised agricultural sector, labour was in seriously short supply. In response, under a National Defence Law passed in 1940, thousands of peasant farmers were drafted for forced labour in the Zonguldak coal mines. Factories could oblige their workers to undertake compulsory work and overtime, and they were not allowed to leave their place of employment. This naturally caused intense resentment among those affected, but was also indicative of the severe setbacks suffered in the wartime economy.[38] Inevitably, the National Defence Law and other restrictions increased the role of the state in the national economy at the expense of the private sector, with the output of the State Economic Enterprises increasing by almost 50 percent between 1939 and 1945, compared to a rise of only 7 percent in that of the mechanised private sector.[39] Apart from their easier access to capital, the State Economic Enterprises also enjoyed special privileges in the allocation of foreign exchange, import licences and access to raw materials.[40]

These problems were worsened by mistaken government policies. In wartime conditions, government expenditure exceeded revenue by a wide margin. The state attempted to plug the gap with loans, but only about 10 percent of these were taken up by the public, with the rest absorbed by the banking system, primarily the Central Bank. Deficit financing of the State Economic Enterprises worsened these inflationary pressures. The resulting increase in the money supply produced a rise in the cost-of-living index from a base of 100 in 1938 to 354 in 1945.[41] Since wages failed to keep pace, urban workers experienced a serious drop in living standards. Overall, GNP at constant prices is calculated to have fallen from just over TL 2 billion in 1939 to TL 1.38 billion in 1945 – a drop of almost one third – bringing Turkey's national income back to about where it had been in 1933–34.[42] The sole gain for Turkey was that, thanks to the involuntary restriction of imports, it had built up substantial foreign exchange reserves by the end of the war. This did not mean any immediate benefit for the Turkish people, however. Although İnönü's government could reasonably claim that the economy had been an inevitable victim of wartime conditions, economic losses and the heavy hand of the state had seriously undermined the CHP's public support and thus its political future.

Debate and Transition, 1945–49

In November 1945, worried that the continuation of the single-party regime would effectively cut Turkey out of the post-war international system, President İnönü took the momentous step of announcing that he favoured the establishment of an opposition party. In response, the Democrat Party (DP) was set up by three prominent members of the ruling CHP, Adnan Menderes,

Celal Bayar and Refik Koraltan. Rigged elections kept the Democrats out of power in 1946, but in 1950 they reversed this by winning a massive majority in Turkey's first free general elections. Meanwhile, faced with the threat of territorial aggression by a resurgent USSR, Turkey urgently sought diplomatic and military support from the western powers. This was partly achieved in 1947, when President Truman announced his initial programme of aid to Greece and Turkey under the 'Truman Doctrine', to be followed in 1948 with Turkey's incorporation into the Marshall Aid programme. It culminated in the admission of Turkey and Greece to NATO in 1952.[43]

These changes had fundamental effects on the direction of economic and industrial policy. On the one hand, the DP enjoyed and encouraged the support of a large number of private entrepreneurs who looked for more liberal economic policies and – in some cases, paradoxically – had benefitted from wartime shortages by speculation in commodities. Internationally, also, there was strong pressure for economic liberalisation. In 1950, at the invitation of the government, the International Bank for Reconstruction and Development (IBRD) sent a mission to Turkey, which issued its report in 1951. Apart from the extensive reorganisation of the SEEs, including the delegation of more authority to managers of individual enterprises and better coordination of investment decisions at the top level, the mission recommended measures to encourage the growth of the private industrial sector. It criticised the existing family-owned private firms for acting like merchants more than industrialists, looking for quick speculative profits rather than long-term investment commitments. However, it also urged that the government should clearly define the limits of the state sector, be prepared to privatise some of the SEEs, putting state and private sectors on an equal footing by abolishing special privileges enjoyed by state enterprises and ending direct controls over business and workers' organisations.[44]

Criticisms of the state's role in industrial development went further in another report, this time for the Twentieth Century Fund, prepared by Max Weston Thornburg (a senior executive of Standard Oil of California and adviser to the US State Department) together with Graham Spry and George Soule, and issued in 1949. Thornburg and his colleagues were more trenchant in their criticisms of etatism, claiming that in the 1920s private enterprise had hardly been given a fair trial: 'private enterprise did not fail – it was deliberately discouraged'.[45] During the 1930s, so Thornburg claimed, the government had been under heavy influence from the USSR and Germany and had actively obstructed the growth of private industry.[46] The Karabük iron and steel works came in for very harsh criticism, being dismissed as 'an economic monstrosity' and 'industrial Moloch', in the wrong location and producing the wrong products.[47] In conclusion, Thornburg recommended that US aid should be based on the principle of 'recognition of the right of the individual to both economic and political freedom', and that '[g]overnment funds should not be used in commercial undertakings for which private capital is available with equal or better effect', although private investment could be 'supplemented by state economic activities where necessary' (without giving specific details or examples).[48]

In the post-war years, the nascent Democrat Party's proposals reflected these ideas (whether they had actually helped to inspire them is an open question). The party's programme for 1946 stated that it considered private enterprise to be one of the 'principal elements' of the economy, that the SEEs should not be granted special advantages, and that the limits of the state sector should be clearly defined. In 1947, the ruling CHP tried to follow suit by issuing a 'Turkish Plan for Economic Recovery', expected to run from 1948 to 1952. With a view to enlisting the support of peasant farmers, most of whom favoured the Democrats, this covered agriculture and transport as well as mining and manufacturing. Equally significant was its commitment to the principle that 'private enterprise shall be left free to thrive in all safety in whatever economic spheres it may elect'.[49] The plan even proposed that the state sector should be limited to coal and lignite mining, larger electric power plants, iron and steel, as well as railways and navigation, with all other industries left to private capital, with the existing SEEs to be privatised 'in due course'.[50] The plan was potentially significant, but remained a dead letter. The CHP's eleventh-hour conversion failed to convince the voters, and when Turkey went to the polls on 14 May 1950, the Democrats scored a landslide victory, with Celal Bayar becoming president[51] and Adnan Menderes his prime minister.

The Failed Liberalisation, 1950–60

In their initial wave of public support, Adnan Menderes and his colleagues were committed to the goal of liberalising and expanding the Turkish economy, but with no clear programme for achieving it. Given the conditions at the time, this was not too surprising. As the well-informed observer Dwight J. Simpson remarked in the mid-1960s, the processes of economic development were barely understood in 1950. 'Massive injections of capital, the importation of a few squads of foreign technicians and advisers, forced draft industrialization and of course the creation of great amounts of the evidence of development or of a developed nation: factories, roads, public buildings etc'[52] was thought to be sufficient. Menderes and his team were staunch opponents of economic planning, which the prime minister described as a 'Communist principle'.[53] Initially, his approach was not likely to be rejected by the US authorities who now became Turkey's main military and economic backers. This external support brought with it substantial inflows of foreign aid, mainly from the US government and other US-backed institutions, for the first time in Turkey's history.

In the early years of Democrat rule, Turkey's economic performance started off strongly, as the country benefitted from favourable global and local conditions, as well as increased international assistance. Buoyed by these economic successes, the Democrats retained their majority in the general elections held in 1954 and 1957. Thanks to the substantial foreign exchange reserves built up during the war, followed by a rise in the prices of its main agricultural exports caused by the Korean War, Turkey was able to increase imports from an annual USD 286 million in 1950 to USD 498 million in 1955. Over the same period, the cumulative deficit in the current account came to USD 860 million, with USD 415 million of this being covered by official project and programme aid, and most of the remainder by a drawdown of reserves and increase in the external debt.[54] Aided by good harvests, GNP at constant prices increased at an annual average of 11.5 percent per annum during 1951–53: due to poor weather conditions, GNP fell by 8.8 percent in 1954, before resuming growth at 4.9 percent in 1955.[55]

Thereafter, however, the Turkish economy began to run out of steam. With falling growth, but a savings rate quite inadequate to sustain its investment programme, the government resorted to deficit financing to cover shortfalls in the budget and the SEEs.[56] The increase in the money supply combined with lower increases in output resulted in the rise of the price index from a base of 100 in 1950 to 130 in 1954, and 266 by 1960.[57] Ineffective price controls were introduced in 1955. Government policy worsened these problems by maintaining an artificially high exchange rate for the Lira, holding back exports and meanwhile restricting imports through quotas. This led to a flourishing black market in smuggled goods and an unofficial (in effect, black market) exchange rate several times the official rate.[58] By 1957, a crisis point had been reached, with the foreign debt standing at USD 1,011 million, or over three times the export earnings for that year.[59] In 1958, under pressure from the IMF, the government was finally forced to swallow the bitter pill, by announcing a devaluation of the Lira from TL 2.80 to TL 9.00 to the dollar. Domestically, it was also forced to restrict commercial and Central Bank lending, to raise the prices of SEE products, and withdraw the price controls of 1954. In return, Turkey's main international creditors arranged to reschedule the repayment of USD 422 million of the existing debt over the following eleven years, while Turkey also received USD 359 million in additional credits, mainly from the US.[60] This allowed it to increase import quotas, leading to some economic revival, but the economy was still not out of the woods when the Menderes government was overthrown by a *coup d'état* on 27 May 1960.

Turning to industrial policy, the Democrats' economic liberalisation programme had four main components: first, a commitment to privatising parts (albeit not all) of the state economic sector; second, to 'save productive life from the harmful interferences and bureaucratic obstacles of the state';[61] third, greater freedom for the SEEs to set their own prices and investment programmes, allowing them to behave more like private firms; and fourth, and overall, a greater emphasis on the private sector as the agent of industrial growth, with an increase in foreign direct investment.

On the first score, almost nothing was achieved. In 1951, the State Maritime Lines shipping line was turned over to the Maritime Bank (*Denizcilik Bankası*), but it was reported that by 1958 only a small proportion of the bank's shares had actually been passed to private investors.[62] Far from reducing state interference in private economic activity, the Democrat governments increased it, by controlling the distribution of domestic raw materials, granting import licences, subsidies and price supports to favoured firms.[63]

In their policies towards the SEEs, the Democrats significantly failed to adhere to their liberal, market-oriented principles. Although the state enterprises were supposed to be free to determine their own prices, in practice the government frequently fixed these at artificially low levels. The resulting deficits, as well as finance for new investments, were made good by Central Bank credits.[64] Overall, the direction of state industrial development was determined largely by political considerations. Due to the weakness and fluidity of party allegiances, patron–client relations,[65] rather than economic rationality, became the basis of investment allocations. Frequently, state factories were located far from raw materials, markets or transport links, but where the government needed to bolster its support. Political favourites were appointed to top management positions, and SEEs took on more workers than they needed, so as to boost local support for the government, with some departments in the Sümerbank textile mills recruiting at least twice as many men as they required. In the quest for increased output, two successful import-replacement industries, sugar and cement, in which state and private firms competed, production exceeded domestic demand by a wide margin, so that surpluses had to be dumped on export markets at a loss. In textiles, in which state and private firms again competed, there was also a substantial surplus capacity which was left idle as export markets were undeveloped. The Karabük iron and steel works – the show-case project of the pre-war etatist programme – also operated at well below capacity, as its prices were higher than competitive imports.[66] Overall, at the beginning of the decade, in 1950, private industrial investment accounted for 57 percent of the total, but by 1959 this proportion had fallen to 38 percent, with a consequent rise in that of the state sector – the very opposite of the Democrats' original declared intention.[67] With output growth slower than in the first half of the decade, the conclusion is that increased state industrial investment was yielding steadily lower returns over time.

In an attempt to attract foreign investment, the Industrial Development Bank of Turkey (*Türkiye Sinai Kalkınma Bankası*, or TSKB) was set up in 1950, as a private institution, with support from the World Bank, but foreign exchange resources for investment were limited. Beginning in 1954, a series of laws was passed to encourage private foreign investment, providing for unlimited transfer of profits and capital, but this failed to produce the desired results, as total foreign private investment for 1950–60 inclusive only amounted to USD 101 million, or an annual average of USD 9.2 million. Foreigners' reluctance to invest was explained by the country's economic instability, cumbersome bureaucracy and difficulties in obtaining raw materials and spare parts – problems similar to those faced by Turkish firms.[68]

Meanwhile, the expectation that private firms would necessarily be more efficient than the SEEs was not necessarily born out in practice. As already noticed, in leading industries such as textiles, sugar and cement, privately-owned factories – and there were also many state-private partnerships – were as prone as the state establishments to over-production and idle capacity. As in previous years, the private sector was dominated by small firms. In 1959, it was calculated that the average number of workers in private firms employing ten or more workers was sixty-seven (as compared to 575 in the case of state enterprises), and there were an estimated 60,000 firms employing less than ten workers. Private industrial firms were mostly family-owned, with the families jealously guarding their control and often reluctant to adopt efficient management practices. The lack of a capital market was another serious handicap.[69]

This said, the growth of the private sector could not be ignored and had a critical role in enhancing human capital, by aiding the rise of a technocratic-*cum*-entrepreneurial middle class, with important implications for subsequent development. The SEEs trained their employees in the most advanced production techniques, who were then attracted to private firms with higher salaries.[70] During the decade, family-owned firms which later became the giants of Turkish industry, moved from trading into large-scale manufacturing – notable examples include the Sabancı company which in this period established the corner-stone BOSSA textile factory in Adana with finance from the Industrial Development Bank, and the Koç company which established the Otosan plant to assemble Ford vehicles, as the start of Turkey's now-flourishing automotive industry.[71] In 1989, of the 405 firms which were members of the Turkish Association of Industrialists and Businessmen (Tüsiad), representing the large enterprises in Turkish industry, forty-nine had been set up during the 1950s, compared to just nineteen during the previous thirty years.[72] The Democrat Party's industrialisation policy, such as it was, had been erratic, unpredictable and flawed by serious errors in economic policy generally. Yet, it showed results that helped to lay some of the foundations of a modern industrial economy.

The Second Planning Period: Progress, Adaptation and Collapse, 1960–80

With the *coup d'état* of 27 May 1960, Turkey's domestic politics experienced an abrupt change of direction, with the apparent return to power of the military-*cum*-bureaucratic élite which had dominated Turkish politics prior to 1950. Within the military junta which ruled the country until November 1961, there was a radical group of younger officers who apparently aimed to institute a long-term military regime, but these were ousted in November 1960. This cleared the way for a return to elected civilian government, but only after the execution of Menderes and two of his colleagues on very dubious grounds in September 1961. On the positive side, Turkey was invested within a democratic constitution providing, *inter alia*, for enhanced civil liberties, and a two-chamber legislature with a mainly-elected senate. A new electoral law also introduced proportional representation for national elections, the first of which were duly held on 15 October 1961.[73]

Sadly, hopes that this would provide for stable democratic government were left unrealised. At the centre of Turkish party politics, the two dominant identities of the pre-coup years continued, with the statist-modernist alignment represented by the Republican People's Party (CHP) led by the veteran İsmet İnönü, and the liberal-conservative Justice Party (*Adalet Partisi*, or AP), set up in 1961 as the successor to the Democrat Party, led from 1964 onwards by Süleyman Demirel. However, the change in the electoral system also allowed a host of smaller parties to win seats in parliament. These included Islamist, socialist and ultra-nationalist parties, besides splinter groups based on personal rivalries, or local power-brokers. To add to the confusion, elements in the military had never accepted the restoration of civilian rule in 1961 and were ready to make a further bid for power. Within the Justice Party, Demirel provided continuity of leadership, but the CHP was split between an older etatist-nationalist element and a younger group who wished to re-orient the party in a socialist or social-democrat direction. As party leader, İnönü accepted the adoption of a 'left of centre' programme in 1965, but this split the CHP and led to his ouster in 1972, as well as his replacement by the younger and more identifiably leftist Bülent Ecevit. Ecevit gave the party a more dynamic leadership but was unable to re-establish it as a stable party of government.

Contrary to the expectations of the junta, the CHP failed to win a majority in the first post-*coup* elections held in October 1961, and İnönü was forced into an unwieldy coalition government with the Justice Party. Predictably, this fell apart in June 1962, leaving İnönü with the only other option of a minority government, in coalition with the minor New Turkey Party, and independents. When this collapsed in February 1965, a caretaker government was formed under the independent Senator Suat Hayrı Ürgüplü, pending general elections held in the following October. These were won by the Justice Party with a convincing majority. His successful performance as premier allowed Demirel to win a second election victory in October 1969. By 1971, however, the government was running into serious security problems, with a wave of strikes and terrorist attacks by ultra-leftist groups, as well as growing opposition within the military establishment. On 12 March, in a successful bid to head off a coup by radicals from within their own ranks, the commanders of the armed forces issued a 'memorandum', forcing Demirel to resign, giving way to a supposedly 'supra-party' civilian government which followed the off-stage directions of the military chiefs.[74]

During the summer of 1973 the '12 March regime' fell apart, following disagreements among the military commanders, and general elections were held on 14 October. Unfortunately, these failed to result in stable and effective government, with both the CHP and AP leaders forced to form coalitions from among a host of minor parties. Among these were the National Salvation Party, Turkey's first overtly Islamist political party to win parliamentary representation which, like other small political parties, switched sides between the CHP and AP. The next elections were held in June 1977, but with a similar outcome. The result was that between January 1973 and the end of 1979 Turkey had no less than seven successive governments and long periods under caretaker governments with no parliamentary mandate. Meanwhile, terrorism and political instability almost brought the country to its knees. By the end of the decade, Turkey seemed to be drifting into systemic disintegration, with gun-slinging militants of both left and right taking over whole city districts and a death toll of 898 between December 1978 and September 1979 steadily rising to 2,812 during the following twelve months. The economic collapse, which is explained below, must be seen against this background of political paralysis, leading to Turkey's third military takeover on 12 September 1980.

The beginning, and eventual collapse, of industrial planning in Turkey was fundamentally affected by these changing political fortunes. The planning principle was the child of the military regime of 1960, and its belief that the economic chaos of the late Menderes years could be cured by a more rational and coherent approach to both state and private investment. There was also broad international support for the planned approach to economic development, born essentially from experiences since the great depression and post-war reconstruction. In this way, 'planning' referred not just to industrial development, but a planned approach to the economy as a whole (See Box 2.1: 'The SPO: The Early Years').

Such was the initial confidence in its efficacy that the planning concept was actually written into Turkey's new constitution of 1961 in which Article 129 stated that 'economic, social and cultural development is based on a plan. Development is carried out according to this plan'.[75] In fact, in September 1960, the military-controlled government had already issued a Law concerning the Establishment of the State Planning Organisation (SPO) (Law No. 91). Under this legislation, the SPO was to be attached to the Prime Minister's Office and headed by the Under-Secretary for Planning. Its top decision-making body was the High Planning Council, consisting of the prime minister (or his deputy), three other cabinet ministers, the under-secretary and the three heads of the Economic Planning, Social Planning and Coordination Departments of the Central Planning Organisation of the SPO. The required procedure was that the High Planning Council would first decide on the general strategy of the plan, which would be submitted to the cabinet for approval, and then elaborated by the Central Planning Council. The final draft of the plan would then be sent to the cabinet and the parliament for final approval, being considered binding for the government and public administration. In this way, authority over the provisions of the plan was effectively divided between the government and the technocrats of the SPO, with the former given the final say.[76]

From the start, the SPO was expected to prepare a series of three Five-Year Economic Development Plans, to run from 1963 to 1967, 1968 to 1972 and 1973 to 1977, within the framework of a fifteen-year 'perspective plan'.[77] In formulating the plans, increasing GNP by 7 percent per annum was posited as the major target and independent variable of their model, with all other magnitudes adjusted accordingly.[78] Since Turkey's population was now growing at an annual rate of around 2.75 percent,[79] the creation of extra productive employment opportunities was cited as the second objective, followed by the ambitious aim of eliminating the balance of payments deficit, the realisation of social justice and the reduction of regional imbalances, particularly between south-eastern Anatolia and the rest of the country.[80] The planners used a Harrod-Domar growth model, calculating the marginal capital-output ratio, times the required level of investment to reach the required growth rate. The level of savings needed to realise this investment was then calculated as expected domestic savings, plus the external resource requirement (that is, foreign aid plus private investment). Having calculated the planned total investment and output targets, their distribution between different sectors was then determined as the value added within each sector plus the inputs from other sectors, with the marginal capital-output ratio for each sector then used to calculate the level of investment required. Projects which would meet each of the sectoral targets were finally evaluated, with constant trial and error adjustments made to correct earlier calculations.[81]

Central to the planning process was its approach to the respective roles of the state and private sectors in industrial development. According to the 'Objectives and Strategy' of the First Plan the 'Turkish economy is a mixed economy, where public and private enterprise function side by side. The planning activities should exploit all the opportunities provided by the mixed economy and the rules of this system shall be applied'.[82] However, it did not say what the 'rules' were: as R. Hammaş has remarked, 'is there such a system and are there any such rules?'[83] A crucial aspect of the plan was the proposed treatment of the State Economic Enterprises. On this score, the 'Objectives and Strategy' of the First Plan required the SEEs to be 'fund producers' – that is, sources of revenue which could then be used for investment. Essentially, the plan repeated the provisions of Law No. 3460 of 1938, by requiring them to be managed autonomously, adding that 'new arrangements will be made which will promote unity in working and control methods and other administrative matters',[84] but again without saying how these apparently conflicting objectives were to be realised.

The first plan also envisaged an expansion of private investment, at the annual rate of 11 percent, so as to reach 8 percent of GNP by 1967 (the target for the state sector being 10.6 percent). It expected the private business sector to shift away from housing construction to productive industries, concentrating on those industries specified in the plan. The government could not force the private sector to comply with these expectations, but had various means of influencing private industrial development, primarily through import measures, not just through tariffs but more particularly import quotas. In this way, new industrial developments were primarily aimed at import substitution.

However, the planners still stopped short of defining any boundaries between state and private enterprise, claiming that 'it is neither necessary nor possible to draw a definite line between the activities of the public and private sectors'.[85]

Needless to say, implementation of the plans was seriously affected by the changing political environment. Although Süleyman Demirel and his colleagues did not reject the planning principle as such, the Justice Party appealed primarily to those who had supported Menderes to the end. For the party's grassroots supporters, the SPO and all its works were essentially seen as the work of the military junta and thus regarded with grave suspicion. In his introduction to the second plan, issued in 1967, Demirel stated that it would be 'imperative' for the public sector, but have a purely 'indicative character' for private entrepreneurs. The plan document also stated that the plan would enable private business to take over the development of the manufacturing industry 'in the long run', although not specifically saying that the SEEs would be privatised.[86]

By the mid-1970s, the entire planning process was being fundamentally affected by political instability, followed by external shocks and chronic mismanagement by the succession of weak coalition governments. During the first two planning periods, annual GNP growth, at 6.7 percent and 7.1 percent, respectively, came close to (in the second case slightly above) the planners' 7-percent target. During the third plan period (1973–77), the annual target was raised to 7.9 percent. This compared to an actual growth rate of 6.5 percent – short of the target, but still an apparently respectable performance.[87] The fourth plan period should have begun in 1978, but due to disagreements within Demirel's government and its succession by another feeble coalition led by Ecevit, its appearance was delayed. Accordingly, an interim plan for 1978 was issued, to be followed by a fourth plan, expected to run from 1979 to 1983.[88]

While aggregate growth appeared to be broadly in line with the plan targets during the first three plan periods, there were still some serious miscalculations and upsets as well as basic strategic mistakes. The achieved aggregate GNP growth rate hid the fact that in the vital industrial sector – expected to be the main generator of growth – output was consistently below the plan targets,[89] with the gap made good by house construction and services – the opposite of the plan's stated objectives. In 1970, Demirel's government was faced with the prospect of a large budget deficit as the result of civil service reform, and a serious foreign exchange shortfall. It sought to meet the challenge by a round of tax increases, combined with a 66-percent devaluation of the Lira (See Chapter 3) and measures to incentivise exports. These needed changes were eventually implemented, but they provoked a widespread rebellion by Justice Party supporters in the private sector, who splintered from the party to join what became known as the National Order Party (later re-named National Salvation Party),[90] led by Necmettin Erbakan. With its somewhat odd mixture of Islamist-populism and a commitment to state-led industrial growth, Erbakan's party ended the Justice Party's domination of the conservative stream in Turkish politics, becoming a major cause of the intense political instability of the 1970s, hence of a near-collapse of state power, and the later wave of terrorist attacks by political extremists.[91]

Growing political paralysis was exacerbated by external shocks and serious policy failures. At the beginning of 1974, thanks to a temporary boom in exports following the 1970 devaluation, plus a fortuitous inflow of remittances from expatriate workers who had begun to flow into West Germany and other European countries in the 1960s, Turkey's foreign exchange reserves reached a record high.[92] Turkey, like other oil-importing countries, was then hit by the oil price explosion of 1974, followed by a further round of price hikes in 1979. Energy consumption had meanwhile been growing apace, particularly that of oil, of which Turkey had very limited domestic supplies. By 1975, the bill for oil imports was equivalent to just under 30 percent of total export earnings, plus emigrants' remittances, rising to 44 percent in 1978. Rather than devalue the Lira, the government maintained an artificially high exchange rate, which discouraged exports while artificially reducing the prices of imports. Following the devaluation by Demirel's government in 1970, until 1978 the official exchange rate was held at around TL 14 to TL 19 to the dollar, but in the meantime its purchasing power parity (that is, roughly, the free market rate) increased from TL 21 to TL 42 to the dollar.

There were subsequent devaluations of the Lira, but these failed to keep pace with the collapse of its free market value, so that by 1980 the disparity was almost 100 percent (TL 169 compared to an official rate of TL 79). The result was a huge increase in the current account balance of payments deficit, from USD 720 million in 1974 to USD 3,426 million in 1977, before import restrictions produced an enforced reduction of the deficit to USD 1,420 million in 1978 and USD 1,800 million in 1979. To cover these deficits, the government had to resort to massive foreign borrowing, often at high interest rates. From around USD 1,9 billion in 1970, the total outstanding foreign debts rose to USD 14.6 billion in 1979. By the time the last Demirel government took over in October 1979, it found that the Central Bank's disposable cash reserves stood at USD 30 million, or just enough for two days' worth of imports. With the enforced restriction in imports and the general loss of business confidence, industrial output fell in 1979 and 1980, producing an absolute fall in GNP of 0.6 percent and 2.4 percent in each of the two years. Meanwhile, flimsy governments tried to shore up their electoral support by running budget deficits and covering losses in the SEEs by Central Bank lending. The resultant increase in the money supply, combined with the fall in constant-price GNP, produced runaway inflation, with the GNP deflator rising from just above 16 percent in 1976–77, 48 percent in 1978 and almost 70 percent in 1979–80.[93] The government attempted to soften the blow for consumers by price controls, but these simply drove goods into the black market, as producers could not cover their costs at the officially fixed prices. By the winter of 1979, the economy was in a state of virtual paralysis, as drivers waited in long queues for the scanty supplies of fuel, and families shivered in their homes, bereft of heating oil.

Some Conclusions and Implications

The crisis of the late 1970s, together with Turkey's overall experiences since World War II, highlight important features of Turkish society and political culture, as well as fundamental shortcomings of the way in which import-substitution industrialisation strategy had been implemented, with little focus on exports and a mixed economy which had been applied since the 1930s. From the Ottoman Empire Turkey inherited the tradition of a strong and autonomous state, unchallenged by a feudal landowning aristocracy or a powerful mercantile class.[94] Hence, the state retained a powerful economic role, even when governments were supposedly committed to reducing it, as under the Democrats in the 1950s. However, this historical legacy meant that institutions mediating between the state and business remained weak and dependent on personalised patronage relations. Equally, the argument that the state opposed the development of a free market economy, advanced by

Thornburg and others, is contradicted by the experiences of Turkey's leading industrialists, which suggests something of a symbiotic relationship between private business and the state, with large firms looking to the state for privileges as well as markets. For business, with the exception of a few periods such as the 1960s, the problem was not that the state played a powerful role in economic development, but that it lacked a coherent or systematically planned strategy for achieving it, frequently and arbitrarily changing track for short-term political gains by the politicians who controlled it and failing to draw any clear frontier between areas of activity for which either the state or the private sector would be responsible.[95] These problems came to the fore by the end of the 1960s. Although Demirel and his government paid lip service to the planning principle, in practice the provisions of the plan were increasingly ignored in the process of economic decision-making.[96] In its place, with crucial decisions made by politicians rather than state bureaucrats, they were made purely *ad hoc* and often on the basis of outright favouritism. The associated uncertainty that this created undermined long-term investment for industrial development. This is a key theme of this study, which will be also seen in later years, suggesting that the problem is not one of 'how much' state intervention in the economy but 'how the government intervenes and for what purpose' (See Chapter 1).

The second theme of this study, as shown in the analysis within this chapter, consists of the problem of industrial development paradigms becoming trapped in dichotomies, such as import-substituting versus export-oriented industrialisation. In Turkey's case, the problem with the pursuit of import substitution was that it was not at the same time combined with policies incentivising business towards export orientation, as happened in the Asian economies at that time. ISI had managed to establish a reasonably diverse industrial base for Turkey, composed of state-owned heavy industry and private sector led consumer goods industries – but it was not globally competitive. Moreover, industry remained highly import-dependent on capital goods – a problem that became increasingly difficult to overcome. A strategic missed opportunity was that the devaluation in 1970 and the export-incentivising measures adopted were not followed through (more on this in Chapter 3). Instead, import-substituting industrialisation strategy with its elaborate apparatus of protection for infant industries, fixed exchange rates and foreign currency controls, protective tariffs and import quotas, price controls and subsidisation of favoured industries, was continued on its own. The fault was not entirely on the government side, since Turkey's infant industries were also very reluctant to get up out of their prams, preferring rent-seeking behind protective barriers to the rigours (and possible benefits) of competing in global markets with exports. To set up a new factory, the first thing an entrepreneur needed to do would be to persuade the government to put up protective barriers against the import of competitive products. Having done so, he could be assured of a comfortable domestic market, regardless of his cost base. If he needed to import certain intermediate products, then the overvalued Lira meant that he could obtain them at artificially low cost.[97] Domestic consumers were thus left with artificially expensive products, perhaps of low quality. As Henri Barkey has commented, 'the reaping of economic rents cushioned everyone, especially industrialists, from the vagaries of international competition and prevented the formulation of new ideas in favour of maintaining the status quo'.[98] By 1979, in the face of the general economic collapse, even parts of the business community, notably the bigger firms that were members of Tüsiad, were re-considering their support for import-substitution policies.[99] In this way, some time before the *coup d'état* of 12 September 1980, the ground was already being prepared for a radical change in Turkey's industrialisation strategy.

Box 2.1 SPO: The Early Years . . . An Insider's View

Brian Beeley (OECD Research Fellow, SPO 1962–64)

The State Planning Organization (Devlet Planlâma Teşkilâtı), established in Ankara only four months after the coup of 27 May 1960, was a remarkable venture in comprehensive national development. It was distinguished by its commanding position in the hierarchy of authority – reporting directly not only to the Prime Minister, but also to the Grand National Assembly through the High Planning Council. The pre-eminent status of the SPO in its early years was visibly underscored by its very location within the buildings of the Parliament (*Meclis*), looking down to Ataturk

Boulevard and the spread of ministries and agencies. SPO workers at their desks during the 1960s were supplied with tea and toast by soldiers of the parliamentary guard while one might receive a 'Good Morning' from Prime Minister İnönü in a corridor or meeting room.

Also remarkable was the working atmosphere within the SPO where young Turkish planners brought their enthusiasm and their qualifications back from Europe and North America to work alongside established members of the civil service. To this mix were added foreign specialists from the United States – notably the Agency for International Development (AID), the United Nations, the Paris-based Organization for Economic Cooperation and Development (OECD) and many other agencies and governments. Some of these 'consultants' might be found working late into the night with their Turkish counterparts. All this seemed consistent with the national mood of a westward-looking, industrialising Turkey in the 1960s and 1970s with a dash of Turkish hospitality enabling non-Muslim foreign experts to receive gifts – and the day off – on 25 December. SPO cooperation also developed with local institutions, most notably universities such as the new Middle East Technical University.[100]

Much was made of the need to strengthen the role of private business initiative in the comprehensive development scheme – especially by AID – but there was also a sense in Ankara during the 1960s that the first priority was to get a state-led system mobilized and 'to promote social welfare'.[101] At the same time much was heard about industrialisation and impressive rates of economic growth. One element of this was concern about the range of State Economic Enterprises. This proved to be one of the areas where SPO proposals for reorganization were rejected by the High Planning Council.[102]

The role and special status of the SPO were publicized by government, particularly after work began on the First Plan. Turkish and foreign planners explained what they were doing on radio and in the press. Such was the image of the SPO that its members might expect quick attention when they visited ministries in search of information or to discuss plan priorities and procedures. Perhaps it was the success of image-building of the Plan which led a farmer, from a village near Antalya, to visit the SPO one day in

1964 to ask when 'development' was likely to arrive in his home area. His appearance prompted a small group of startled planners to meet with him.

A key feature of the Plan model was the trio of departments, economic planning, social planning, and coordination. The equality of status of the 'social' reflected a recognition of the impact of the changes increasingly evident in Turkish society at this time when Turks were looking to Europe. Would-be workers in search of visas lined up outside the German and other embassy offices in central Ankara. Signs of the rural-urban migration which was to come were apparent. Most obvious to the planners were the disparities in material well-being between sections of society and parts of the country. Perhaps a major concern was the divide between the conservative elements which had supported the administration displaced in 1960 and the modernisers who represented the new Turkey.

Planners discussed the implications of regional aspects of development aware of the paradox that return on investment can be expected to be greater where there is already an infrastructural basis for growth. How to match this with the much-publicized removal of unequal access to national wealth? Some saw the system of provinces (*iller*) as restricting the extent to which plans could be based on local realities rather than administrative boundaries, given the direct links between individual provinces and Ankara. SPO thinking was to build cooperative 'regional' schemes linking provinces-and even parts of provinces. Inevitably such research produced factual survey data plus identification of needs which differed according to particular local development potentials. Areas surveyed included Antalya (with UN Food and Agriculture Organization, FAO, input), Eastern Thrace (OECD), the Çukurova (AID, SPO and others) and the ambitious Keban study from 1964 in south-east Turkey (SPO and local planners). In the case of the Zonguldak study, led by the Ministry of Reconstruction and the SPO in the early 1960s, there was a special focus on industrial potential (coal, iron, steel).

The range of pre-investment surveys and local 'plans' quickly pointed up the need for broad-ranging and consistent data collection and sophisticated analysis. Soon planners thought up approaches which moved away from existing structures to involve schemes for 'growth hubs', 'central villages' etc. Community development at village level was tried in some places, with help from the United Nations, while the Ministry of Village Affairs, set up in 1964, aimed to target rural-urban imbalances. Meanwhile, in those same early SPO years, some influential figures remained doubtful about the very notion of 'regionalism', concerned that it might be a route to separatism. Indeed in 1965 activities were moved from the Social to the Economic branch of the SPO and words such as 'environmental', for some time, replaced concern with regions *per se*.[103]

From the 1970s it was increasingly recognized that the pattern of uneven development across Turkey was geographically complex. Parts of more 'developed' provinces were clearly not so, while there were evident pockets of progress in the east of the country. One response was to identify provinces and parts thereof as 'underdeveloped' and to allocate them special investment, tax holidays, and other support. It was hoped that visible improvement in such – mainly rural – areas would reduce levels of migration to burgeoning towns and cities.

Turkish planners were keen to be involved in international research initiatives. Just one of these was the Mediterranean Regional Project,[104] coordinated by the OECD, in which young planners from a range of countries and training backgrounds combined to find ways to forecast the skill levels required to meet planned development objectives. The SPO, representing Turkey, was among countries taking part and welcomed planners from Canada, Italy, France and the United Kingdom to work alongside Turkish colleagues. Part of this work in the SPO involved identifying the future need for training establishments which would produce the vital cadres of graduates. Immediately, such an approach to planning highlighted the likelihood that changes in the political, ideological or economic basis of government would make it unlikely that a scheme requiring predictable investment levels over a decade or more could work reliably.

Much of the routine work of the SPO involved the collection of the survey data and reports in a significant library, along with work on the ongoing debates about planning methodology. One important spin-off of this effort was improvement in the State Institute of Statistics (Devlet İstatistik Enstitüsü). Hitherto checks on the accuracy of collected data had often been inadequate; frequently figures in reports from government agencies for personnel numbers had been the 'official' staffing levels rather than the real ones. The same applied to inventories of equipment and property. Having said that, the plans themselves sometimes retained a certain aspirational optimism in place of verifiable measurement.

As the working systems of the new SPO developed there was special excitement about the compilation of the First Plan itself and its translation into English. Here some of the anglophone staff were called on to assist. Turkish colleagues faced the additional requirements from the Turkish Language Organization (Türk Dil Kurumu) for elements of language reform. Most notable were proposals to replace words of Arabic origin with authentic Turkish forms. For example, the word *ziraat* for agriculture was to be restricted to the name of the eponymous bank and was to be replaced more generally by *tarım*. The new word *tarım*, along with many other changes, *then* required explanation to local officials when they were handed a printed survey about agricultural extension staffing levels and problems in south-eastern Anatolia!

The innovative, outward-looking 'think-tank' nature of the SPO was largely true of the 1960s and into the 1970s. In those years the mix of Turkish and foreign staff working across the organization produced a special energy and enthusiasm. One of the visiting consultants, Professor Jan Tinbergen, from the Netherlands, acquired a particularly high measure of respect enabling him to work across the departments of the SPO. For the younger staff, he and others like him provided something of the constructive support one might expect in a university.

But, even in those early years, there were inevitable problems in the function of the new SPO. Most fundamental was finance – or the shortage of it. Early during the period of the First Plan the heads of the three departments resigned (with much publicity) because of concerns about financial priorities – although they were replaced, and the work of the Plan continued. It was also clear at the time that the very special status and relative autonomy of the SPO was not to the liking of some established elements in the civil service who resented it as an imposition and an intrusion on civil service custom. Some civil servants brought with them experience in the previous decade where there was no SPO-equivalent. Others resented the role of younger planners and foreign consultants.

The five-year plans continued to appear during the 1970s and subsequently, but the SPO lost much of that which had made it original. Its commanding status in the government system was changed. It moved down from its offices in the parliament buildings to a typical ministry-style location. Planning continued mostly as an aspirational document and without the authority and pivotal role of the early SPO. The national planning function was shunted around from one ministry to another and ultimately subsumed in the Ministry of Development set up in 2011. But this too was terminated in 2018 and responsibility for the five-year plans transferred to the Strategy and Budget Committee of the Presidential Administration. But the recognition of the merits of comprehensive planning sporadically reappears with calls for the re-establishment of the SPO.

Was the very nature of coordinated, multi-sector planning a step too far in the 1960s? Was the special, authoritative status of the SPO in its early years at odds with the conventional structure of the Turkish civil service and state agencies? Or were changes in national political and ideological priorities too frequent to allow measures planned for fifteen or more years to achieve their objectives? Certainly, the Turkey of the 1960s and 1970s had a more coherent orientation towards Europe and the West than in recent years. Within the country the state-private sector balance has evolved. It might be hard to envisage today the kind of open-door think-tank combination research and priority-setting unit which was the SPO in its early years.

Notes

1. Ayşe Buğra, *State and Business in Modern Turkey: A Comparative Study* (Albany: SUNY Press, 1994), p. 11.
2. The writer has given a fuller account of events in this section in William Hale, *The Political and Economic Development of Modern Turkey* (Beckenham: Croom Helm, 1981; repr. Abingdon: Routledge, 2014), pp. 33–52. For the full text of Atatürk's speech, see Gündüz Ökçün, *Türkiye İktisat Kongresi 1923 – İzmir* (Ankara: Ankara University Political Science Faculty, 1968), pp. 243–56.

3. William Hale, *The Political and Economic Development of Modern Turkey* (Beckenham: Croom Helm, 1981; repr. Abingdon: Routledge, 2014), p. 36.

4. That is, the First and Second Balkan Wars (1912–13), the World War I (1914–18) and the Greek-Turkish War (1919–22).

5. Approximate estimates by the writer, from data in T. Lefebre, 'La densité de la population en Turquie en 1914 et en 1927', *Annales de Géographie*, Vol. 37, No. 210 (1928), p. 520, and Ahmet İçduygu, Şule Toktaş and B. Ali Soner, 'The Politics of Population in a Nation-Building Process: Emigration of Non-Muslims from Turkey', *Ethnic and Racial Studies*, Vol. 31, No. 2 (2008), pp. 363, 368.

6. Ahmet İçduygu, Şule Toktas and B. Ali Soner, 'The Politics of Population in a Nation-Building Process: Emigration of Non-Muslims from Turkey', *Ethnic and Racial Studies*, Vol. 31, No. 2 (2008), p. 368. According to the Republic's first census, carried out in 1927, the Armenian population of Turkey stood at 77,000; ibid.

7. Ayşe Buğra, *State and Business in Modern Turkey: A Comparative Study* (Albany: SUNY Press, 1994), p. 39.

8. *Treaty of Peace with Turkey and other Instruments signed at Lausanne on July 24, 1923: Commercial Convention* (London: HMSO, 1923), p. 157.

9. Şevket Pamuk, 'Turkey's Response to the Great Depression in Comparative Perspective, 1929–1939', European University Institute, Florence, EUI Working Paper No. 2000/21, 2000, p. 8.

10. An exception was that of the Greek minority in Istanbul, which was originally excluded from the population exchanges. This largely survived until the 1950s.

11. According to several accounts, the capital was derived from part of the funds originally sent by the Indian Muslims to aid the nationalists in the war against the Greeks: see Lord Kinross, *Ataturk: The Rebirth of a Nation* (London: Weidenfeld and Nicolson, 1964), p. 448, and Ünal Somuncuoğlu, 'Atatürk'ün Vasiyeti, İş Bankası Hisse Senetleri ve Cumhuriyet Halk Partisi', http://www.unalsomuncuoglu.net/ataturkun-vasiyeti-is-bankasi-hisse-senetleri-ve-cumhuriyet-halk...

12. Korkut Boratav, *Türkiye'de Devletçilik* (Istanbul: Gerçek Yayınevi, 1974), pp. 31–34, 37, 115–17; Z. Y. Hershlag, *Turkey: An Economy in Transition* (The Hague: van Keulen, 1958), pp. 66–67.

13. Korkut Boratav, *Türkiye'de Devletçilik* (Istanbul, Gerçek Yayınevi, 1974), pp. 111–20. For the later development of the tobacco monopoly, see Özgür Burçak Gürsoy, 'Struggle over Regulation in the Turkish Tobacco Market: The Failure of Institutional Reform, 1936–1960', *Middle Eastern Studies*, Vol. 16, No. 4 (2015), pp. 588–607.

14. Korkut Boratav, *Türkiye'de Devletçilik* (Istanbul, Gerçek Yayınevi, 1974), pp. 31–34, 115–17.

15. Data based on estimates by Tuncer Bulutay, Nuri Yıldırım and Yahya S. Tezel, *Türkiye Milli Geliri (1923–1948)* (Ankara University, Political Science Faculty, 1974), Tables 8.2c and 8.1: see William Hale, *The Political and Economic Development of Modern Turkey* (Beckenham: Croom Helm, 1981; repr. Abingdon: Routledge, 2014), pp. 46, 47–48.

16. Şevket Pamuk, 'Turkey's Response to the Great Depression in Comparative Perspective, 1929–1939', European University Institute, Florence, EUI Working Paper No. 2000/21, 2000, p. 8; Z. Y. Hershlag, *Turkey: An Economy in Transition* (The Hague: van Keulen, 1958), p. 82.

17. Text in İlhan Tekeli and Selim İlkin, *1929 Dünya Buhranında Türkiye İktisadi Politika Arayışları* (Ankara, Middle East Technical University, 1977), pp. 229–559.

18. Şevket Pamuk, 'Turkey's Response to the Great Depression in Comparative Perspective, 1929–1939', European University Institute, Florence, EUI Working Paper No. 2000/21, 2000, p. 7.

19. William Hale, *The Political and Economic Development of Modern Turkey* (Beckenham: Croom Helm, 1981; repr. Abingdon: Routledge, 2014), pp. 72–73.

20. From Atatürk's Preface to the Second Industrialisation Plan, reprinted in Afet İnan, *Türkiye Cumhuriyetinin İkinci Sanayi Planı* (Ankara, Türk Tarih Kurumu, 1973), page following p. ix.

21. This argument raised a theoretical problem – if Turkey did not have a class-divided society, then why was a non-capitalist development path required to prevent it? This principle was given legal force when Article 141 of the Penal Code was extended by a clause making it illegal to engage in any activities aiming to 'establish the hegemony or domination of a social class over the other social classes, or eliminate a social class, or overthrow any of the social or economic orders established within the country' (this clause was not withdrawn until 2005). 'Etatism', along with 'populism', as two of the 'six arrows' of the CHP's ideology, was written into the constitution in 1937. The author has discussed these and other ideological issues a greater length in William Hale, 'Ideology and Economic Development in Turkey, 1930–1945', *British Society of Middle Eastern Studies Bulletin*, Vol. 7, No. 2 (1980), pp. 103–8, 110–13,

22. For details of the plan, see Afet İnan, *Devletçilik İlkesi ve Türkiye Cumhuriyetinin Birinci Sanayi Planı, 1933* (Ankara: Türk Tarih Kurumu, 1972).

23. Since the two banks did not have to pay dividends to the government (receiving, in effect, a large state subsidy), almost all profits should have been available for reinvestment.

24. International Bank for Reconstruction and Development [IBRD], *The Economy of Turkey: An Analysis and Recommendations for a Development Program* (Baltimore: Johns Hopkins Press, for IBRD, 1951), pp. 152–55.

25. Ibid., pp. 152–53, 156. H. Hammaş, 'The Plan and the State Economic Enterprises', in S. İlkin and E. İnanç, eds, *Planning in Turkey (Selected Papers)* (Ankara: Middle East Technical University, Faculty of Administrative Sciences, 1967), p. 137. Different arrangements applied to what were known as Annexed Budget Institutions, such as the state railways administration (TCDD) and the state monopolies, which were taken over by the government from the previous foreign concessionaires. These were attached directly to the Ministry of Communications and the Ministry of Customs and Monopolies, with their revenues turned over to the Treasury. Their operational expenditures, depreciation and investments were voted for annually in an Annexed Budget attached to the government's general budget, so that they effectively operated as government departments; see William Hale, *The Political and Economic Development of Modern Turkey* (Beckenham: Croom Helm, 1981; repr. Abingdon: Routledge, 2014), pp. 41–42.

26. Tuncer Bulutay, Nuri Yıldırım and Yahya S. Tezel, *Türkiye Milli Geliri (1923–1948)* (Ankara: Ankara University, Political Science Faculty, 1974) Tables 8.2c and 8.1; see William Hale, *The Political and Economic Development of Modern Turkey* (Beckenham: Croom Helm, 1981; repr. Abingdon: Routledge, 2014), p. 76.

27. Şevket Pamuk, 'Turkey's Response to the Great Depression in Comparative Perspective, 1929–1939', European University Institute, Florence, EUI Working Paper No. 2000/21, 2000, Table 2, p. 24.

28. Max Weston Thornburg, Graham Spry and George Soule, *Turkey: An Economic Appraisal* (New York: The Twentieth Century Fund, 1949), p. 278, Table 31.

29. For further details and discussion, see William Hale, 'Ideology and Economic Development in Turkey, 1930–1945', *British Society of Middle Eastern Studies Bulletin,* Vol.7, No.2 (1980), pp. 105–8.

30. Şevket Pamuk, 'Turkey's Response to the Great Depression in Comparative Perspective, 1929–1939', European University Institute, Florence, EUI Working Paper No. 2000/21, 2000, p.11.

31. Z. Y. Hershlag, *Turkey: An Economy in Transition* (The Hague: van Keulen, 1958), p. 120.

32. Ayşe Buğra, *State and Business in Modern Turkey: A Comparative Study* (Albany: SUNY Press, 1994), pp. 70–77.

33. Murat Korutürk, 'Karabük Demir-Çelik İşletmeleri', *Atatürk Ansiklopedisi*, www.ataturkansiklopedisi.gov.tr/bilgi/katrabuk-demir-celik-isletmeleri/.

34. See Afet İnan, *Türkiye Cumhuriyeti'nin İkinci Sanayi Planı* (Ankara: Türk Tarih Kurumu, 1973).

35. See William Hale, 'Turkey and Britain in World War II: Origins and Results of the Triple Alliance, 1935–40', *Journal of Balkan and Near Eastern Studies*, Vol. 23, No. 6 (2021), pp. 835, 839.

36. Ibid., p. 827.

37. William Hale, *The Political and Economic Development of Modern Turkey* (Beckenham: Croom Helm, 1981; repr. Abingdon: Routledge, 2014), p. 73.

38. Caroline E. Arnold, 'In the Service of Industrialization: Etatism, Social Services and the Construction of Industrial Labour Forces in Turkey (1930–50)', *Middle Eastern Studies*, Vol. 48, No. 3 (2012), pp. 364, 366, 371; Can Nacar, '"Our Lives Were not as Valuable as an Animal": Workers in State-Run Industries in World War II Turkey', *International Review of Social History*, Vol. 54, Supplement S16 (2009), [n. p., online].

39. William Hale, *The Political and Economic Development of Modern Turkey* (Beckenham: Croom Helm, 1981; repr. Abingdon: Routledge, 2014), p. 59, based on estimates by Vedat Eldem.

40. International Bank for Reconstruction and Development [IBRD], *The Economy of Turkey: An Analysis and Recommendations for a Development Program* (Baltimore: Johns Hopkins Press, for IBRD, 1951), p. 167.

41. E. R. Lingeman, *Turkey: Economic and Commercial Conditions in Turkey* (London, HMSO, 1948), p. 30.

42. Estimates by Tuncer Bulutay, Nuri Yıldırım and Yahya S. Tezel, *Türkiye Milli Geliri (1923–1948)* (Ankara University, Political Science Faculty, 1974), Tables 8.2c and 8.1.

43. For further details, see, for example, Ekavi Athanassopoulou, *Turkey-Anglo-American Security Interests* (London: Cass, 1999).

44. Afet İnan, *Türkiye Cumhuriyetinin İkinci Sanayi Planı* (Ankara: Türk Tarih Kurumu), pp. 158–59, 160–67.

45. Max Weston Thornburg, Graham Spry and George Soule, *Turkey: An Economic Appraisal* (New York: The Twentieth Century Fund, 1949), pp. 33–34.

46. Ibid., pp. 34, 38–41.

47. Ibid., pp. 108–11.

48. Ibid., p. 211.

49. Quoted in E. Günce, 'Early Planning Experiences in Turkey', in S. İlkin and E. İnanç, eds., *Planning in Turkey (Selected Papers)* (Ankara: Middle East Technical University, Faculty of Administrative Sciences, 1967), p. 22.

50. Quoted in ibid.

51. At the time, the political power of the president was limited, with executive power in the hands of the prime minister. Presidents İnönü and Ataturk had exercised full power because they were also chairmen of the single ruling party.

52. Dwight J. Simpson, 'Development as a Process: The Menderes Phase in Turkey', *Middle East Journal*, Vol. 19, No. 2 (1965), p. 142.

53. Quoted in Feroz Ahmad, *The Turkish Experiment in Democracy* (London: Hurst, for Royal Institute of International Affairs, 1977), p. 127.

54. Calculated from Morris Singer, *The Economic Advance of Turkey, 1938–1960* (Ankara, Turkish Economic Society, 1977), p. 392.

55. Data from ibid., Ch. 4, Table 4.

56. James A Morris, 'Recent Problems of Economic Development in Turkey', *Middle East Journal*, Vol. 14, No. 1 (1960), p. 11.

57. William Hale, *The Political and Economic Development of Modern Turkey* (Beckenham: Croom Helm, 1981; repr. Abingdon: Routledge, 2014), p. 102.

58. Dwight J. Simpson, 'Development as a Process: The Menderes Phase in Turkey', *Middle East Journal*, Vol. 19, No. 2 (1965), pp. 147–48: Osman Cenk Karaca, '1950–1960 Arası Türkiye'de Uygulanan Sosyo-Ekonomik Politikalar', *Mustafa Kemal University Journal of Social Sciences Institute*, Vol. 9, No. 19 (2012), pp. 56–58: Anne O. Krueger, *Turkey, Foreign Trade Regimes and Economic Development Series* (London and New York: Columbia University Press, 1974), pp. 21, 82, 272, 302.

59. Osman Cenk Karaca, '1950–1960 Arası Türkiye'de Uygulanan Sosyo-Ekonomik Politikalar', *Mustafa Kemal University Journal of Social Sciences Institute*, Vol. 9, No. 19 (2012), pp. 58–59; Anne O. Krueger, *Turkey, Foreign Trade Regimes and Economic Development Series* (London and New York: Columbia University Press, 1974), p. 21.

60. Anne O. Krueger, *Turkey, Foreign Trade Regimes and Economic Development Series* (London and New York: Columbia University Press, 1974), pp. 71–81.

61. In its own words, as quoted in Osman Cenk Karaca, '1950–1960 Arası Türkiye'de Uygulanan Sosyo-Ekonomik Politikalar', *Mustafa Kemal University Journal of Social Sciences Institute*, Vol. 9, No. 19 (2012), p. 53.

62. Ibid., p. 55.

63. James A Morris, 'Recent Problems of Economic Development in Turkey', *Middle East Journal*, Vol. 14, No. 1 (1960), p. 4.

64. Morris Singer, *The Economic Advance of Turkey, 1938–1960* (Ankara: Turkish Economic Society, 1977), pp. 351–55.

65. For further discussion, see Sabri Sayarı, 'Clientelism and Patronage in Turkish Politics and Society', in Faruk Birtek and Binnaz Toprak, eds, *The Post-Modern Abyss and the New Politics of Islam: Assabiyah Revisited – Essays in Honour of Şerif Mardin* (Istanbul: Istanbul Bilgi University Press, 2011), pp. 81–94.

66. Morris Singer, *The Economic Advance of Turkey, 1938–1960* (Ankara: Turkish Economic Society, 1977), pp. 264–66, 269–72, 275–76, 279–80, 282, 302.

67. Osman Cenk Karaca, '1950–1960 Arası Türkiye'de Uygulanan Sosyo-Ekonomik Politikalar', *Mustafa Kemal University Journal of Social Sciences Institute*, Vol. 9, No. 19 (2012), p. 55.

68. Ibid., p. 392; James A Morris, 'Recent Problems of Economic Development in Turkey', *Middle East Journal*, Vol. 14, No. 1 (1960), pp. 4, 7.

69. Morris Singer, *The Economic Advance of Turkey, 1938–1960* (Ankara: Turkish Economic Society, 1977), p. 263.

70. Ibid., p. 302.

71. Ayşe Buğra, *State and Business in Modern Turkey: A Comparative Study* (Albany: SUNY Press, 1994), pp. 81, 83–84.

72. Ibid., p. 55.

73. The writer has explored these and subsequent political developments in greater detail in William Hale, *Turkish Politics and the Military* (Abingdon: Routledge, 1994), pp. 119–245, on which this account is based.

74. See ibid., pp. 184–93.

75. Text in 'Constitution of the Republic of Turkey', *Islamic Studies*, Vol. 2, No. 4 (1963), p. 505.

76. O. N. Torun, 'The Establishment and Structure of the State Planning Organisation', in S. İlkin and E. İnanç, eds, *Planning in Turkey (Selected Papers)* (Ankara: Middle East Technical University, Faculty of Administrative Sciences, 1967), pp. 58–63: C. H. Dodd, *Politics and Government in Turkey* (Manchester: Manchester University Press, 1969), pp. 232–34, 245–46.

77. O. N. Torun, 'The Establishment and Structure of the State Planning Organisation', in S. İlkin and E. İnanç, eds, *Planning in Turkey (Selected Papers)* (Ankara: Middle East Technical University, Faculty of Administrative Sciences, 1967), p. 64.

78. Z. Y. Hershlag, *Economic Planning in Turkey* (Istanbul: Economic Research Foundation, 1968), p. 36.

79. Calculations by the author, allowing for net international migration; see William Hale, *The Political and Economic Development of Modern Turkey* (Beckenham: Croom Helm, 1981; repr. Abingdon: Routledge, 2014), p. 18.

80. Y. Küçük, 'The Macro-Model of the Plan', in S. İlkin and E. İnanç, eds, *Planning in Turkey (Selected Papers)* (Ankara: Middle East Technical University, Faculty of Administrative Sciences, 1967), pp. 80–81.

81. This outline of the methodology must be regarded as a very brief general summary. For further details, see Küçük, 'Macro-Model' and 'Sectoral Programming in the Plan', and J. Tinbergen, 'Methodological Background of the Plan', all in S. İlkin and E. İnanç, eds, *Planning in Turkey (Selected Papers)* (Ankara: Middle East Technical University, Faculty of Administrative Sciences, 1967), and Mete Durdağ, *Some Problems of Development Financing: A Case Study of the Turkish First Five Year Plan* (Dordrecht: D. Reidel Publishing Co., 1973), pp. 27–45.

82. Quoted in H. Hammaş, 'The Plan and the State Economic Enterprises', in S. İlkin and E. İnanç, eds, *Planning in Turkey (Selected Papers)* (Ankara: Middle East Technical University, Faculty of Administrative Sciences, 1967), p. 140, note 5.

83. Ibid.

84. Quoted in ibid., p. 142.

85. I. Ongut, 'The Private Sector in the Five Year Plan', in S. İlkin and E. İnanç, eds, *Planning in Turkey (Selected Papers)* (Ankara: Middle East Technical University, Faculty of Administrative Sciences, 1967).

86. State Planning Organisation, *Kalkınma Planı, İkinci Beş Yıl, 1968–1972* (Ankara: SPO, 1967), pp. iii, 101.

87. Data from William Hale, *The Political and Economic Development of Modern Turkey* (Beckenham: Croom Helm, 1981; repr. Abingdon: Routledge, 2014), p. 147, following SPO and other sources.

88. Ibid., p. 143.

89. That is, for the first plan period, 9.7 percent compared with 12.3 percent; for the second plan period, 9.9 percent compared with 12.0 percent; for the third plan period, 9.4 percent compared with 11.3 percent. Ibid., p. 147.

90. *Milli Nizam Partisi, Milli Selamet Partisi.*

91. To be fair, Erbakan and his parties were not directly responsible for the violence, but the political fragmentation which they helped bring about fatally weakened the state, with the consequent rise in armed attacks by extremists.

92. Henri J. Barkey, *The State and the Industrialization Crisis in Turkey* (Boulder: Westview Press, 1990), p. 98.

93. William Hale, *The Political and Economic Development of Modern Turkey* (Beckenham: Croom Helm, 1981; repr. Abingdon: Routledge, 2014), pp. 162, 230, 241–43. Exchange rate from Henri J. Barkey, *The State and the Industrialization Crisis in Turkey* (Boulder, Westview Press, 1990), p. 94.

94. See, for example, Ayşe Buğra, *State and Business in Modern Turkey: A Comparative Study* (Albany: SUNY Press, 1994), pp. 18, 31. A classic discussion of this issue is that of Metin Heper, *The State Tradition in Turkey* (Beverley: Eothen Press, 1985) and *Strong State and Economic Interest Groups: The Post-1980 Turkish Experience* (Berlin, Walter de Gruyter, 1991). Against this, Başak Kuş has argued that in the 1930s the adoption of etatism was due to the weakness, rather than strength of the state, which 'lacked the governance capacities' such as 'the capacity to define and enforce property rights, tax, or collect information' necessary for the formation of a thriving market economy. 'Failing to subject the newly emerging class of domestic capitalists to a formal regulatory framework, state elites began to view them as a serious threat not only to their political authority but also to public morality, and swiftly moved to assert its overarching control over the economy'. However, this remains a minority view; as she admits later, 'that is not to say that other factors do not matter'. Basak Kus, 'Weak States, Unruly Capitalists, and the Rise of Etatism in Late Developers: The Case of Turkey', *British Journal of Middle Eastern Studies*, Vol. 42. No. 3 (2015), pp. 358–59, 374.

95. Ayşe Buğra, *State and Business in Modern Turkey: A Comparative Study* (Albany: SUNY Press, 1994), pp. 23, 32, 51, 64, 97, 106, 135, 137, 256–59.

96. Ibid., p. 138.

97. Henri J. Barkey, *The State and the Industrialization Crisis in Turkey* (Boulder: Westview Press, 1990), pp. 113–18.

98. Ibid., p. 117.

99. Ibid.

100. A comprehensive account of the SPO is in Günal Kansu, *Planlı Yıllar: Anılarla DPT'nin Öyküsü* (İstanbul: Türkiye İş Bankası, 2004).

101. State Planning Organization, *First Five Year Development Plan 1963–1967* (Ankara: Prime Ministry, 1962), p. 3.

102. Attila Sönmez, 'The Re-Emergence of the Idea of Planning and the Scope and Targets of the 1963–1967 Plan', in Selim İlkin and E. İnanç, eds, *Planning in Turkey* (Ankara: Middle East Technical University, 1967), p. 41.

103. İlhan Tekeli, 'Regional Planning in Turkey and Regional Policy in the First Five Year Development Plan', in Selim İlkin and E. İnanç, eds, *Planning in Turkey* (Ankara: Middle East Technical University, 1967), pp. 257–58.

104. OECD, *The Mediterranean Regional Project: Turkey* (Paris: OECD, 1965).

3

INDUSTRIAL POLICY DEMOTED, 1980–2000

This chapter examines the paradigmatic shift in Turkish political economy and the changing parameters of industrialisation and state intervention after 1980, in line with the global trends that saw the replacement of import-substituting industrialisation by the new 'Washington Consensus'. Turkey's transition to neoliberalism following the military coup in September 1980 was driven by a new policy framework constructed on the free-market paradigm and export-led growth that culminated in Turkey joining the World Trade Organization (WTO) and the EU customs union by the mid-1990s. In this period, industrial policy was demoted and re-framed in line with the 'limited state' paradigm that dominated policy circles. However, Turkey's transition to neoliberalism was 'heterodox' in the sense that the state remained an important economic actor. The state policies during the neoliberal era mostly created an adverse impact that exacerbated macroeconomic instability and uncertainty in the market.

The modality of state intervention did change with the liberalisation of finance and trade in comparison to the planning era in the 1960s and 1970s. Yet, Turkey's integration with the global economy in the absence of an effective institutional and regulatory framework further weakened the market-steering capacity of the Turkish state. Turgut Özal's restructuring of the government bureaucracy did not include a comprehensive institutional reform to bring it in line with market liberalisation (which came after the 2001 crisis).

Instead, there were *ad hoc* measures and frequent prime-ministerial decrees which increased discretionary policy-making. This began a process of gradual demotion of industrial policy, as the framework provided by the Five-Year Plans for industrial development was replaced by an extensive, *ad hoc* mix of export incentives, extra-budgetary funds and market-distorting state–business relations. The State Planning Organisation (SPO) was a major victim of the weakening institutional quality. Despite these problems, the Turkish industry was integrated into the global economy in these years, with the share of exports and imports in GDP more than doubling. Combined with the membership obligations of the WTO and EU customs union, these trends reinforced the transition from state-led heavy industry and protectionist industrial policy to a pragmatic neoliberal programme that would be implemented by the AKP in the early 2000s.

This chapter begins with a brief review of global trends in industrial policies and the bumpy trajectory of the Turkish economy in the 1980s and 1990s, focusing on the two defining reforms of the era – namely, liberalisation of trade and capital account.[1] A discussion of the impact of financial liberalisation on manufacturing investment and the emergence of a new business elite in Anatolian mid-sized towns follows. The third section focuses on the weakening of institutions and the transformative role of the state with the demotion of industrial policy, the side-lining of the SPO and the problems with the privatisation of state enterprises. Section four contains an assessment of Turkish industry in the second half of the 1990s and a renewed framework for a more limited industrial policy in line with the WTO and EU customs union regulations. The chapter ends with Box 3.2, comprising in-depth information on the automotive sector tracing the rise, retreat and return of industrial policy in the Turkish context.

Industrial Policy Reframed: The Washington Consensus and the Global Integration of the Turkish Economy

The international economic crisis of the late 1970s and the emerging market debt crisis of the 1980s brought a dramatic shift in the conditions attached to development and balance of payments finance by international financial institutions (IFIs). The import-substituting industrialisation (ISI) model was replaced by market-led, export-oriented industrialisation (EOI) policies codified in the Washington Consensus. Industrial policy was reframed around the neo-classical critique of state intervention: that the costs of government failure outweighed the costs of market failure. 'Vertical' policies that prioritised specific sectors with a transformative objective were discouraged because of the inability of the state to 'pick winners'. But 'horizontal' measures were promoted to allow market forces and comparative advantage to determine sector choice (see chapter 1).

Dependent on external finance and with an uncompetitive state-dominated industrial base draining public finances, Turkey was one of the early adopters of this approach, which set new goals for industrial policy. These included the reform of state-owned enterprises (SEEs) to improve efficiency and promote manufacturing exports; to increase the share of the private sector in manufacturing investment and production; and to reduce government interference in the SEEs and the wider economy, with a greater focus on market signals. The IMF agreements negotiated in 1980 encapsulated these objectives in what was called 'supply side' measures: reduction of import tariffs and quotas to improve the competitiveness of the domestic industry and the lifting of decade-long controls over interest rates, exchange rate and the prices of basic industrial and agricultural products produced by SEEs. Meanwhile, with the commercialisation and privatisation of the SEEs, the state was to reduce its activities on the production side of the economy. These policies meant that the previous approach to industrialisation, led by an industrial policy targeting strategic sectors in the framework of Five-Year Development Plans, was largely abandoned. Public investment in industry declined, and entities such as the SPO were side-lined. In their place was a frequently changing mix of 'horizontal' investment incentives that became allocated on an increasingly discretionary basis from 'extra-budgetary funds' that lacked public oversight and provided scope for corruption and rent-seeking.

The switch to export-oriented industrialisation was equally fraught. The 1980s reforms required an abrupt shift in Turkish industry from its inward-looking focus on the domestic market towards exports. The Turkish governments had delayed policies to encourage export orientation in the 1970s, due to opposition from protectionist private interests.[2] This was in contrast to successful industrialisers such as South Korea and Taiwan, where the export orientation and competitiveness of industry had been established during the

1970s while import and capital account protection was still maintained. As Evans has pointed out with reference to the case of Taiwan, 'what distinguishes K. Y. Yin's program from typical Latin American support for import-substituting industrialisation is that it was not captured by the entrepreneurs it had created'.[3] The challenge that several Latin American countries faced is also valid for the Turkish case at the time, as a form of 'state capture' led to significant delay in the new phase of industrial transformation attempts.

An early attempt to shift Turkish policy towards export orientation came in August 1970, with a devaluation of the long-overvalued Lira to resolve foreign exchange shortages combined with trade measures to encourage non-traditional manufacturing exports.[4] In 1971, import liberalisation began with the signing of the European Community Additional Protocol. These policies, as well as an upsurge in civil unrest, triggered a major political rupture in the Justice Party and the resignation of Prime Minister Demirel when presented with a military memorandum (see Chapter 2). Thereafter, the reforms lost momentum under the military-backed governments in 1971–73. In addition, an unexpected increase in foreign currency inflows from workers' remittances that delivered a historically rare current account surplus in 1973 gave a false sense of security and reduced the pressure for policy-makers to focus on exports. Thus, policy remained stuck in the import-protectionist versus export-oriented dichotomy, rather than pursuing both in a judicious combination. This was an opportunity missed to begin the transformation to a globally competitive industry early, with a head start in global trade.[5] Thus, the economy was left unprepared for the shock-increase in oil prices that followed in 1974–79, leading to a deep foreign payments crisis.

The severity of the late-1970s crisis was such that the political resistance to the trade liberalisation reforms was weakened, but not so to other aspects of the reforms, which saw the state continue to play a reduced but still significant role in the economy. Wide political opposition to the privatisation of SEEs left key industrial sectors in state hands through the 1990s. Contrary to the new stance against the state 'picking winners', there were continued public investments in 'strategic sectors' such as defence. Indeed, what decline was achieved in the role of the state was mostly driven by fiscal constraints and, from the mid-1990s onwards, to comply with the WTO and the EU customs union rules restricting the use of 'state aids'. As seen previously in the 1950s

Menderes era, the 1980s reforms once more illustrated the paradox of Turkish 'economic liberalisation': despite the measures to reduce the role of the state, government intervention in the economy remained extensive.[6]

But the role of the state was now less coherent and more discretionary. The centralisation of executive power during the Özal years and the increased recourse to *ad hoc* prime ministerial decrees retained a large degree of state control over resource allocation, and this had the adverse effect of increasing uncertainty for investors. The reforms that lifted state controls over finance and capital account also weakened the market-steering and transformative capacity of the state as globalisation took off. Combined with domestic political instability, the result was more economic instability and uncertainty for business.[7]

Although the liberalisation era since the 1980s downplayed the role of industrial policies, there was a partial international revival of interest in industrial policies in the late 1990s in response to what was then called the 'new economy'. Drawing on the 'endogenous growth theory', this approach emphasised human capital and innovation and promoted public investment in education and scientific research.[8] In Turkey, the Fifth Five-Year Plan (1985–89) had already signalled the need to increase research and technology to 'prepare' the domestic-market-oriented Turkish industry for the 'opening-up' to global competition and export growth.[9] A report prepared by the Scientific and Technological Research Council of Turkey (TÜBİTAK) in 1993 had proposed the opening up of the telecommunications sector to competition through privatisation of the state's Post, Telegraph, and Telephone (PTT) monopoly, which was slow to respond to the demands of the Information and Communications Technology sectors (see Chapter 4).[10] But this would be repeatedly postponed for another decade.

The liberalisation reforms and integration into world markets proceeded in this half-prepared way, despite the relentless series of external shocks in the 1990s. Domestic conditions were also difficult. Fiscal deficits returned in the 1990s, as weak short-lived populist governments opted for increased budget spending to support their electoral constituencies (see Box 3.1: Elections and Coalition Governments in the 1980s–90s). By the end of the decade, with export growth also faltering, the build-up of macroeconomic imbalances had left the economy vulnerable to rising international interest rates and the spillovers from a series of emerging market crises.

There were two major sets of liberalisation reforms achieved in these two decades: the easing of government controls over trade and finance in the 1980s, which in the 1990s was followed by the lifting of controls over international capital flows. The trade liberalisation was painful but mostly met its objective of increasing manufactured exports. The liberalisation of the financial sector also increased competition and mobilised new sources of funds, but was undermined by weak regulation, leading to the financial crisis of 2000–1. Hence, the lifting of capital controls was badly timed. It took place in the context of extremely volatile global conditions exposing the Turkish economy to fluctuations in international capital flows and increased macroeconomic fragility. The next two sections focus on the defining reforms of this era: the trade and capital account liberalisation that began the global integration of the Turkish economy but also, given the context of weak institutions and state capacity, reduced the policy space for Turkish industrialists.

Box 3.1 Elections and Coalition Governments in the 1980s–90s

- **September 1980–83:** Military rule, previously existing political parties dissolved. Ultra-nationalist, Islamist and centre-right forces gathered in the Motherland Party (*Anavatan Partisi*, ANAP) led by Turgut Özal.
- **November 1983 general election:** ANAP government led by Turgut Özal.
- **September 1987:** Bans lifted on pre-1980 political leaders, including Süleyman Demirel, Bülent Ecevit, Necmettin Erbakan and Alparslan Türkeş, leading them to form new parties.
- **November 1987 general election:** ANAP government led by Turgut Özal.
- **October 1989:** Turgut Özal succeeds Kenan Evren as president; Yıldırım Akbulut (ANAP) appointed as prime minister, replaced by Mesut Yılmaz in June 1991.
- **October 1991 general election:** Coalition government of Süleyman Demirel's centre-right True Path Party (*Doğru Yol Partisi*, DYP) and the centre-left Social Democrat Populist Party (*Sosyaldemokrat Halkçı Parti*, SHP) led by Erdal İnönü.

- **May 1993:** Turgut Özal dies of a heart attack, succeeded by Süleyman Demirel as president; Tansu Çiller becomes leader of the DYP and Turkey's first woman prime minister.
- **December 1995 general election:** No party wins the majority; Necmettin Erbakan's pro-Islamist Welfare Party (*Refah Partisi*, RP) emerges as the biggest party with 21.4 percent of the popular vote; centre-right vote split between ANAP and DYP, centre-left between the now divided SHP into Bülent Ecevit's Democratic Left Party (*Demokratik Sol Partisi*, DSP) and a revived Republican People's Party (CHP) led by Deniz Baykal. This led to a series of short-lived coalition governments:
  - **March-June 1996:** ANAP/DYP, led by Prime Minister Mesut Yılmaz of ANAP.
  - **July 1996-June 1997:** DYP/RP, led by Necmettin Erbakan of RP as prime minister collapses due to secular opposition and military pressure; closure of RP by the Constitutional Court in 1998; RP revived as Virtue Party (*Fazilet Partisi*, FP).
  - **June 1997-January 1999:** Mesut Yılmaz forms right-left coalition of ANAP/DSP/DTP (*Demokratik Türkiye Partisi*, DTP: Democratic Turkey Party, split off from the DYP).
- **April 1999 general election:** Bülent Ecevit's DSP, revived MHP (*Milliyetçi Hareket Partisi*, Nationalist Action Party) under new leader Devlet Bahçeli and ANAP form a broad left-right coalition led by Ecevit as prime minister. Virtue Party closed by the Constitutional Court in June 2001.

This decade of fragmentation of party structures and short-lived coalition governments (with an average lifespan of 449 days) created a political context of 'polarised pluralism'.[11] Parties competed for votes, with pre-election wage increases for public sector workers, agricultural subsidies for rural voters, investment incentives and state bank credits for the private sector and reduced retirement age for pensioners. The 1980s and 1990s were transitional years during which political support for state-led heavy industry and protectionist policies gradually gave way to a grudging acceptance of markets that was reinforced by Turkey joining the WTO and the EU customs union. One of the political shifts that supported this transition came from the Islamist-inspired political parties which switched to a pragmatic neoliberal economic programme as their business support base of SMEs grew into large conglomerates. This was the political legacy that shaped the policies of the newly formed AKP that came to power in 2002 on the back of weakened public confidence in the existing parties, high-profile cases of corruption revelations and the deep economic crisis of 2001.[12]

From Import-substituting Industrialisation to Export-oriented Industrialisation

The veteran planner Günal Kansu in his book *Planlı Yıllar* has located the end of ISI and the planned period to 1977, during the Third Five-Year Plan. This was when the build-up of payments arrears on the foreign debt sent Turkey to the IMF and the OECD's Turkish Consortium to reschedule the foreign debt.[13] The 1979 oil price shock led to the suspension of two IMF programmes, requiring a new agreement in January 1980. By the time of the military *coup* in September 1980, Turkey was in the midst of its second year of economic contraction, accelerating inflation, shortages of basic goods and services, trade union strikes and violent street clashes. Against this background, the liberalisation attempts gained currency as a reaction to the massive problems of the 1970s.

The radical reforms undertaken in the 1980s are associated with Turgut Özal. From 1979 onwards, Özal first acted as the economy minister negotiating the IMF agreements in the coalition government of Prime Minister Süleyman Demirel, then as deputy prime minister during the military regime, and as prime minister and leader of the ANAP until 1989, when he became president. The IMF agreements consisted of standard measures to stabilise the balance of payments: suppressing domestic demand with interest rate rises and fiscal austerity and supporting exports with a currency devaluation. There was also a supply-side aspect that embodied the new revamped industrial policies. Such stabilisation measures usually imply a period of slow growth, if not recession. But annual growth averaged around 5 percent, peaking at 9 percent in 1987. As Ayşe Buğra has explained, '[l]ater it became quite clear that the program implemented at least between 1983–87 was an expansionist program with heavy state investment in infrastructure acting as the main engine of growth'.[14] Growth was also supported by the rise in off-budget spending from extra-budgetary funds that financed investment and export incentives. As fiscal discipline was relaxed in the lead up to elections, the wider public sector deficit was back up to 7–8 percent of the GNP by the end of the decade, while public debt doubled to over 50 percent. Price stabilisation proved elusive, fuelled by currency instability and Central Bank and state bank lending. Contributing to inflation were price adjustments by SEEs, in line with commercialisation reforms to reduce their reliance on budget transfers. Inflation was back up to 60–70 percent by the end of the 1980s. For wage-earners – the biggest losers from these early reforms – it seemed that the scarcity of goods in the late 1970s were now replaced by unaffordable goods.[15]

However, the export-oriented industrialisation objective to increase manufacturing exports was achieved and brought a rare period of stabilisation to the balance of payments. Exports benefited from investment and incentives that helped raise the share of manufactures from 36 percent of total exports in 1980 to 75.3 percent in 1985. The restructuring of the foreign debt, strong export growth and a slow start to the reduction of import tariffs contained the annual current account deficit to USD 2–3 billion. Also supporting the export boom were the thriving Middle Eastern markets. Including services exports such as contracting, transport and tourism, as well as remittances from Turkish workers in the Gulf states, the Middle Eastern markets accounted for around half of total export receipts in the early 1980s.[16]

The stabilisation of foreign payments, however, did not last. Export incentives – such as export tax rebates that had doubled in 1985–89, when compared to the previous five years – had to be wound down due to extensive corruption. Policies to support export growth began to be abandoned from 1988 onwards, as governments increasingly relied on an overvalued Turkish Lira in an attempt to contain inflation. Given this background, the First Gulf War in 1990–91 hit exports to the Middle Eastern markets. These conditions exposed the weak foundation of Turkey's export leap in the 1980s, which had taken place on the basis of mostly existing industrial capacity and technology. These weaknesses, combined with capital account and trade liberalisation in these decades, set the scene for the mini-crisis of 1994.

Capital Account Liberalisation amidst Multiple External Shocks in the 1990s

Whereas Turgut Özal had been the man of the 1980s, it was the veteran politician Süleyman Demirel of the True Path Party (DYP) who would come to define the 1990s as prime minister in 1991, then as president from 1993 until 2000. A self-described 'infrastructure man', Demirel had been an effective head of the State Hydraulic Works (*Devlet Su İşleri*, DSİ) in the 1950s, which gave him an understanding of the Turkish bureaucracy. In an interview by this author in 1986, at his house on Güniz Sokak, in a study room with books piled high all the way from the floor and still banned from participating in politics, Demirel said that he did not disagree with the overall programme and aims of Turgut Özal's policies; where he differed was with the speed and manner with which they had been implemented. But Demirel's aspirations to deliver a stable policy and macroeconomic environment failed. The 1990s were characterised by more instability, as the fragmentation of the political party structures yielded weak, short-lived governments unable to manage the Turkish economy under the volatile global conditions. Demirel took over the government with its institutional fabric weakened and key policy instruments to direct the economy abandoned. This was the case with the lifting of capital controls. As one of his last decrees before moving to the presidency, Turgut Özal had liberalised the capital account abruptly on 11 August 1989, with little consultation with the business community. It was also against the advice of the Central Bank and the SPO. This lost Turkish policy-makers a crucial buffer against volatile capital flows and 'market sentiment' in this new era of rapid globalisation, increasing the risks facing Turkish investors and exacerbating macroeconomic instability and uncertainty.

This became evident during the 1994 crisis when Tansu Çiller, as the economy minister in 1991 (and prime minister from 1993 onwards), underestimated the new fragilities of the Turkish economy with an open capital account. A series of policy mistakes in 1993, including cancelling several treasury bill auctions to reduce market interest rates, public criticism of the tight monetary policy of the Central Bank when inflation reached triple digits and the fiscal profligacy of the DYP-SHP coalition taking the public-sector borrowing requirement (PSBR) to 14.6 percent undermined policy credibility. These conditions, combined with a downgrade of Turkey's sovereign ratings in early 1994, brought sharp capital outflows, currency depreciation, loss of foreign currency reserves and yet another IMF agreement.[17]

The 1994 crisis should be understood in the context of the volatile international markets in the 1990s. Turkish governments had to cope not only with domestic pressures, but also with major external shocks, including a sharp volatility of capital flows in what came to be called 'sudden-stop' crises. The decade began with the First Gulf War and ended with the devastating Istanbul earthquake in 1999. In between were a series of emerging market crises – the 1994 Mexican crisis and the 1997 Asian crisis, triggered by interest rate hikes by the US Federal Reserve, and the 1998 Russian debt default.[18] Meanwhile, in the first half of the 1990s, Turkey was also involved in long-running negotiations to wrest open European markets for Turkish exports. It was an uphill battle. In 1991, for example, the *Financial Times* reported that 'Turkey was cited in more EC anti-dumping investigations than any other country'.[19]

Despite all this, there was no going back. By 1995, in line with WTO obligations, Turkey had cut (output-weighted) average import tariffs on manufacturing imports to 20.7 percent, compared to 75.8 percent in 1983. In 1996, the EU-Turkey customs union decision came into force and Turkey's candidacy for EU membership – having been lodged over a decade ago, in 1987 – was finally acknowledged in 1999. In terms of investments, the 1990s saw annual FDI inflows rise somewhat to USD 609 million per year, from very low levels of USD 168 million in the 1980s. For Turkey, arguably the policy reforms with the biggest long-term impact in this period were the lifting of capital controls in 1989 and the liberalisation of trade. This would enable those internationally competitive sectors of the Turkish economy to participate in the new era of globalisation. But it would also constrain the policy space to pursue long-term industrial policies.

A Bumpy Start: Reducing the State Role in Finance and Increasing Long-term Funding

Financial sector liberalisation was a major tenet of the 1980s reforms aimed at increasing competition and developing capital markets to support the private-sector contribution to long-term funding for industry and infrastructure investments. This required a radical overhaul of the existing financial structure that was state-dominated. Investment in industrialisation during the planned period was mostly budget-funded and supported by state banks with sector specialisation. Halk Bank prioritised lending to small and medium-sized enterprises (SMEs), Ziraat Bankası to agriculture, Etibank to mining and Sümerbank to textiles and consumer goods. Also, many of the private banks were associated with large conglomerate holdings. The Central Bank was a major source of credit to state enterprises, with the authority to extend medium-term loans to industry since the late 1970s (Law No. 1211). Long-term funding was also available from the Industrial Development Bank of Turkey (TSKB). The TSKB had been set up in 1950 with private and public participation to allocate the Marshall Plan funds and played a major role in the import-substituting industrialisation process (see Chapter 2).

The liberalisation effort began badly. In mid-1980, before legal or regulatory reforms were introduced, deposit rates were abruptly deregulated, lending rates freed, and several new banks and brokerage entities were allowed to enter the market. After decades of control, this unleashed a price war for deposits offered by banks, brokerage houses and unofficial money-lenders. This inevitably ended with the 1981–82 'bankers' crisis' or the Kastelli crisis (referring to the biggest broker), which caused many bankruptcies and loss of savings of hundreds of thousands of people.[20] In response, the Central Bank had to rescue several banks and re-regulate deposit interest rates in 1983.[21]

This crisis revealed at the time the lack of appreciation for market regulatory structures. The regulatory framework for a deposit insurance scheme was rushed through in the midst of the 1983 crisis (replaced by the Savings Deposit Insurance Fund, SDIF, in 1985). This was belatedly followed up with a new Banking Law (Banks Act No. 3182) in 1985. The institutional framework to establish a capital market was better prepared. A Capital Market Law was passed in 1981, followed by a Capital Market Board in 1982, and in 1983 the Istanbul Stock Exchange (ISE) was established (although the ISE did not begin fully functioning before 1986). A major step towards reducing the creditor role of the Central Bank was the establishment of the government securities market in 1985, the interbank money market in 1986, and the open market operations by the CBT in 1987. In the 1990s, other regulations to diversify financial products as well as to tighten regulatory controls – such as an insider-trading law in 1992 — were also introduced.

These measures succeeded in boosting asset growth and reducing concentration in the sector. Bank assets to GNP rose to 71.3 percent by 1999, from only 26.7 percent in 1979; the number of banks had doubled to eighty-one, of which fifty-two were privately owned, and included nineteen development and investment banks. Among the new development and investment banks were Islamic banks known as Special Financing Institutions (see below, Anatolian SMEs), although their legal basis remained weak. However, progress on financial deepening – that is, diversifying the supply of funds beyond banks – was slow. The stock market capitalisation to GDP ratio was still only 25 percent by 2000. The delays in the privatisation of the SEEs, some of Turkey's most attractive firms, held back the development of capital markets. Of the securities issued in the bond markets, 80 percent were government bonds and treasury bills. The state role in the credit markets had been trimmed back somewhat from the 1970s, when half the bank lending was to the public sector. But state banks still accounted for 38 percent of banking assets, 34 percent of loans and 40 percent of deposits in 1998.[22] Of the five largest banks, three (Ziraat, Halk and Emlak) were state-owned. The Central Bank was still a fiscal policy tool lending for agricultural support to the Soil Products Office (TMO) – a major component of fiscal deficits in the late 1990s.

There was also the ongoing problem of directed credit requirements for the state banks: 56 percent of total state bank loans in 1997 was still in the form of preferential lending. These obligations led to the build-up of 'duty-losses' on loan write-downs on credits to small business and agriculture, disaster relief operations and rescue of insolvent banks. The several banks that required rescuing in these decades and the populist distribution policies of the fragmented governments in the 1990s soon led to these 'duty-losses' rising to 13 percent of GNP (60 percent held by Ziraat Bank). This and the bankruptcies among the Islamic banks would trigger the banking crisis of 2000–1.[23]

The difficulties in financial-sector reforms, which also hampered industrial development due to inadequate funding allocated to manufacturing firms, have been attributed to the weaknesses in the regulatory framework. Although many state controls had been lifted, the basic structure of the financial sector had not changed. Most of the old issues persisted: banks lent mostly for the short term and at high interest rates; there was little supplier finance or development (long-term) finance; the public sector dominated the utilisation of funds in the capital markets; and banks still held the largest share of financial assets.[24] A major problem was the continued role of the Treasury as the regulator of the banking sector, at a time when government borrowing was at all-time highs. The promises of the liberalisation reforms could not be met while the government continued to dominate financial assets.

The pace and sequencing of the package of reforms was also badly timed – the liberalisation of the exchange rate, the capital account and finance occurred before macro-economic stabilisation was achieved. In this context, the lifting of government controls merely added to the macro-instability of these years and continued to undermine long-term investments needed to support the industrialisation process.

Private Sector Slow to Offset Reduced Public Investment in Manufacturing

The liberalisation reforms of the 1980s were welcomed by the Turkish business community. This included Tüsiad, representing the biggest private industrialists. Even though they had grown during the import-substituting industrialisation era, the bigger entities in Tüsiad were looking to expand into the sectors dominated by these state behemoths. Small business also benefited from reduced barriers to entry, as licensing, foreign exchange requirements and financial controls were eased. In addition, all business had initial favourable conditions to help transition to export-led growth: low real wages, undervalued Lira and generous export and other investment incentives.

The early approval had turned into criticism by the second half of the 1980s, as almost all sectors were hurt by one or another of the reforms. Profitability in the top-500 Turkish firms fell in 1980–86.[25] The private sector had lost two major sources of state support in the 1980s: state-subsidised credit and intermediate inputs from the SEEs. They were also struggling with trade liberalisation. Turgut Özal's application for EU membership in 1987 was met with dismay by some sectors of industry, including the automotive sector, demanding a slower pace of reduction of protective import tariffs. Many SMEs (with fewer than twenty-five employees), which accounted for 80 percent of industrial capacity, could not cope with the high interest rates and went bankrupt. There were also high-profile bankruptcies, such as the Asil Çelik

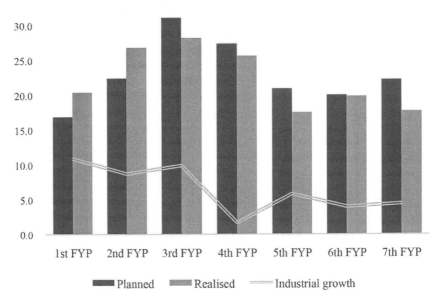

Figure 3.1 Share of manufacturing in total fixed capital investment (1963–2000) (%)
Source: State Planning Organisation.

steel plant in Bursa and textile giant Güney Sanayi in Adana, which had to be rescued by the state in the early 1980s, when they lost the exchange rate guarantee from the government on their imports and were unable to service their debts. Another legacy of the liberalisation was the tenfold increase in external debt (of non-financial corporations) to USD 29 billion by 1999, of which 61 percent belonged to the private sector.[26] As industrial policy measures such as state investment and export incentives were partially wound down from the mid-1990s, private-sector reliance on foreign credits rose, also exposing them to currency risk.

Investment in manufacturing declined in this period from its peak during the Third Five-Year Plan (1973–77; see Figure 3.1), which saw the construction of big industrial projects such as the Aliağa refinery and the İşdemir Iron and Steel complex. Within a decade, the share of investment certificates given to manufacturing fell to 40.3 percent in 1988, from a high of 90.1 percent of the total in 1979. Some public investments continued in the 1980s, but this was mostly 'completion' of already started projects in previously selected 'strategic sectors'.

The private sector was slow to offset the decline in public-sector investment. Macroeconomic instability, cost pressures (SEE price hikes, high interest rates, high import costs) and policy uncertainty held back the private sector from long-term investments. The share of private-sector investment in total fixed investment did not surpass public investment until 1988, when the latter fell due to fiscal constraints and SEE reforms that froze expansion plans. But even then half of private fixed investment was allocated to housing construction, while manufacturing received about 20–25 percent. This problem was amplified by the high real interest rates on the public debt instruments that attracted bank resources, 'crowding out' bank-lending to enterprises. To try and overcome their funding problems, as well as to take advantage of the high returns on government paper, many larger conglomerates had set up their own banks, creating an unhealthy reliance on interest income from government paper held by their related banks. In 1994, the share of non-manufacturing profits in the total profits of Turkey's largest 500 firms had risen to 54.6 percent, from 15.3 percent in 1982.[27] Nor was industry the first choice of sector by foreign investors. Foreign direct investment (FDI) rose in the 1980s. But the share of manufacturing in the FDI's total stock had declined from 87 percent in 1980 to 52.2 percent in 1990, while that of services had risen from 12.5 to 44.7 percent.[28] The automotive sector was one of the few big industrial destinations for FDI in the 1980s. Yet, focused on the domestic market, it remained limited until the second half of the 1990s, when Turkey joined the EU customs union (See Box 3.2 below).

Anatolian SMEs: Tapping New Sources of Finance

The liberalisation of finance had fallen short of several objectives, but it succeeded in mobilising new sources of funds at home and abroad. This and the lifting of state restrictions supported the emergence of the Anatolian SMEs – variously described as 'Anatolian tigers', 'Islamic Calvinists', or 'Network Firms', due to their association with Islamic networks and the newly established Islamist parties. Initially operating as relatively autonomous entities, the Anatolian SMEs grew with the access to new sources of Islamic finance and from the mid-1990s local authority patronage.[29]

The public investment focus on infrastructure in the 1980s also helped improve telecommunications, transport and energy services to mid-sized towns in Anatolia. In addition, they benefited from industrial policies with regional development investment incentives that prioritised the inner-Anatolian provinces – one of the few industrial policy measures that still survived. The formation of new firms was eased by the lifting of barriers to entry, such as import, licensing and foreign currency allocation restrictions that also supported an export orientation. Textiles, furniture and foodstuffs manufacturing businesses sprung up to meet middle-class demand in rapidly growing cities such as Gaziantep, Diyarbakır, Konya and Kayseri.

Moreover, there were new sources of finance available to the newly emerging business groups, including an international angle. The latter included several Middle Eastern banks entering the Turkish market in the 1980s, including the Islamic Development Bank (IDB), Kuwait Turk and Saudi-Arabia-based Faisal Finance and Al-Baraka Group.[30] On the domestic front, new banks called Special Finance Institutions (SFIs) that promised non-interest Islamic banking were established by cabinet decree in December 1983 – one of the first decrees by the incoming Özal government. SFIs managed to pool the 'under the mattress' savings from provincial families and Turkish workers abroad. However, the weak regulatory framework in Turkey meant that these financial flows were mostly through informal channels, with entities that were often not registered with the Capital Markets Board – a problem that would be exposed in the 2000–1 banking crisis.

All this had a political dimension. By the end of the 1980s, these business networks helped propel the Islamist parties into the national political sphere (see Box 3.1). With only a 21.4-percent share in the highly fragmented result of the 1995 election, the Welfare Party (RP) became the biggest party in parliament, placing Necmettin Erbakan as prime minister in the coalition government formed in July 1996. This process transformed the policies of the RP from an Islamic social-welfare-inspired, protectionist, state-led heavy-industry focus towards a neoliberal programme backing private entrepreneurship and export growth, emulating successful majority Islamic economies in Asia, such as Malaysia. This was also in line with the associated business groups that defined themselves as self-made entrepreneurs waging a battle for 'economic democratisation' and forming the Independent Industrialists and Businessmen's Association (*Müstakil Sanayici ve İş Adamları Derneği*, Müsiad) in 1990, with the stated aim of focusing on 'competitive engagement with the global economy'.[31]

This 'independence', however, was overstated and belied the increased blurring of boundaries between business and state. The Özal government actively supported the establishment of SFIs. Local authority support came with the control of several metropolitan municipalities newly empowered by the ANAP after the 1984 elections, and by the RP after the 1994 local authority elections including Istanbul (where Recep Tayyip Erdoğan became mayor). These links raised the customary levels of patronage in Turkey to new levels, with the new entrepreneurs tapping local authority funds for state procurement contracts in lucrative *rent-thick* sectors, such as construction and real-estate development. By the end of the 1990s, the number of 'network firms' in the national top-500 firms had risen to over a hundred from a handful a decade ago. Many had become holdings setting up their own Islamic finance arms and operating in diverse sectors, such as Server Holding and İhlas Holding.

These developments were interrupted when the Refah-Yol (RP-DYP) coalition led by Prime Minister Necmettin Erbakan fell apart in mid-1997, as pressure increased from the Turkish military, alarmed that the country's secular structures were being threatened. Pressures from the military came to a head at a National Security Council meeting on 28 February 1997 – known as the 'February 28 crisis' and seen as a 'post-modern coup'. In the aftermath, the closure of the RP and regulations restricting the SFI's financial links abroad followed, triggering several bankruptcies. The Banking Law of 1999 belatedly incorporated the SFIs into the national deposit insurance scheme and strengthened the legal basis of the Islamic finance sector. Yet, this could not prevent the collapse of the biggest, İhlas Finans, which accounted for around 40 percent of SFIs assets; this collapse became one of the triggers of the 2001 banking crisis.

This was a difficult but temporary setback for these new business and political forces. From their beginnings as self-reliant SMEs, over beneficiaries of government-backed Islamic bank funding in the 1980s, to local authority patronage in the 1990s, Islamic business–state relations were to be brought even closer in the 2000s during AKP rule. These early trends during the 1980s and 1990s succeeded in mobilising new sources of funds and brought much-needed social mobility and economic dynamism to inner Anatolia. The downside was that the lack of transparency and the dangerous blurring of the boundaries between economic, religious and political interests in the nexus of Islamic charities-business associations-political parties would come to undermine Turkey's democratic and secular institutions in the 2000s.

Özal's Parallel Bureaucracy: Increased Rent-seeking, Weakened State Capacity and SEEs in Limbo

The prevalent Washington Consensus in the 1980s saw 'economic policy' measures as key to development and macro-stabilisation: lifting government restrictions and liberalising regulations were considered as sufficient to let the market do the rest. The recognition of the importance of 'institutions' came after the 1997 Asian crisis in what was called the 'post-Washington Consensus' (See Chapter 4). Hence, the Turkish 1980 liberalisation reforms had no systematic focus on the overall institutional framework, and there was insufficient appreciation of the need for market regulatory institutions. That would come later, after the 2001 crisis. Thus, the 1980s saw abruptly implemented reforms (such as the overnight lifting of capital and other financial controls, as discussed above) followed by *ad hoc* administrative restructuring and belated regulation to try to bring some stability to the markets.

Turgut Özal combined this approach with increased centralisation of executive control with ministerial decrees. A number of functional commissions (*kurullar*) were established to exercise greater control over policy and to supervise the implementation of the liberalisation reforms, such as the Money and Credit Commission (Para ve Kredi Kurulu) and the Capital Markets Commission (Sermaye Piyasası Kurulu). They were positioned above the relevant minister and reporting to the prime minister. A second major change in the government administration in these years was increasing recourse to the use of decrees (*kanun hükmünde kararnameler*), by-passing lengthy parliamentary debates. From 1982 to 90, there were 305 decrees, compared to only seventeen from 1972 to 1978.[32] Another series of administrative reforms aiming to reduce central government bureaucratic restrictions and break down 'ministerial fiefdoms', particularly those exercised by the Ministries of Interior and Public Works and Resettlement, were the municipalities reforms. In 1984, a series of administrative reforms to the metropolitan municipalities took place, including several new acts to increase their revenue-raising and spending powers.[33]

These reforms did not work as planned. Despite attempts to by-pass parliament with decrees, many reforms were challenged in the constitutional court and overturned – especially when it came to SEE privatisation. As for the commissions that aimed at centralising authority, in practice, the frequent establishment and closure of commissions as well as confusion about the lines of ministerial authority compounded these difficulties. Similar to the local authority reforms, without independent institutions to exert controls and transparency, these changes partially re-allocated the source of patronage from the centre to the regions. These organisational changes, which were made to speed up reforms, hollowed out the existing institutional structures and weakened state capacity. It also increased unpredictability in the investment environment creating adverse incentives and rent-seeking by the private sector.[34] Even when legislation was – often belatedly – introduced, professional, technical and institutional capacity to implement them were often lacking.

All these administrative measures created almost a 'dual' or 'parallel bureaucracy'. The power of the civil service and the ministers were reduced, with authority shifting to metropolitan mayors, technocrats and high-level executives whom Turgut Özal had appointed to key positions, such as the head of public-sector banks – who came to be known as 'Özal's princes'. Nevertheless, the crucial broader democratic checks and balances still functioned in this period, with parliament, the judiciary, the Constitutional Court and the presidency retaining their spheres of authority, as well as vocal media.

Radical changes in the Turkish economic orientation led by Turgut Özal were unique in the post-World War II history of Turkey. State intervention did begin to decline in industry, and state controls over prices, trade and finance were eased. However, the reforms were – perhaps inevitably, given the deep structural and institutional changes required – only partly successful and brought more rent-seeking and corruption in the absence of the needed institutional reforms of the state bureaucracy, privatisation of SEEs and establishment of market regulators. The state's role in the economy remained significant, with the instruments of intervention taking a different form – what some call 'liberal interventionism'.[35] The industrial policy instruments which defined this period were those industry-related extra-budgetary funds and investment and export incentives which would become mired in corruption. Meanwhile, the main institution that defined the 'hey-day of industrial policies', the State Planning Organisation, became increasingly side-lined, while the problems with the privatisation of the SEEs left them in limbo. In what follows we cover these developments, which, along with a declining state capacity, failed to orient investments in industry towards high-tech sectors in the last two decades of twentieth-century Turkey.

The Rise and Fall of Extra-budgetary Funds and Export Incentives

Extra-budgetary funds were a key component of the increase in executive power under Özal. They were also a major source of the decrease in government transparency as, initially, they were not subject to parliamentary control. The discretionary allocation of these funds became the source of political meddling and uncertainty in the business environment. Although extra-budgetary funds had previously existed, with revenues coming from ear-marked duties and taxes, they tended to be on cross-party matters of long-term national importance, such as the Earthquake Fund set up in 1972. In the 1980s, the number of funds doubled to around a hundred. Those relating to industrial policy included the Apprentices Fund, Defence Industries Fund, Small Business Support Fund and Export Promotion Fund. Among the biggest were those involved in the privatisation of the SEEs, the Public Participation and Mass Housing Fund.[36]

With special surcharges on finance and trade, large revenues began to accumulate in these funds separate from the government budget. By 1986, fund revenues relative to the total central government budget revenues rose to 31 percent, creating a national outcry.[37] At a conference organised by the Association of Public Supervisors (Devlet Denetim Elemanları Derneği, DENETDE), the government was criticised for failing to 'account for fund spending' and for use of the funds for pet projects rather than longer-term investments.[38] New measures to increase transparency followed, including in 1987 placing the funds under the scrutiny of the Parliamentary Planning and Budget Committee and attaching them to the relevant ministries (Law No. 3346). From 1988 onwards, they were also obliged to transfer 30 percent of their revenues to the central government budget. By the early 1990s, extra-budgetary revenues were still high, at around 3 percent of GNP, but they also had deficits of 1.6 percent of GNP.[39] Following the 1994 crisis, measures were taken to bring them back into the official budget process. However, the discretionary spending of these funds and associated patronage weakened the legitimacy of Özal's reforms, creating a strong public perception of corruption and sleaze in the ANAP government, resulting in the loss of the 1991 elections. Of the extra-budgetary funds that continued to operate in the 1990s, some, such as TOKİ, would be revived in the 2000s and once again become a controversial source of discretionary governance and patronage.

The other key instrument of industrial policy in this period were the incentives to boost private-sector exports. Consisting of tax rebates, favourable credit terms and exemptions from customs, stamp and other duties, these incentives for export industries were not new. In the late 1970s, the share of eligible exports for export tax rebates had risen to around 50 percent, but it declined to 24.6 percent by 1980. The incentives schemes were expanded and took on a new significance after the Özal government came to power in 1983. An 'Export Promotion Decree' attached responsibility for the incentives to the Prime Minister's Office and widened the benefits to include low-interest credit from the Export Promotion Fund, increased access to the allocation of foreign exchange and tax rebates of up to 20 percent of tax liabilities. By 1984, 64 percent of total exports were benefiting from these incentives, and the volume of business had led to the emergence of Japanese-style Foreign Trade Companies that could take advantage of scale economies in marketing.[40]

Given the lack of proper performance measurement criteria and the perseverance of rent-seeking state-business networks, these instruments were far from ideal for effective export-led industrial transformation. Soon, significant levels of illicit transactions emerged around these programmes, which also caused international concern. Export growth had become so dependent on these subsidies that, when one of the incentive measures, the Resource Utilisation Support Premium payments, was abolished to comply with the GATT subsidy code that Turkey signed in 1985, exports fell by almost 10 percent in 1986. Unofficial reports suggested that some 15 percent of export revenues in 1980–87 could consist of 'fictitious exports', where export prices and volumes were falsely exaggerated to take advantage of the incentives.[41] By 1988, the export-tax rebates schemes had been phased out in a multi-stage process.

There were similar policy zigzags in several aspects of trade reforms, including legislation around Foreign Trade Companies and repeated changes in the list of commodities benefiting from export promotion and import liberalisation. These zigzags in trade incentives policies had a high cost. Business representatives complained about the frequent changes in policy – such as changes to export liberalisation lists – as a major source of uncertainty that undermined their longer-term investment plans. But the governments argued that these frequent adjustments were in response to speculative, rent-seeking activities by the private sector. This tension reflects the weakness of state capacity in Turkey, which lacked effective market regulating institutions to monitor performance and prevent abuse of the incentives policies. It also reveals the inability of the government, facing populist pressures, to discipline the highly fragmented business community and to cut support when private firms failed to improve their export competitiveness. This stands in contrast to the industrialisation experience of the East Asian economies that took place under authoritarian corporatist relations between the state and business. Furthermore, Turkey's investment and export incentives policies would undergo several changes in the 1990s, with the closure and redesign of several incentive programmes. Repeated efforts from the late 1980s onwards to try to increase transparency and reduce graft were reinforced by the requirements of the GATT subsidy rules and compliance with the EEC customs union state-aid regulations that brought a significant change in the form of industrial policies.

The SPO Side-lined

The centralisation of power in the executive during the Özal years also affected the State Planning Organisation, reducing its relative autonomy and its capacity to direct industrial policies. The SPO represented the height of industrial policy in Turkey in the 1960s (see Chapter 2, Box 2.1: 'SPO: The Early Years . . . An Insider's View'). Over these years, there were three waves of 'planners'. First there were the early academics, engineers and technocrats, as well as foreign advisors such as Jan Tinbergen and Jagdish Bhagwhati. Most of this group had left by the late 1960s, weakening the coherence of the plans. The second group were the statist-minded planners associated with the left-of-centre Bülent-Ecevit-led CHP (Republican People's Party), and a third intake of people was associated with the leadership of the SPO under Turgut Özal (1967–71) and later Necmettin Erbakan (1974–78).

Günal Kansu, one of the 'early generation of planners' as head of the Economic Planning Department during the First Five-Year Plan, describes a politically divided entity reflecting the dominant political trends in Turkey. As these shifted, the planning teams were purged, or many resigned (Kansu resigned when Turgut Özal took over the SPO). Between 1960 and 1980, the SPO had eleven presidents and thirteen directors of the Economic Planning

Department. This turn-over of expertise, with waves of resignations and sharp conflict between planners and ministries, was a peculiarity of the SPO and had not been previously seen in the Turkish bureaucracy, which had mostly been subservient to politicians. Efforts to strengthen the bureaucracy came in the aftermath of the 1960 coup that largely represented the interests of the military and civil bureaucracy, having concluded that the economic problems of the late 1950s were due to 'planlessness [. . .] and investment decisions [. . .] made piecemeal'.[42] The establishment of the SPO and the exceptional powers it was initially given reflected this view. Although the SPO was given exceptional powers, 'the mechanisms [. . .] to enforce the executive's compliance with the plan were not at all well-defined'.[43] This would become a source of ongoing political conflicts between the technical approach of the planners and the ruling governments.

Turgut Özal was already familiar with these problems as previous head of the SPO. As prime minister in the 1980s, he 'solved' this problem by installing many loyal new hires and increasing centralisation in a personalised way that, inadvertently, further undermined the planning institution. In 1980, 183 new planners were hired – that is, over half the number of existing staff. This intake was seen by the SPO's old guard of mostly left-leaning, secular, state-interventionists as a tactic to ensure its dominance by 'conservative pious liberals' (*mukaddesatçı muhafazakar liberaller*), unleashing a round of 'culture wars'.[44] The old guard planners mostly lost the debate in the 1980s.

The SPO's role and functions had seen several changes since its early days when it was established as a technical planning body. In 1967, it was made responsible for administering investment incentives and import policies. The importance of the latter function declined with the liberalisation of imports in the 1980s. However, the SPO still administered the incentive system, allocating state funds to private-sector investments, in line with the Five-Year Plans. This already had a history of political patronage. A Development Fund (Kalkınma Fonu) had been previously established in 1967 by Turgut Özal, to avoid the interminable approval rounds of the ministries. It soon transpired that the Development Fund was in reality 'Özal's fund' allocated on his discretion, and hence it was shut down by the Constitutional Court in 1969. However, this authority was returned to the SPO in 1979, when Özal became Economy Minister, as a separate entity called the Teşvik ve Uygulama Başkanlığı (Incentive Administration Secretariat), which, with Özal's loyalists appointed, functioned largely under his control. This feature of Turkey's industrialisation efforts is captured in a UNIDO report comparing Turkey, Brazil, India, Mexico and South Korea where the 'ad hoc nature of decision making' in the SPO in Turkey is noted.[45]

SPO authority was further restricted in the 1980s, when a new entity, the Undersecretariat of Treasury and Foreign Trade (Hazine ve Dış Ticaret Müsteşarlığı, HDTM), was formed to take over the roles of the Ministry of Finance and the SPO. This reduced the role of the SPO in long-term planning and policy. The SPO's next demotion took place when the head of the SPO was no longer a voting member of the High Planning Council (Yüksek Planlama Kurulu, YPK) reporting to the Prime Ministry (after protests, they were allowed to attend). As a final sign of side-lining, once the ANAP lost power in 1991, the Incentives Administration Secretariat was transferred to the HDTM. The Five-Year Development Plan exercise would still continue over the decades to come, but its directive authority was mostly lost, as it was shunted from one ministry to another.

State Enterprises Left in Limbo

While the SPO had provided the framework and long-term plans for industrialisation, it was with the State Economic Enterprises (SEEs) that the plans were achieved. The aim of the SEEs from the start was to provide private enterprise with subsidised inputs, with the long-term objective of returning them back to the private sector. The liberalisation reforms set out to do just that. But the country did not seem to be ready politically, legally, or institutionally for this radical transformation, leaving the SEEs in limbo by the end of the 1990s.

SEEs ranging from consumer industries, over heavy and intermediate industries, to agro-industry were the core of the Turkish industrial structure, providing 53 percent of value added in manufacturing by the early 1960s.[46] They held monopoly positions in defence, rail, air, ports, most mining, and post and telecommunications. SEEs had the advantage of economies of scale greater than the private sector and, in the 1960s, of being more technologically advanced. As a group, they had been in aggregate net profit in most years from 1960 to 1974. But the dual shocks of the mid-1970s oil price rises and the rise in international interest rates had increased cost pressures, initiating an inflationary wage/price spiral and, from 1977 onwards, an increase in SEE losses.[47] Contributing to this commercial deterioration was overstaffing – an essential social function in a country that had rudimentary unemployment insurance. The number of the total employed doubled during the 1970s, to more than 700,000. By the end of the 1970s, the SEE borrowing requirement had reached 8 percent of GDP. There was an urgent need to address the SEE losses and their fiscal burden.

But this did not happen right away, and not in all sectors. From 1980 to 1983, under military rule, there was a big expansion of public investment in defence-related state enterprises. Following the US arms embargo after the 1974 Cyprus crisis, the military had concluded that Turkey needed to build up its own defence industries. State entities such as Tüsaş in aviation, Temsan in electrical machinery, Tümosan in automotive, Testaş in electronics, Aselsan in defence electronics, MKEK in munitions production and Petlas in tires all saw more investment financed from military funds and OYAK, the army pension fund. Public investments also continued in already initiated projects in energy (hydro) and transport, as well as in sectors that were deemed 'strategic' to the industrialisation strategy – such as chemicals and iron and steel.

Thus, the reforms of the state enterprise sector did not begin until there was a civilian government in 1983, with Turgut Özal as prime minister. Reforms to improve the 'efficiency' of the SEEs and to stem losses began with a 1983 law (No. 2929, overridden by the 1984 Law No. 233) that reclassified the entities into two groups. State-owned enterprises (KIT) were to operate on a commercial basis with deregulated prices in preparation for privatisation. The second group – including state firms in power, transport, communication, fertilisers and agricultural agencies – were to remain under direct government control. By 1986, the initial objective of privatisation to increase efficiency was expanded to include 'ownership dispersion' and the development of a capital market. But in the 1990s, as government fiscal constraints mounted, budget revenue generation became the major driver of the privatisation process.

The government agency charged with privatisation, set up in 1984 in a somewhat make-shift apartment block in the Çankaya hills in Ankara (when this author visited), was the Housing Development and Public Participation Administration.[48] The privatisation team included enthusiastic professionals who had returned from positions abroad to undertake nothing less than the transformation of the fundamental structure of the Turkish economy. Directly charged with privatisation was an ex-J. P. Morgan employee, Cengiz İsrafil. The strategy that he presented at the World Economic Forum in 1987 began with the sale of minority state shares in eight profitable enterprises already listed in the Istanbul Stock Exchange.[49] The objective of these 'easy' privatisations was to test the market and train personnel. He also prophetically announced a plan for a stabilisation fund that could intervene in the stock market to prevent manipulation. İsrafil would resign after the first public float of 22 percent of the shares in the telecom equipment firm Teletaş in 1988 tanked in the thinly traded Istanbul Stock Market.[50]

Meanwhile, after deep wage and labour cuts brought a brief period of profitability in the early 1980s, SEE losses had returned. Contributing to the loss of efficiency was a lack of investment for modernisation. A report in 1988 lamented that the iron and steel industry was not ready for European Economic Community membership, citing the example of fifteen-year-old technology at the İskenderun Demir Çelik.[51] Nor had ministerial interference in price-setting been much reduced. An OECD report noted: 'In 1987 more than one-fifth of the largest SEEs reported operating losses [. . .] there is a degree of synchronisation between the largest public and private firms: profits of the former increase when profits of the latter decrease and vice versa [. . .] This seems to reflect [. . .] inadequate adjustment to inflation'.[52] The 'inadequate adjustment to inflation' was the price freeze in the lead up to the November 1987 election.

These dependencies between the government, SEEs and the private sector, as well as the conflicting social and commercial aims of these entities, prevented effective 'commercialisation' of the state enterprises in the 1980s. Despite the cuts in employment to almost half peak levels, SEE deficits persisted, with a financing requirement of 5.7 percent of GNP in 1991. During the 1990s, the new government of Prime Minister Süleyman Demirel of the DYP – with a centre-left coalition partner, the SHP, opposed to privatisation –

was also unable to make much headway. Given the entrenched patronage networks built around every SEE, a wide cross-party political support for privatisation remained lacking.

Privatisation revenues in 1986–94 amounted to only USD 2.1 billion, including the block sales of the five cement plants of Çitosan to Ciments Francais in 1989, 38 percent of Turk Kablo (cables) to Nokia in 1991 and 70 percent of USAŞ (airport handling) to Scandinavian Airlines (SAS).[53] A report by the Capital Markets Board noted in 1996 that domestic interest came from local entrepreneurs acquiring regional entities of importance to their area – such as milk processing, cement and animal feed factories – while the bigger holdings and foreign investors seemed to be waiting for the larger assets to come to market.[54] Holding back interest was also the formidable legal challenges led by a former constitutional lawyer, Mümtaz Soysal, a DSP (Democratic Left Party) MP, whose foundation, the Public Entrepreneurship Development Centre (KIGEM), had launched seventy lawsuits against agreed sales, which resulted in nine cancellations by the Constitutional Court.

Following the 1994 crisis, new enabling legislation was passed to overcome the technical, legal and administrative problems. A Privatisation High Council reporting to the prime minister and a new executive body, the Privatisation Administration, were established. Preparations were made for big-ticket privatisations, such as Türk Telekom, Erdemir, Tüpraş and Petkim. But by the end of 1997, the whole effort had yielded only USD 3.4 billion of privatisation revenues from the sale of many small entities and state shares in some of the bigger ones.[55] Reviewing the 1990s, the veteran economist, Merih Celasun has concluded that 'the commercialisation and/or privatisation of the SOE sector should squarely face the political task of transferring non-commercial functions (mainly income support schemes and job creation) to the general government [. . .] This point has been totally missed'.[56] That was not all, as the reform process in Turkey 'has been hampered by ad hoc approaches to legal arrangements, heavy reliance on statutory decree with the force of law and insufficient dialogue with labour unions, political opposition and local business communities'.[57] It would require more public discussion, a deep financial and banking crisis, and a constitutional amendment before major privatisations would go ahead in the 2000s.

Box 3.2 Automotive Sector: The Rise, Retreat and Return of Industrial Policy in Turkey

The automotive sector in Turkey illustrates the changes in industrial policy over the years. Despite the story of the Devrim cars covered in the introduction to this book, the automotive sector became a success story of the liberalisation era –building on the foundations that had been laid in the 1960s and 1970s. Early investments had focused on small-scale production of agricultural machinery, buses and trucks. This changed with the first Five-Year Development Plan (1963–67) that saw the automotive industry as a strategic sector driving 'import-substituting industrialisation' and encouraging the growth of other industries such as glass, textiles, chemicals, iron and steel, and rubber. Investments during the 'planned years' of the 1960s and 1970s included a USD 600 million joint venture between Karsan and Hyundai to produce buses in Bursa in 1966, followed by Mercedes Benz, Mann Truck and Fruehauf/ Otokar. Attracted by the growing urban middle-class demand for cars, global auto firms began to enter the market, beginning with Renault in a USD 323 million joint venture with OYAK in Bursa in 1971. The same year, a joint venture investment of USD 500 million with Koç and Fiat, forming Tofaş, also in Bursa, established the city as an automotive production centre.

Production in these years began as assembly operations under licence to foreign auto firms and focused on the domestic market protected by import barriers. The licence agreements also tended to bring outdated and lower technology models and some prohibited exports.[58] Exports would have been difficult at any rate, since the small scale of production was not internationally competitive. The large number of firms relative to the size of the domestic market meant that they were unable to benefit from economies of scale. In addition, wage levels in Turkey still remained high when compared with Asia and failed to offer sufficient incentives for an Asian-style 'export platform' type of FDI into manufacturing in Turkey. Nevertheless, import controls, investment incentives and local content rules encouraged the emergence of an extensive spare-parts manufacturing industry by the mid-1970s.[59] The automotive sector as a central focus of industrial policies in the Five-Year Plans were abandoned in the 1980s. However, the liberalisation of imports forced a process of restructuring and efficiency improvements with technology upgrades, mergers and new foreign partnerships (such as the USD 350-million joint venture investment by Ford/Otosan in 1983) that also increased economies of scale.[60] The automotive firms began to export the additional output, also taking advantage of the lucrative export-incentives in the 1980s. Turkey joining the EU customs union brought a new phase in the development of the sector as exports took off in the late 1990s. The customs union restrictions on imports of Asian cars into Turkey prompted the Asian car giants to invest in production facilities in Turkey to export to the EU and other regional markets. This included Japan's Toyota, with an initial investment of USD 150 million, Honda with USD 180 million and South Korea's Hyundai with USD 670 million.

It was the export dynamic that was to attract further investment in the decades to come. Automotive sector production peaked in 2017, with 1.75 million units (65 percent passenger cars) of which 1.35 million were exported (68 percent passenger cars), amounting to 15 percent of total exports. The three biggest producers are Ford/Otosan, Oyak/Renault and Tofaş. At that point, including the support industries, the sector employed around 76,000 workers – but this is an underestimation, as it does not take into account the several rings of suppliers, service centres, car mechanics and so on, with varying degrees of informality. But crises in the Middle East and the slowing demand for cars in Europe have resulted in a decline in production since 2017.

The automotive sector has once more become the focus of attention for new industrial policies since the global financial crisis (see also Chapter 5). These have focused on the technological upgrade and reduction of the high import dependence of the automotive sector. A state-supported project to build an all-Turkish electric vehicle – TOGG – has been initiated. Increased state investment incentives have prompted several automotive firms to establish R&D centres. The boundaries of local automotive technology are also being pushed forward by the defence industry vehicles sector.

EU Customs Union and WTO Membership: A New Framework for 'Horizontal' Industrial Policy

How did these changes in the 1980s and 1990s impact the structure of the Turkish economy? The crisis of the late 1970s led to abandoning the inward-looking ISI strategy and replacing it with an export-led growth model in the 1980s. The trade and financial liberalisation reforms of the 1980s began the process of global integration of the Turkish economy, raising the share of exports and imports to 46 percent of GDP on the eve of joining the EU customs union in 1996, compared to only 20 percent in 1980. Over the same period, there was also deep structural change in the overall economy, with the share of agriculture down to 15 percent of GDP (constant 1987 prices, factor cost) from 25 percent, while services rose from 46.5 to 50.7 percent; and the share of the industrial sector (including construction and utilities) rose from 28.4 percent in 1980 to 34.3 percent in 1995. Meanwhile, the share of manufacturing initially rose from 17 percent in 1980 to 23 percent by 1989, but it remained at 21–23 percent in the 1990s.

As discussed above, while public investment in the SEEs declined, the private sector was initially slow to step up its investment in manufacturing in the 1980s, showing a preference for housing investment and rent-seeking activities. Macroeconomic instability, neglect of the institutional basis for market reforms and delays in the privatisation of state enterprises resulted in only patchy progress in industrial restructuring and in technological and skills upgrading. Of the top-ten biggest enterprises in 1995, there were only two – Arçelik (Koç Holding, white goods producer) and Tofaş (automotive, Koç/Fiat joint venture) – that were privately owned. According to SPO figures, almost 60 percent of the Turkish industrial sectors still maintained an oligopolistic character in the 1990s, mostly dominated by SEEs.[61]

There was, however, in preparation for the EU customs union, a strong investment and production spurt in 1995–97. This raised the annual average growth of manufacturing output to 5 percent in 1980–99, although this was still only around half the rate of the 1960s and 1970s. And there was another crucial difference from the previous decades. The late 1990s investment spurt was private-sector-led; combined with the struggling public-sector manufacturing, this reduced the relative share of SEEs in manufacturing value added down to 22 percent – at half their levels in the early 1980s.[62]

The EU customs union deal and the WTO regulations in the 1990s, once again, showed the importance of the global context in informing the nature and scope of Turkish industrial policies. Yet, how ready was Turkey for the full exposure to competitive forces that came with the EU customs union? The general opinion was that Turkish industry had sufficient flexibility and dynamism to adapt to the challenges posed by the customs union.[63] This was the view from the big business association, Tüsiad, but those representing smaller entities were more cautious, if not outright opposed.[64] The sector leading Turkey's joining was textiles and clothing, as the customs union would abolish EU textile quotas.[65] Accounting for over 30 percent of exports and 12 percent of the manufacturing sector output, in the mid-1990s it stood trapped between low-cost Asian suppliers and EU import quotas. Other sectors in favour were those already exporting to the EU, including white goods and consumer electronics producers, construction materials (ceramics as the third-largest producer in Europe, cement as the second-largest in Europe).[66] The chemicals industry, too, seemed prepared with ongoing technology upgrades and joint ventures with foreign investors.

On the less enthusiastic side was the automotive sector, which gave qualified support with various demands, including bans on second-hand car imports from the EU. The electronics sector was under-prepared and lacking a domestic supplier base that could compete with the Asian suppliers of the EU producers. Pharmaceutical producers were also wary, as it would require the tightening of previously lax patent laws. Sector spokesmen complained that they were handicapped by the macroeconomic instability, including the high real interest rates and given the depreciating Lira, as well as the rising energy and raw material import costs.[67] The biggest negative impact was expected to be on state monopolies such as Tekel in tobacco and Seka in paper and pulp. The customs union also brought added urgency to the restructuring and privatisation of public-sector giants, such as Tüpraş, Petkim and Türk Telekom.

Turkey was the EU's tenth-largest export market at the time of negotiation of the customs union deal, and it was the EU that was expected to be the principal winner from the agreement. The removal of Turkish tariffs on EU products and the adoption of the common external tariff on non-EU products was expected to double EU exports to Turkey within five years. Yet, Brussels was doing its usual hard-grinding bargaining. One sticking point was the Mass

Housing Fund which relied on an import surcharge for its revenues. Seeing this as an indirect import tariff, the EU demanded that it be closed; in the end, it was agreed to reduce the number of products on which the surcharge would be levied. Japanese car imports to Turkey were also a sticking point for the EU side.[68] Agriculture and services were left out of the agreement. A separate agreement with the European Iron and Steel Community brought restrictions on state aids. Amongst the many prerequisite regulatory requirements for Turkey was a Competition Regulator which was met with the Anti-Monopoly Act in 1995 and the rules of the Agreement on Trade-Related Aspects of Intellectual Property Rights (TRIPS) concerning copyright, patent and industrial design protection, with which Turkey would comply by 1999.

Turkish economists warned that no other EU member had joined the customs union before they had been full members with access to EU financial transfers to support the costs of the transition. The reduction of the customs duties and the Mass Housing Fund levy alone amounted to a loss of around USD 2.5 billion of fiscal revenues, estimated at 1.4 percent of GDP. Turkey asked for USD 6 billion to cover the costs of adjustment (including 1,634 legal and institutional changes to comply with EU regulations); it received ECU 1.5 billon over a five-year period, mostly in the form of loans from the European Investment Bank.[69] Meanwhile, the EU was yet to release the ECU 600 million previous commitments under the Association Agreement's fourth financial protocol; and the previously agreed-upon free circulation of labour was postponed again. There were concerns that, by locking itself into the EU single market, Turkey was restricting its geostrategic advantages to reach other regional markets.[70] In the end, it did not seem as if this was a 'good deal' for Turkey. But it went ahead because it was not a 'new' deal. It was the completion of a 1973 'Additional Protocol' to the 1963 Association Agreement.[71] At that time, the European Economic Community had abolished all customs duties on industrial products imported from Turkey (there were not many), and Turkey was expected to reciprocate over a period of twenty-two years to join the customs union as a step towards full membership. Hence, the Turkish side accepted the completion of the customs union based on the assumption that full membership would soon follow.

The Turkish private sector rose to the occasion. Manufacturing growth picked up in the second half of the 1990s; output almost doubled in 1994–98

in the machinery and transport equipment sector.[72] Despite the caution-
ary debates, by the end of the 1990s, the EU customs union had resulted in
increased trade in both directions. As expected, EU exports to Turkey grew
faster than Turkish exports to the EU. The share of the EU in Turkey's total
trade rose from 46 to 53 percent. Also as expected, and despite some teething
problems, Turkish textiles and clothing exports increased the most in absolute terms. This was achieved even though the global economic instability at
the end of the 1990s and Turkey's 2001 crisis limited the rate of growth of
trade and held back FDI inflows.

Not surprisingly, studies that examined the impact of trade liberalisation
in Turkey comparing import-competing, export-oriented and non-traded
industries, found that productivity growth and export growth was highest in
import-competing sectors, especially so after the customs union deal.[73] This
was seen in the white goods, brown goods and automotive sectors in the early
2000s, which turned to exports to offset weak domestic demand. For example,
automotive exports rose from USD 200 million in the early 1990s to USD 1.5
billion in 2000. This changed the composition of Turkey's exports to the EU,
moving it up on the technology ladder. The relative share of textiles and clothing in total exports declined, as other medium-technology exports grew, such
as automobiles, machinery, and iron and steel, boosted by a reduction in trade
costs and the emergence of integrated production networks between Turkish
and EU firms.[74]

Industrial Policies Adapt to WTO and EU Customs Union Rules

One of the main changes brought by the WTO membership and EU customs
union entry came with the regulatory requirements of the agreements. This was
especially so with EU rules on state aids that affected Turkish industrial policies. Until the late 1980s, private-sector investors could still rely on state support,
through the investment incentives programmes. These were important policy
instruments, not only for raising the level of investments, but also for directing
investments to particular sectors by specifying a 'positive list' of sectors that were
eligible for the incentives. During 1981–90, the number of investment certificates had risen to 25,000, from 4,802 in 1968–80.[75] However, as discussed above
in the sections on extra-budgetary funds and export incentives, the rapid expansion of these programmes, lack of transparency and discretionary allocation of

funds by Özal's increasingly centralised and personalised regime had created major problems.

Attempts to deal with these problems in the late 1980s were reinforced by the requirements of Turkey's new international trade treaties signed with the WTO and the EU, which brought restrictive rules on industrial policy measures and wider state-aid policies. The WTO rules on Subsidies and Countervailing Measures (SCM) prevented measures based on export performance or measures that discriminate in favour of domestic production. Moreover, measures that targeted specific products or sectors would be 'actionable' and could be subject to legal challenges. Meanwhile, the EU customs union required that state aid be harmonised with EU rules (which at any rate allowed large amounts of state aid to EU firms) and that public procurement legislation did not discriminate between EU and Turkish nationals.[76]

These rules changed the form of Turkish industrial policies away from direct sectoral targeting to a greater focus on 'horizontal' criteria that were allowed: support for SMEs, environmental protection, support for R&D, regional development, employment creation, technology upgrade and foreign currency earning investments. For exports, direct export subsidies had to be phased out, but incentives to support participation in trade fairs, certification and product and brand promotion were still allowed. Although compliance with these treaties increased the administrative burden, they supported the already existing (not always successful) efforts to improve transparency and reduce the *ad hoc* nature of the incentives process.

The value of state incentives granted also fell, but this had more to do with fiscal constraints in Turkey. The value of incentive certificates was already declining by the early 1990s, as those most open to corruption and abuse – such as the export-tax rebates – had been closed. For example, the Resource Utilisation Support Fund set up in 1984 was one of the few entities from which cash support was granted to investments; its use declined, as fiscal constraints increased by the end of the 1980s, and it was discontinued in 1991. Thereafter, the incentives system relied more on tax exemptions and credits from state banks. From the mid-1990s, fiscal spending, including spending associated with industrial policies, was tightened further. The annual value of incentives certificates peaked in 1995 and fell throughout the rest of the 1990s (see Figure 3.2), with the share of manufacturing down to 43.4 percent in 1999. The 1995

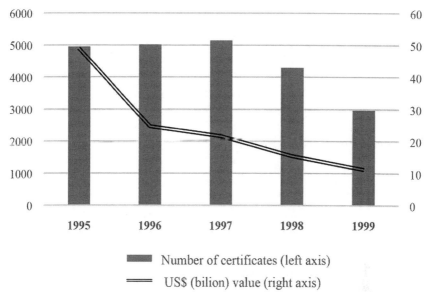

Figure 3.2 Number and value of incentive certificates (1995–99)

Source: State Planning Organisation, Seventh Five-Year Plan.

peak reflected the major investment push to upgrade the textile, chemicals and ceramics sectors in preparation for the start of the customs union.

These years also saw a debate regarding the effectiveness of investment incentives, which questioned their efficacy. Atiyas has quoted studies examining the impact of incentives programmes in 1980–2000 that showed *no impact* of the volume of investment certificates on the actual volume of investment; other surveys have indicated that 64 percent of respondents would have decided to invest even if no incentives had been offered.[77] These studies, along with the discussion above, have suggested significant capacity problems. They show the low social 'embeddedness' of how incentives were designed and allocated, which in turn reflected the weakening of the transformative element in state capacity.

By the end of the 1990s, there was increased recognition of the need for a new approach in state–business relations, as noted in the Seventh Five-Year Plan (1996–2000) to free business '*from knocking on the door of the state*' (italics added). In terms of 'autonomy', the personalised decision-making practices during the Özal period and the fragmented political environment in the 1990s undermined merit-based institutional procedures in economic bureaucracy.

As a result, there emerged a greater understanding of the need for independent regulatory and supervisory agencies. Already in 1997, plans were being discussed to establish the independence of the Central Bank – one year prior to the 1998 IMF stand-by, and four years before it came into law. Similar discussions were taking place on institutional reforms which would be implemented following the 2001 crisis.

Conclusion: The High Cost of Industrial Policy Dichotomy Traps

This chapter has examined the demotion of industrial policies in Turkey, as the global development paradigm shifted from import-substituting industrialisation to an export-oriented one. Although the reforms of the 1980s did reduce the role of the state in trade and finance and lifted many controls over business, limited progress in the privatisation of state enterprises and large budget deficits ensured that the state remained a significant actor in resource allocation.

What industrial policies remained, along with state intervention generally, had become less coherent and more discretionary. The reliance on off-budget funds that lacked public oversight for investment and export incentives – which were allocated on an increasingly discretionary basis – increased uncertainty for private investors. Thus, business success remained dependent on relations with political and bureaucratic actors, fostering corruption and cronyism. The *ad hoc* and particularistic interventions of the Özal regime that undermined existing institutions such as the SPO also weakened the capacity of the state to guide industrial transformation. This stood in contrast to the previous approach to industrialisation, led by active industrial policies targeting strategic sectors in the framework of Five-Year Development Plans. Active industrial policies were further demoted in the late 1990s, by fiscal constraints as well as the WTO and the EU customs union regulations restricting state aids. Instead, industrial policies were reshaped around a frequently changing mix of 'horizontal' investment incentives.

Despite the success of the export-oriented policies in increasing manufactured exports in the 1980s and the breakthrough sectors such as automotives in the 1990s, the economic environment deteriorated, with a severe rise in macroeconomic instability. Amplified by exposure to volatile international capital flows, these unstable conditions would lead to a major payments crisis in 2001. Turkey had missed the opportunity in the early 1970s to shift to export orientation earlier, a move that could have begun to establish a more resilient and competitive industrial base prior to the trade and capital account liberalisation of the 1980s. This could have reduced the rise in import dependence and the associated macro-instability.

These developments in the 1980s and 1990s confirm the main theses of this book – that is, industrial development depends not so much on the size of the state, but on its effectiveness to manage industrial policies. Second, as seen with the struggles of the private sector to offset the decline in public investment in manufacturing, macroeconomic instability and the associated uncertainty for investors became major impediments to long-term investment. Finally, the missed opportunity in the early 1970s to pursue export growth and the lack of support for the 'new economy' sectors in the late 1990s (see Chapter 4) illustrate the need to avoid the dichotomies in industrial policy, between export-oriented versus import-substituting industrialisation or horizontal versus vertical measures. As suggested in Chapter 1, these need to be pursued together within a proper institutional context.

Notes

1. These trends have been extensively and authoritatively studied. Key sources, also consulted for this chapter, include Annual OECD Economic Surveys of the Turkish economy from the 1990s; TÜSİAD Annual Reports: *The Turkish Economy*; State Planning Organisation, Five-Year Development Plan reports; Ayşe Buğra, *State and Business in Modern Turkey: A Comparative Study* (Albany: SUNY Press, 1994); Ziya Öniş and Süleyman Özmucur, *Supply Side Origins of Macroeconomic Crises in Turkey*, Boğaziçi University Research Papers, 1988; Tosun Arıcanlı and Dani Rodrik, eds, *The Political Economy of Turkey: Debt, Adjustment and Sustainability* (Basingstoke: Palgrave Macmillan, 1990); Ümit Sönmez, *Piyasanın İdaresi: Neoliberalizm ve Bağımsız Düzenleyici Kurumların Anatomisi* (İstanbul: İletişim Yayınları, 2011); Fikret Şenses, ed., *Recent Industrialisation Experience of Turkey in a Global Context* (Westport: Greenwood Press, 1994); Yakup Kepenek, *Gelişim, Üretim Yapısı ve Sorunlarıyla Türkiye Ekonomisi* (Ankara: Teori Yayınları, 1983). In addition, the material incorporates the author's own work drawing on original public reports by ministries, interviews with senior policy-makers and political figures, and the Economist Intelligence Unit Special Report No. 1136: Mina Toksöz (with a contribution by David Barchard), *Turkey to 1992: Missing Another Chance?* EIU Economic Prospects Series, September 1988.

2. Dr Demir Demirgil, who taught economics at Bosphorus University for many years, listed among the costs of postponing the Lira's devaluation in the late 1960s the requirement of 'stronger and stronger controls on foreign trade and foreign exchange' to manage the foreign currency shortage; Class Notes for Economy 204: 'Growth Performance of the Turkish Economy 1950–70', 1973.

3. Peter Evans, *Embedded Autonomy: States and Industrial Transformation* (Princeton: Princeton University Press, 1995), p. 57.

4. Ali Tekin, 'Turkey's Aborted Attempt at Export-led Growth Strategy: Anatomy of the 1970 Economic Reform', *Middle Eastern Studies*, Vol. 42, No. 1 (2006), pp. 133–63. On the structure of the manufacturing sector and the missed opportunity of the early 1970s reforms, see Mina Toksöz, *Turkey to 1992: Missing Another Chance?* EIU Economic Prospects Series, September 1988, 'Chapter 4: Context of the 1980s Reforms'. See also Gülten Kazgan, *Ekonomide Dışa Açık Büyüme* (İstanbul: Altın Kitaplar Yayınevi, 1984), pp. 318–43.

5. Ziya Öniş, 'The State and Economic Development in Contemporary Turkey: Etatism to Neoliberalism and Beyond', in Vojtech Mastny and Craig Nation, eds, *Turkey Between East and West* (Boulder: Westview Press, 1996), pp. 155–78.

6. For an extensive analysis, see Ziya Öniş, *State and Market: The Political Economy of Turkey* (Istanbul: Boğaziçi University Press, 1998).

7. For an extensive analysis on the state in Turkey as a source of uncertainty for the business environment, see Ayşe Buğra, *State and Business in Modern Turkey: A Comparative Study* (Albany: SUNY Press, 1994).

8. Ricardo Hausmann and Dani Rodrik, 'Economic Development as Self-Discovery', *Journal of Development Economics*, Vol. 72, No. 2 (2003), pp. 603–33.

9. State Planning Organisation, *V. Beş Yıllık Kalkınma Planı Döneminde Sektörel Gelişmeler (1985–89)* (Ankara: SPO, 1985), p. 48–49.

10. TÜBİTAK, *Turkish Science and Technology Policy: 1993–2003* (Ankara: TÜBİTAK, 1993). In 1994, PTT was divided into two firms, one providing postal service and the other serving as Türk Telekom.

11. Mustafa Kutlay, *Crisis and Change: The Political Economies of Turkey and Greece* (London: Palgrave Macmillan, 2019), p. 39.

12. William Hale, 'Democracy and the Party System in Turkey', in Brian Beeley, ed., *Turkish Transformation, New Century, New Challenges* (Huntingdon: Eothen Press, 2002).

13. Günal Kansu, *Planlı Yıllar: Anılarla DPT'nin Öyküsü* (İstanbul: İş Bankası Kültür Yayınları, 2004). Although the 'planned' period has ended, Five-Year Development plans continue to this day, with the latest (Eleventh) Five-Year Plan published in 2019.

14. Ayse Buğra, *State and Business in Modern Turkey* (Albany: SUNY Press, 1994), p. 146.

15. By 1986, the share of wages and salaries in total incomes had halved from their peak of 36.8 percent in 1977, according to Ziya Öniş and Süleyman Özmucur, *Supply Side Origins of Macroeconomic Crises in Turkey*, Boğaziçi University Research Papers, 1988, p. 65.

16. Yıldız Atasoy, *Turkey, Islamists and Democracy* (London: I. B. Tauris, 2005), p. 152. Remittances from the Turkish migrant workers in the Middle East doubled from USD 983 million in 1978 to USD 2.2 billion in 1982; by 1986, the cumulative value of Turkish construction firm contracts in the Middle East amounted to USD 17 billion.

17. In fact, what was thought to be an alarming 'six-fold increase in the external current account deficit to about 5% of GNP' estimated by the IMF turned out to be a manageable 2.6 percent of GNP, once the informal 'shuttle trade' exports (with the former Soviet Union) were included. The alarming estimate can be found in the IMF Press Release No. 94/48, 'IMF Approves Stand-By Credit for Turkey', 8 July 1994. On the shuttle trade impact, see IMF, *Turkey: Recent Economic Developments and Selected Issues*, No. 97/110, November 1997, p. 30.

18. Mina Toksöz, *The Economist Guide to Country Risk* (London: Profile Books, 2014), p. 61.

19. John Murray Brown, 'Promises of a Better Life', *FT Survey: Turkish Finance Investment & Industry*, 17 December 1991.

20. These bankruptcies related to the issuing of 'certificates of deposits' (CDs) which offered high interest rates to attract '*yastık altı*' (under the pillow/mattress) savings into the official banking sector. The banks outsourced the marketing of these CDs to brokers called *borsa bankeri* (market bankers) who added an extra premium (for which the brokers were responsible) to the interest rates set by banks. Soon joining these relatively established brokers were numerous self-appointed *köşebaşı bankerler* (kerb-side-bankers), offering increasingly unrealistic interest rates and creating a ponzi-scheme bubble. Belated attempts at regulation by the Ministry of Finance in late 1981, requiring ministry-licensing of the brokers and minimum capital requirements, triggered the bankruptcy of a few small brokers. But this was enough to alarm some 300,000–400,000 savers into panic withdrawals that began in March 1982. In the midst of the panic, Cevher Özden, the owner of Banker Kastelli, the biggest broker, had to flee to Switzerland. For details see, Arslan Başer Kafaoğlu, *Bankerler ve Kastelli Olayı* (İstanbul: Alan Yayıncılık, 1982).

21. These included İstanbul Bankası, Hisarbank, Bağbank, Odabank and İşçi Kredi Bankası, which later closed down and transferred their liabilities to state-owned

or stronger private banks. See İzak Atiyas, 'The Private Sector's Response to Financial Liberalisation in Turkey: 1980–82,' World Bank, Working Papers WPS147, 1989.

22. Data on the banking sector in the 1990s is from *OECD Economic Surveys, Turkey*, 1999, p. 126.

23. World Bank, *Turkey Country Economic Memorandum: Structural Reforms for Sustainable Growth*, Report No: 20657-TU, 15 September 2000, p. 96.

24. Mehmet Sami, *Developments in Turkish Capital Markets* (Istanbul: ATA Securities, 1996).

25. Süleyman Özmucur, 'Productivity and Profitability in 500 Largest Firms of Turkey 1980–1990', *Yapı Kredi Economic Review*, Vol. 5, No. 2 (1992), table 16, p. 68.

26. Ziya Öniş and Fikret Şenses, eds., *Turkey and the Global Economy: Neoliberal Restructuring and Integration in the Post Crisis Era* (London: Routledge, 2009), p. 18.

27. Although lucrative, this was a precarious existence: of the twenty-two new banks established in the 1990s, only thirteen would survive by the end of the decade. See Galip Yalman, 'The Neoliberal Transformation of State and Market in Turkey: An Overview of Financial Developments from 1980 to 2000', in Galip Yalman, Thomas Marois and Ali Rıza Güngen, eds, *The Political Economy of Financial Transformation in Turkey* (London: Routledge, 2019), p. 72.

28. State Planning Organisation, *Yabanci Sermaye Raporu*, June 1990, p. 10; Tüsiad, *The Turkish Economy*, 1990, p. 168.

29. This section draws on the work by Ishac Divan, Adeel Malik and Izak Atiyas, eds, *Crony Capitalism in the Middle East* (Oxford: Oxford University Press, 2019); Gül Berna Özcan and Hasan Turunç, 'Economic Liberalisation and Class Dynamics in Turkey: New Business Groups and Islamic Mobilisation,' *Insight Turkey*, Vol. 13, No. 3 (2011), pp. 63–86; Gül Berna Özcan, *Small Firms and Local Economic Development: Entrepreneurship in Southern Europe and Turkey* (Aldershot: Ashgate, 1995); Yıldız Atasoy, *Turkey, Islamists and Democracy* (London: I. B. Tauris, 2005); European Stability Initiative, 'Islamic Calvinists, Change and Conservatism in Central Anatolia', 19 September, 2005, https://www.esiweb.org/publications/islamic-calvinists-change-and-conservatism-central-anatolia.

30. The latter had close personal connections to the government via Turgut Özal's brother Korkut Özal, who had previously been a consultant to the Islamic Development Bank and founding member of Al-Baraka Türk.

31. There was also ASKON, formed in 1998, and TUSKON, formed in 2005. The latter was shut down after the attempted coup in 2016; associated prominent firms – such as the Boydak Group, Koza İpek and Bank Asya – were taken over by the state, with their assets transferred to the Savings Deposit Insurance Fund (TMSF).

32. Ümit Sönmez, *Piyasanın İdaresi: Neoliberalizm ve Bağımsız Düzenleyici Kurumların Anatomisi* (İstanbul: İletişim Yayınları, 2011), pp. 145–86.

33. This took place just prior to the local elections where the big municipalities were won by ANAP candidates. Metin Heper, ed., *Democracy and Local Government: Istanbul in the 1980s* (Huntingdon: Eothen Press, 1987), p. 3.

34. Mustafa Kutlay, *Crisis and Change: The Political Economies of Turkey and Greece* (London: Palgrave Macmillan, 2019), p. 35.

35. Ayşe Buğra, *State and Business in Modern Turkey* (Albany: SUNY Press, 1994), p. 121.

36. Oğuz Oyan, 'An Overall Evaluation of the Causes of Use of Special Funds in Turkey and Their Place in the Economy', *Yapı Kredi Economic Review*, Vol. 1, No. 4 (1987), pp. 83–116.

37. OECD, *Economic Surveys, Turkey*, 1989/90, p. 70.

38. 'Fon Uygulamaları Ekonominin Makro Dengelerini Bozuyor', *Dünya*, 14 May 1987.

39. IMF, 'Turkey: Recent Economic Developments and Selected Issues', *IMF Staff Country Report No 97/110*, November 1997, table A24.

40. Ziya Öniş and Süleyman Özmucur, *Supply Side Origins of Macroeconomic Crises in Turkey*, Boğaziçi University Research Papers, 1988, Table 5.10, p. 88.

41. Mina Toksöz, *Turkey to 1992: Missing Another Chance?* EIU Economic Prospects Series, 1988, p. 51.

42. Anne O. Kruger and Baran Tuncer, 'Industrial Priorities in Turkey', in *Industrial Priorities in Developing Countries* (New York: UNIDO, 1979), p. 133.

43. Ayşe Buğra, *State and Business in Modern Turkey: A Comparative Study* (Albany: SUNY Press, 1994), p. 159.

44. Günal Kansu, *Planlı Yıllar: Anılarla DPT'nin Öyküsü* (İstanbul: İş Bankası Kültür Yayınları, 2004), p. 160.

45. Ibid., p. vii.

46. Kamil Yılmaz, 'Industry', in Metin Heper and Sabri Gultekin, eds, *The Routledge Handbook of Modern Turkey* (London: Routledge, 2012), chapter 33.

47. The data on SEEs in this section are derived from OECD, *Country Surveys, Turkey*, 1981, 1989–90, and 1999; see also World Bank, *Turkey: State Owned Enterprise Sector Review*, Report No 10014-TU, 3 March 1993.

48. In 1990, the HDPPA was split into two separate agencies: the Housing Development Administration responsible for mass housing development, and the Public Participation Fund in charge of privatisation and large project finance.

49. Cengiz Israfil, 'The Privatisation Program in Turkey,' presentation at the World Economic Forum National Meeting on Turkey, 1 May 1987, İstanbul.

50. This was a public disaster, as the shares were offered through 4,800 bank branches across Turkey and bought by 42,000 retail investors.

51. Nurhan Yönezer, 'Demir Çelik Sektörü AT Üyeliğine Hazır Değil', *Dünya*, 11 July 1988. Today, İsdemir is part of the Oyak holding group and the biggest iron and steel complex in Turkey.

52. OECD, *Economic Surveys, Turkey*, 1989/90, p. 100.

53. Public Participation Administration, *Privatisation in Turkey*, Ankara, January 1992. Usas and Çitosan sales were promptly challenged in the administrative courts and cancelled; the government appealed, leading to a prolonged legal process before the sales were eventually finalised.

54. Capital Markets Board, *Turkish Capital Markets*, May 1996. The one exception of interest by large holdings in privatisations was Rumeli Holding (of the collapsed Uzan Group), which bought several cement firms and two regional electricity firms (Çukurova, Kepez) in the early 1990s.

55. OECD, *Economic Surveys, Turkey*, 1999, p. 21.

56. Merih Celasun, ed., *State Owned Enterprises in the Middle East and North Africa: Privatisation, Performance, and Reform* (London: Routledge, 2001), p. 243.

57. Ibid., p. 249.

58. Murat A. Yülek, Kwon Hyung Lee, Jungsuk Kim and Donghyun Park, 'State Capacity and the Role of Industrial Policy in Automobile Industry: A Comparative Analysis of Turkey and South Korea', *Journal of Industry, Competition, and Trade*, 20 (2020), pp. 307–31.

59. Hacer Ansal, 'International Competitiveness and Industrial Policy: The Turkish Experience in the Textile and Truck Manufacturing Industries', in Fikret Şenses, ed., *Recent Industrialisation Experience of Turkey in a Global Context* (Westport: Greenwood Press, 1994), p. 184.

60. Erol Taymaz and Kamil Yılmaz, *Political Economy of Industrial Policy in Turkey: The Case of the Automotive Industry*, Global Development Institute, The University of Manchester, ESID Working Paper No. 90, September 2017.

61. State Planning Organisation, *7th Five Year Plan*, Ankara. Out of eighty-three sectors surveyed, forty-eight had 50 percent of the total output produced by the top four firms.

62. Kamil Yılmaz, 'Industry', in Metin Heper and Sabri Gultekin, eds, *The Routledge Handbook of Modern Turkey* (London: Routledge, 2012), chapter 33.

63. Mükerrem Hiç, *Turkey's Customs Union with the EU*, Stiftung Wissenchaft und Politik, September 1995.

64. 'Gümrük Birliği İçin Teşvik İstemiyoruz, Önlem Alınsın', *Dünya*, 3 August 1993.

65. In the early 1990s, the Turkish textiles sector production was one of the biggest in Europe, with 90 percent in the private sector. The sector contained large competitive firms producing for export. But many producers – especially the SMEs – had fallen behind their competitors in Asia and Southern Europe in installing new technology developed in the 1970s and 1980s: some 80 percent of the machinery was older than ten years, compared to 40–60 percent in Spain, Brazil and South Korea, for example. Çiğdem Kılıçkaya, 'Tekstil Sektörünün Yapısı ve Türkiye'de Tekstil Sektörü', *Hazine ve Dış Ticaret Dergisi*, Vol. 16, No. 1 (1993), p. 62.

66. Safa Ocak, 'General Outlook of the Turkish Industry and Competitiveness of the Private Sector', *Istanbul Stock Exchange Review*, Vol. 11, No. 1 (1997), p. 7.

67. 'Sanayiciden Birlige "Şartlı Evet"', *Dünya*, 3 July 1993.

68. At the time, Japan had agreed to a voluntary export restraint on car exports to the EU markets, but this was not universally accepted by all EU members, with Germany, the UK and the Netherlands disagreeing with the rule.

69. In a sign of the future pattern of EU–Turkey political relations, the ECU 375 million portion of the agreed-upon assistance that was to come from the community budget was frozen in the first year of the customs union coming into effect. This was done by the European Parliament, citing human rights violations.

70. This was one of the main arguments against the EU customs union made by Islamist parties, including the Welfare Party (RP). But the RP dropped this demand during its coalition government with the DYP in 1996. This warning also came from unexpected quarters, including the veteran World Bank economist Anne Kruger in her speech to YASED (Association for Foreign Capital Coordination) in Istanbul, on 15 November 1989.

71. For a critical examination of Turkey–EU relations during the Cold War era, see Mehmet Ali Birand, *Türkiye'nin Ortak Pazar Macerası, 1959–1985* (İstanbul: Milliyet Yayınları, 1987).

72. Industrial Production Index 1992=100, weighted by value added; OECD, Economic Surveys, *Turkey*, 1999, p. 162.

73. İzak Atiyas and Ozan Bakış, 'Structural Change and Industrial Policy in Turkey', *Emerging Markets Finance and Trade*, Vol. 51, No. 6 (2015), p. 1224.

74. European Commission, 'Study of the EU-Turkey Bilateral Preferential Trade Framework Including the Customs Union, and an Assessment of its Possible Enhancement,' Final Report, 26 October 2016.

75. Erinç Yeldan, 'The Economic Structure of Power under Turkish Structural Adjustment: Prices, Growth and Accumulation', p. 84; and Fikret Şenses, 'The Stabilisation and Structural Adjustment Program and the Process of Turkish Industrialisation: Main Policies and Their Impact', p. 59, both in Fikret Şenses, ed., *Recent Industrialisation Experience of Turkey in a Global Context* (Westport: Greenwood Press, 1994).

76. In the early 1990s, state aid in EU members averaged just under 4 percent of total public spending, with Germany and Italy spending around 5 percent. See Chris Rumford, *State Aid to Industry: Turkey and the Customs Union* (Istanbul: Intermedia Publications, 1997).

77. İzak Atiyas and Ozan Bakış, 'Structural Change and Industrial Policy in Turkey', *Emerging Markets Finance and Trade*, Vol. 51, No. 6 (2015), p. 1222.

4

INDUSTRIAL POLICY IN RETREAT, 2001–9

This chapter covers industrial policy from the 2001 Turkish economic crisis to the 2008 global financial crisis, which saw a rare period of macroeconomic stability following the 2001 crisis. Inflation was reduced to single digits after a long time, and economic growth remained robust until the global financial crisis. The reforms following the 2001 crisis were designed in line with the post-Washington Consensus paradigm and its emphasis on institutions – not only curbing the role of the state in the economy, but also re-positioning it as a 'regulatory state'. The 2001 crisis poses a turning point in Turkish political economy, as it enabled the establishment of independent regulatory institutions, including central bank independence. The long-overdue economic transformation in this period, however, was lacking a proper industrial policy pillar, leading to lost opportunities and significant challenges in the decade to follow.

The Turkish economy had staggered through the 1990s, buffeted by volatile international capital flows. Short bursts of growth had been driven by fiscal and credit stimulus and foreign borrowing that brought rising non-performing loans and state-bank duty-losses and unsustainable foreign debt levels. Meanwhile, liberalisation reforms to reduce the state role in the economy had sidelined the institutions that had delivered industrialisation in the 1960s, replacing them with increasingly erratic, reactive and discretionary government policies. Combined with macroeconomic and political instability, this had created a volatile business environment. It took a multi-dimensional crisis in 2000–1 before the country could overcome the political fragmentation that blocked the deep reforms needed.

With the Justice and Development Party (AKP) coming to power in 2002, and the twin anchors of the IMF and the EU candidacy, the post-Washington Consensus was further consolidated during an exceptionally favourable period of the global economy. Unlike in the previous two decades, the mass privatisation of SEEs also gained momentum, attracting high levels of foreign direct investment. There were break-through sectors, such as the automotive sector, that benefited from integration with EU supply chains within the customs union. The post-2001 crisis measures also included banking sector restructuring and radical reforms in agriculture. The fiscal space gained from the decline in inflation and interest rates allowed for a major increase in infrastructural, health and other social investments that also involved private sector participation. However, this chapter makes the point that, in contrast to the state's improved regulatory capacity, its capability to guide industrial transformation remained erratic and weak in the early 2000s. The demotion of 'vertical' industrial policies lost the opportunity to support the emergence of higher-technology 'new economy' sectors in this period. Turkey, as a result, was integrated into the global economy in the wake of the twenty-first century, with an industrial structure mostly dominated by low- and middle-technology sectors with high import dependence.

The virtuous growth cycle came to an end with the global financial crisis of 2008–9, followed by increasing instability. This chapter covers Turkey's transition to the new economic paradigm, in line with global trends in early 2000s. The following section reviews the post-Washington Consensus and the associated reforms that paved the way for macroeconomic stability. The third section examines the mass privatisations and their uneven impact on industrial transformation in Turkey, tracing the retreat of industrial policy in this period and the lost opportunity to support the 'new economy' sectors. The fourth section critically assesses the institutional context in the early AKP era, by examining the transformation in regulatory institutions and state–business relations. The chapter concludes with the 'return of crisis of governance', following the 2013 'taper tantrum' – when the US Federal Reserve began to tighten monetary policies – leading to a major withdrawal of capital flows from emerging markets.

The Post-Washington Consensus: Regulatory State and Retreat of Industrial Policy

The neoliberal policies created significant problems for developing countries in the 1990s. A new post-Washington Consensus framework emerged from the lessons of the 1997 Asian crisis, when it was seen that 'inadequate prudential regulation and supervision' during the liberalisation of finance, trade and capital account was associated with more frequent financial crises.[1] While maintaining the market-led orientation of policy and the limited role of the state, the concept of the 'regulatory state' was introduced, with an understanding of the need for independent institutions to regulate markets. Turkey's reforms following the 2001 economic crisis adopted this approach in order to try and repair the institutional deterioration of the previous two decades.[2]

These policies strengthened the much-needed regulatory capacity of the Turkish state (for a while), but its industrial transformative capacity continued to weaken.[3] The state's role in industry retreated, as privatisation finally proceeded and as the banking sector was restructured. Industrial policies had already been pared back in the late 1990s due to fiscal constraints. They were further limited by the WTO and the EU customs union membership and framed in 'neutral' – or 'comparative advantage facilitating' – terms with mixed results.[4] In its place, private-sector growth through 'business environment reforms became the new industrial policy'.[5]

In this changing global setting, still allowed were 'horizontal measures' such as investment incentives for regional development and small and medium-sized enterprises (SMEs). These policies supported the AKP's core constituencies, mostly located in the Anatolian provinces and in low-technology sectors. Conglomerates with close connections to the AKP in construction and real estate emerged on the back of mass housing projects supported by entities such as TOKİ (Mass Housing Fund) and large infrastructure projects through public–private partnerships. Relying on various army funds, a defence and related electronics sector also did well, as did sectors where Turkey had a comparative advantage – consumer durables, automotive, chemicals and iron and steel – which benefited from foreign direct investment inflows and integration with EU supply chains.

The economic policy anchors provided by the start of EU membership negotiations and the IMF stand-by agreement provided a rare period of macroeconomic stability and reduced uncertainty. Also, the favourable global liquidity environment enabled a steady growth of domestic and foreign private investment in 2002–7. However, the appreciating Lira from the mid-2000s eroded competitiveness and increased import dependence, resulting in chronic current account deficits. These problems were revealed by the global financial crisis, leading the AKP to begin to shed its regulatory and economic liberalisation reforms towards a more interventionist approach to industrialisation. This new interventionism of the state – and the return of industrial policy – will be covered in Chapter 5, but first the redefinition and restructuring of the state's role in the economy during the first decade of AKP rule will be examined.

The Twin Crises and the 'Transition Programme Towards a Strong Economy'

The 1990s ended with a badly designed IMF stand-by agreement in December 1999; this was followed by a two-stage crisis in November 2000 and February 2001. The IMF agreement was a recognition by the political and business establishment in Turkey that the accelerating fiscal deficit, debt and inflation could no longer continue. By 1999, the public sector borrowing requirement (PSBR) had reached 11.4 percent of GDP, inflation had been hovering at around 60–80 percent for a decade, and several banks had already needed rescuing. But the 1999 IMF agreement – a three-year exchange-rate-based stabilisation programme – came with a risky, periodically adjusted exchange rate peg.[6] Combined with the fractious debates of the cross-party ANAP, MHP and DSP coalition government at the time and the shadow of the Russian default in international financial markets, the exchange rate peg became a target for currency speculation, as the Lira appreciated following the IMF agreement.

The crisis broke in November 2000, when a mid-sized private bank, Demirbank, went under and set off a liquidity crunch, as the bigger, solvent banks stopped extending credit to smaller banks. The strict monitoring by the recently established Banking Regulation and Supervision Agency had led bankers to become wary of lending to smaller banks, for fear that they could end up in court for lending to a bankrupt bank.[7] But just as this was being contained, a government crisis in February 2001 triggered a big flight from Lira assets. In the market panic that followed with sudden capital outflows, overnight interest rates rose to 5,000 percent, and the Lira-peg collapsed, resulting in a sharp devaluation. This exposed the high 'open-foreign-currency-positions' of many banks, causing further bankruptcies and increasing the risk of debt default. At one level, the 2000–1 crisis for Turkey was a classic combination of banking, political and payments crises. But it also reflected the weakness of state institutions and resulted in the political and business elite accepting that deeper reforms were unavoidable.

Amidst the mayhem, Prime Minister Ecevit requested help from Kemal Derviş, a distinguished economist working at the World Bank as vice president, to take on the role of Minister of Economic Affairs in March 2001; under his leadership, one of Turkey's most transformative reform packages was constructed. The programme, called 'Transition Programme Towards a Strong Economy' – which was approved and supported by the IMF, the World Bank and the EU – consisted of a three-pronged strategy. The first, most urgent task, was to restructure the banking sector and stabilise the financial and currency markets; second was to enact a large fiscal adjustment and a strict monetary policy to reduce inflation; and third was to implement structural reforms to improve competition and efficiency and enhance the role of the private sector. Launched in May 2001, amidst the US Dot-com crisis, the series of laws – which were crucial to releasing funds from the multilateral financial package (of USD 16 billion from the IMF and USD 6.2 billion from the World Bank, plus bilateral loans from allies such as Japan) – were passed at an unprecedented pace, taking the Turkish economy through a shock therapy programme, more associated with transition economies in Eastern Europe.

Box 4.1 Major Institutional Reform Legislation, 1999–2002

- **June 1999:** Banking Law establishing the Banking Regulation and Supervision Agency (BRSA).
- **August 1999:** Constitutional amendment enabling the transfer of public services to the private sector eases the privatisation process.
- **December 1999:** Amendments to the Banking Law to strengthen the independence of the BRSA.
- **March 2001:** Electricity Market Law and the establishment of the Energy Market Regulatory Authority (EMRA).

- **April-May 2001:** Central Bank Law ensuring the independence of the central bank; recapitalisation of state banks and Savings Deposit Insurance Fund (SDIF) under the Banking Sector Restructuring Programme; Law on Individual Retirement Schemes; Sugar Law to enable privatisation of the state sugar firms; Natural Gas Law to liberalise the natural gas market and end BOTAŞ monopoly; Telecommunications Law to liberalise the telecom market.
- **June 2001:** Law enabling the closure of various budgetary and extra-budgetary funds.
- **January 2002:** Tobacco Law providing for privatisation of the state tobacco and alcohol monopoly, TEKEL; New Public Procurement Law.
- **March 2002:** Public Finance and Debt Management Law to bring transparency and accountability.
- **May 2002:** New transitional rules for pension reform.
- **August 2002:** Fourteen-point political democratisation reform package.

The disbursement schedule of the IMF agreement was tight. The Italian IMF representative Carlo Cottarelli (whose comments on football transfers also made headlines) in June 2001 warned that any delays in the privatisation of Türk Telekom could jeopardise the IMF loan disbursement that year. In the event, Türk Telekom privatisation, along with others in the programme, would be delayed yet again. But a debt swap in mid-June 2001 – originally aiming to raise around USD 3–5 billion – raised USD 8.2 billion and provided debt service relief by extending the maturity profile of the domestic debt from a precarious 5.3 months to 37.2 months. Following the 9/11 terrorist attacks in New York, the IMF stand-by was 'augmented', giving Turkey additional financial support to offset the shock to major emerging markets. These and USD 9 billion of IMF funds released in February 2002, as the government succeeded in passing many of the major legislative requirements, helped Turkey avoid debt rescheduling (see Box 4.1).[8]

The reforms also demanded some tough political measures. The improved transparency in public accounts required by the IMF agreement made it imperative for the government to investigate corruption in its ranks. The reform team had to overcome strong opposition to this, including from MHP leader Devlet Bahçeli who accused Kemal Derviş of being 'an IMF bureaucrat [. . .] not experienced in the customary Turkish way of doing politics'.[9] With the energy sector about to begin a radical liberalisation and privatisation drive, corruption investigations cost the Minister for Energy and Natural Resources Cumhur Ersümer and several others their jobs. The privatisation in the telecom sector was the key to attracting large-scale foreign investment, but first the reluctant minister responsible, Enis Öksüz of the MHP, had to go. The domestic political scene became more fragile when the parliamentary commission recommended a corruption investigation into Mesut Yılmaz, the leader of ANAP and deputy prime minister in the coalition government.

Despite these difficulties, the reform effort benefited from a number of factors that enabled the coalition government to implement the programme.[10] The devastation brought by the currency and banking crisis weakened resistance from the private sector to the discipline that the new regulatory institutions would bring. Similarly, political opposition and bureaucratic obstruction was muted by the instability experienced in the 1990s – solutions for which had been discussed for years. Some, such as the Competition Authority, had

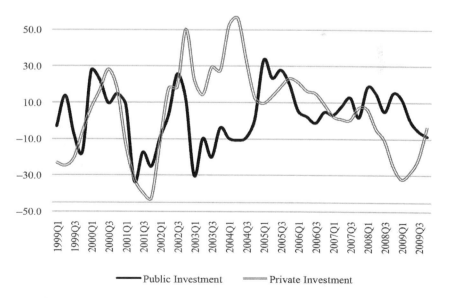

Figure 4.1 Private sector investment-led growth (2002–7)
Source: Institute of International Finance.

already been established before the crisis, and discussion of central bank independence had begun in 1997. Also, there was a positive momentum in the negotiations for EU membership, which had wide public support. In 1999, the EU formally accepted Turkey's membership application, of which these reforms were seen to be a part. Finally, it helped that, once the market volatility from the bursting of the US Dot-com bubble had passed, the global economy had started one of its longest and relatively most stable upswings.

The improvement in macroeconomic indicators was noticeable. The economy soon began to recover, bouncing back from a GDP contraction of 6 percent in 2001 to a 6.3-percent growth in 2002 (2009 base year data), with year-end inflation down to 29.8 percent from 69.4 percent the previous year. The year 2005 would be the peak year for this virtuous cycle, boosted by the start of the EU membership process. FDI (net) rose to an unprecedented 2.5 percent of GDP, privatisations of big-ticket state assets with the revenues from privatisations helped reduce the public sector's budget deficit to less than 1 percent of GDP, year-end inflation was down to 7.7 percent, and the government became a net-repayer of government debt, reducing the total public debt to 68 percent of GDP from its peak of around 100 percent in 2001.[11] More important, the upswing was led by private sector investment growth (see figure 4.1).

Redefining the Role of the State: The Independent Regulatory Agencies

The deep fiscal and financial restructuring and the subsequent economic recovery of this period tend to obscure the essential mission of the 'Transition Programme'. In a short booklet co-authored by Kemal Derviş and published a few years after the crisis, *The European Transformation of Modern Turkey*, the 2001 crisis is described not so much as a financial and economic one, but 'it was in fact a *crisis of governance*, which occurred as a result of the populist, clientelist, and corruption producing nature of Turkish politics in the 1990s. For this reason [. . .] the reform team that took over the reins of the economy in March 2001 [. . .] had as its first aim to restructure the economy and *the relations between the state and economic actors*' (italics added).[12] In this latter sense, the comprehensive reforms that came after the 2001 crisis were the missing piece of the puzzle and the required sequel to the market liberalisation reforms of the previous two decades.

Unlike the liberalisation steps of the 1980s and 1990s, when market regulatory institutions were either missing or haphazardly introduced, the exit from the 2001 crisis included a set of institutional reforms. In line with the post-Washington Consensus, curbing direct state role in the economy also required the state institutions to be re-positioned and, in effect, for the market to be 're-regulated'. A government report in 2003 titled 'The Restructuring of the Public Administration' (Kamu Yönetiminde Yeniden Yapılanma) initiated the process of implementing the reform legislation (see Box 4.1) to facilitate the privatisation process, to make the public sector and the budgeting process more transparent and accountable and to establish the independent regulatory authorities.

Governance measures to discipline the budget process included the closure of many off-budget funds that had been the source of quasi-fiscal activities and abuse in the 1980s and 1990s (see Chapter 3). The 2002 OECD report on Turkey noted that the number of extra-budgetary funds had been reduced from sixty-two to thirteen; the number of revolving funds were down from 2,600 prior to the reforms to 1,400; and the consolidated public accounts also reported on social security institutions, local authorities, SEEs, extra-budgetary funds, revolving funds and contingent liabilities.[13] The Public Finance and Debt Management Law passed in 2003 defined the limits for public sector borrowing and its management to be centralised in a special unit in the Treasury. An autonomous Public Procurement Authority was also set up to ensure that the purchases of the public sector complied with the rules of the 2002 Public Procurement Law.

In addition, the institutional structure of the rule-based market economy required an independent central bank and financial sector regulator, the Banking Regulation and Supervision Agency (BRSA, or BDDK, so the Turkish acronym), which was established in the reform years of 1999–2002. Central bank independence was a rare example of reform that was widely consulted. The discussion began in 1997, when an enquiry to the Constitutional Court gave a positive response on the appropriateness of an independent Central Bank. Discussions were held with employees on the question of 'what kind of Central bank do we want?' This was followed by consultations with the private sector, academics and high-level civil servants, as well as finally the IMF and European Investment Bank.[14] Central Bank independence was a central element of the IMF stand-by agreement, and it delivered the confidence in monetary policy that allowed a rare period of currency and price stability for the Turkish economy.

As privatisation progressed, there was also a need for regulators in sectors where the privatisation of the state entities potentially created private monopolies. Two of the crucial sectors were in telecom, where an Information and Communication Technologies Authority (ICTA, or BTK) was founded, and in the energy sector, where the Energy Market Regulatory Authority (EMRA, or EPDK) was established.[15] There existed also a social agenda with reforms to health as well as social security provision and pension reforms. The latter included a reform of social security pension schemes (SSK, Bağkur and Emekli Sandığı), which had had a deficit of 3.5 percent of GDP in 1999, despite the relatively young age profile of the Turkish population. In addition, a voluntary private pension scheme was introduced. The aim was to improve the low national savings ratio and to help increase the availability of long-term investment funding by encouraging the development of capital markets.

The most central element of these institutional reforms was the *limitation of executive discretion*. The stretching of executive discretion had become a major problem since the 1980s. Although it had been more excessive than previously, this was based on a long legacy of discretionary policy-making in Turkey. Hence, this element of the institutional reforms constituted the one feature that was challenged almost from the beginning. Özel has noted that politicians limiting 'their discretion in economic governance through delegating their authority to agencies endowed with high levels of autonomy was, indeed, a novelty in Turkish governance [...] successive incumbent (politicians) could not bear such a limitation for long'.[16] The AKP governments were no exception and would soon begin the process of deregulating and diluting the independent regulatory authorities, to be discussed below. But first the changes in the state–market relations will be examined, as the privatisation process finally took off with the sale of some of the biggest state enterprises – but not state banks.

The Restructured Banking Sector

Problems in the banking sector that erupted into a full-blown banking crisis in 2000 had been brewing for a few years. Since 1998, a couple of small banks, Bank Express and Interbank, had to be taken over by the Savings Deposit Insurance

Fund (SDIF), set up after the 1994 crisis to guarantee deposits. At the end of 1999, five more banks were taken over, accounting for 5.5 percent of banking sector assets and 7 percent of deposits. The economic crisis was affecting many sectors, causing bankruptcies especially in the leather, textiles and petroleum sectors, with knock-on effects on bank loan balance sheets. As for the looming problem of duty-losses in state banks, the government seemed reluctant to act.

This process took on added urgency after the collapse of Demirbank (later sold to HSBC) and the onset of the first leg of the financial crisis in November 2000. As the interbank market seized up, huge losses affected Ziraat Bank (Agricultural Bank) and Halk Bank – the two biggest state banks. These two were also taken over by the SDIF, and a law was rushed through in November 2000 to prepare them for privatisation. There was also a run on deposits at Islamic banks that were not covered by the deposit insurance scheme, and this led to the closure of one of the biggest, İhlas Finans, by the BRSA in February 2001. The Banking Sector Restructuring Programme, agreed upon in May 2001, would see nineteen banks taken over by the SDIF, as well as several private sector banks closed or merged by the end of July 2001.

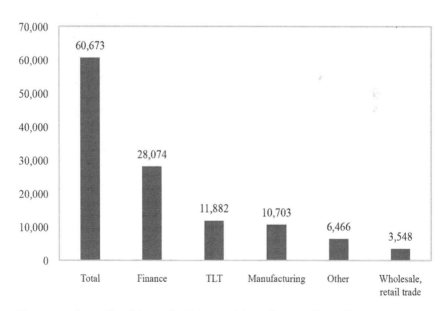

Figure 4.2 Sectoral breakdown of FDI (2003–8) (cumulative, million US$)

Source: Based on the data in Ümit İzmen and Kamil Yılmaz, 'Turkey's Recent Trade and Foreign Direct Investment Performance', in Ziya Öniş and Fikret Şenses, eds, *Turkey and the Global Economy* (London: Routledge), Table 4.2. TLT: transport, logistics, telecommunications.

By 2003, the number of banks had almost halved from eighty-nine prior to the crisis. The 100-percent state guarantee of deposits – which was seen as a major factor behind the risky activities of banks – was gradually reduced. Including the losses of the banking sector due to increased bad loans from the crisis, the devaluation losses, losses from government bond holdings and the duty losses of the state banks, the total cost of re-capitalising and restructuring the banking sector came to USD 53.2 billion, around 36 percent of GDP in 2001.[17]

Despite the heavy cost, the restructuring of the banking sector in 1999–2002 is one of the more effective, long-lasting reforms of this era, generally considered to have been responsible for the relative resilience of the Turkish banking sector during the global financial crisis in 2008–9. Contributing to this resilience was the role of the banking regulator, the BRSA, and Central Bank independence. The BRSA had been set up just before the outbreak of the crisis in 2000, and it was given enhanced supervisory authority never before experienced in Turkey, which included stringent reporting and higher capital adequacy requirements, reworked non-performing loan provisions and strict accounting rules on lending to linked holding groups. The authority of the BRSA increased with the Banking Law (No. 5411) passed in November 2005, as EU accession negotiations began. The Banking Law also transferred the regulation and supervision of non-bank financial institutions from the Treasury to the BRSA, reducing the fragmentation of supervisory authority in the financial sector. The success of the banking sector restructuring was reflected in almost half of the FDI in 2003–8 going into finance (see Figure 4.2), taking the share of banking sector assets by foreign (equity) ownership from 4 percent in 2004 to around a quarter by 2008.[18]

The Commercialisation of State Banks: Limiting Long-term Funding

The restructuring and commercialisation of state banks entailed the securitisation of the 'duty losses' and their recapitalisation with the issue of special government bonds; new management was brought in, and some (such as Emlak Bank) merged with Ziraat Bank. State bank profitability was restored, albeit at the cost of the closure of 800 branches and 30,000 staff laid off from Ziraat Bank and Halk Bank. Although they had been commercialised – as seen with the biggest bank, Ziraat, frequently at the top of banking sector profitability rankings – the privatisation of the three state banks that remained was repeatedly postponed. Even the sale of minority stakes proved difficult, such as the public offering of 25.2 percent of Vakıfbank in 2005, which eventually took place after several legal challenges.

From an industrial policy viewpoint, the restructuring of the banking sector did not ease the dearth of long-term credit for industrial investments. Paradoxically, it was made more acute by the commercialisation of state banks, which restricted bank appetite for more risky long-term funding. By 2008, the share of state banks in total banking sector assets had declined to around 25 percent, from 38 percent in 1998. Contributing to this was the annulling of some hundred regulations in line with EU norms, which had allowed subsidised and directed lending by state banks. This reform aimed to prevent the recurrence of the build-up of 'duty losses'. But attempts to avoid these problems had a price. These measures further curtailed the ability of governments to guide credits in accordance with the objectives of development plans, further limiting the scope for industrial policy in the 2000s.[19] The private business in Turkey also hesitated to invest in 'risky' sectors, such as high technology and innovation, to boost industrial development and sustainable growth.

Long-term funding for investment was also constrained by the slow development of capital markets. The establishment of private pension funds to channel domestic savings as well as an insurance sector to support the growth of institutional investors made slow progress. Early studies showed the big potential: even if only two million people took part in the new pension system in the first year, some USD 10 billion could accumulate in four years.[20] Although the tax and pension reforms passed in March 2001 included provisions for private pensions, it would take longer to establish funded pension plans. Even the government advisor on pension fund reform, Cağatay Ergenekon, admitted that it would take time for these plans to reach a scale sufficient to make a major contribution to the establishment of capital markets and boost the savings/investment trends in the Turkish economy.[21]

Given the decades of high inflation and currency instability, the Turkish public hesitated to make long-term investments. Meanwhile, the government, under strict fiscal constraints, was unable to provide sufficient tax incentives to attract substantial savings into pensions. By 2010, the number of subscribers had only reached 2.3 million people, with the funds amounting to a mere

1 percent of GDP – one of the smallest among emerging market economies.[22] In 2013, with easing fiscal constraints, the scheme was boosted with matching government contributions for participants. But even then the number of participants had only reached around 4 million by early 2014.[23]

While the long-term funding problem of the Turkish financial sector persisted even after the banking sector restructuring, some previously underdeveloped sectors saw major gains. Consumer credit, including mortgage lending, and lending to small and medium-size enterprises (SMEs) – both of which had been neglected in the 1990s – grew rapidly, since banks sought to replace the falling income from government bonds, as interest rates and government borrowing declined. Facilitated by the passage of a new Mortgage Law, a major boom in housing construction took off by 2005, as housing loans rose from 7.4 percent of total consumer lending in 1997, to 48 percent by 2007. Still, this was only some 10 percent of total banking sector credits in 2007; the broader loans to the construction and real estate sectors were a higher 17 percent – still very low, when compared with EU averages. This reflected the constraints of the Turkish financial sector that continued to be dominated by banks with only limited development of capital markets. The banks' reliance on (mostly short-term) deposits restricted the scope for growth of (longer-term) mortgage lending to avoid increased risks of tenor-mismatches on their balance sheets.

In response to these problems, the AKP re-activated the old state intervention instruments of TOKİ (Mass Housing Development Administration) and the Credit Guarantee Fund (KGF). Although the share of state banks in the mortgage lending market was only around 26 percent, state role in housing finance and construction increased in this period with the re-activation of TOKİ. Established in 1984, TOKİ was barely functioning by the late 1990s, having collapsed in a web of corruption. The AKP changed its operations and revived the entity with a lucrative revenue-sharing model, where private shareholders (developers and contractors) could build on extensive tracts of public land apportioned to TOKİ.[24] The Housing Finance Law of March 2007 (Law No. 5582) developed further the legal framework for longer-term mortgage lending. Housing finance was also boosted by the rise of REITs (real estate investment trusts). This has been dominated by the Emlak Konut REIT, which is majority-owned by TOKİ and other entities with close connections to the government.

The KGF had been originally established in 1991 to channel financial credits to small and medium-sized enterprises, by providing partial government guarantees. But with the banking sector focused on lending either to their related corporate holdings or to the government in the 1990s, small enterprise finance had languished. This constituted another impediment undermining effective industrial transformation and technological upgrade, as funding problems for small and medium-sized enterprises persisted in a volatile macroeconomic environment. Weakened by the initial shock of the EU customs union trade liberalisation and politically neglected by governments in the 1990s, the small and medium-sized enterprises became a core electoral support base in bringing the AKP to power in 2002. The AKP re-activated the KGF, with eighteen commercial banks signing up to its protocols from 2003 onwards.[25] This was combined with a major institutional restructuring of KOSGEB, the Small and Medium-Sized Enterprises Development Organisation, which began to provide interest rate support on loans, resulting in a major expansion of its role and membership numbers.[26]

The re-activation of TOKİ and KGF in state-supported finance showed that some previous peculiarities of the Turkish financial sector persisted. There was still the lack of long-term funding, and governments would step in to make funds available to their constituencies. The problem of this dearth of long-term funding was eased somewhat in the early 2000s, with ample FDI inflows that supported private sector investment. But once these declined, business either sought foreign credits or government support. Similarly, at the local authority level, underdeveloped municipal debt markets meant that longer-term funds were mostly available from government sources. *Ad hoc* discretionary measures and favouritism, which increased the longer the party stayed in power, characterised the allocation of these funds by the AKP governments.

Privatisation, 'Neutral' Industrial Policy and Lost Opportunity in the 'New Economy'

The previous section has pointed out that challenges concerning the financing of the industrial sector remained in the first term of the AKP era. In line with the global trends in the development paradigm, in this period, the scope and content of industrial policy also underwent significant transformation – not least in the declared intentions of the state to withdraw from key sectors. The privatisation programme took off towards the end of the 1990s, when a comprehensive legal framework for privatisation was finally in place and a 1999 constitutional amendment reduced the scope for legal challenges. Landmark early privatisations included the public offering of İş Bank shares and licence agreements with the two cellular phone operators Turkcell and Telsim in 1998. The divestment programme gathered momentum in 2000–1, with the sale of assets in the energy and telecom complex: the block sale of 51 percent of Petrol Ofisi, the chain of petrol stations, and a third GSM licence – boosting budget revenues by about USD 3 billion – was desperately needed in the midst of the crisis.

In this sense, 2005–6 saw a major break-through: including the sales of assets taken over by the SDIF during the crisis years, privatisation revenues amounted to some USD 16 billion.[27] Legislation by the AKP government had reduced the power of the judiciary to intervene in the privatisation process, including a 2003 amendment to the 1994 law on privatisation that expanded prime ministerial control over the Privatisation Agency. There were still legal challenges, but these were now more difficult to uphold. These included 51 percent of Tüpraş sold for USD 4.1 billion to Enerji Yatırımları, a consortium led by Koç Holding and Shell, that was contested by the Petrol-İş labour union taking it to the Danıştay (High Administrative Court). It was subsequently cleared. The passage of the 2005 Banking Law paved the way for acquisitions with foreign partners in the banking sector. One of the biggest in 2005 was Koç Financial Services – a joint venture between Koç Holding and Italy's Uni-Credit, acquiring 57.4 percent of Yapı Kredi Bank (formerly owned by Çukurova Holding; see below) for USD 1.4 billion from the SDIF. But this was only approved after parliament overrode the veto by President Ahmet Necdet Sezer who had questioned its constitutional compliance.

From 2005 to 2008, some USD 26 billion were raised in privatisation revenues. But the privatisation programme that was implemented in this period was mostly driven by fiscal imperatives and political drivers that overrode the basic economic justification for privatisation of increasing competition and productivity. The recovery from the 2000–1 crisis in the framework of the IMF stabilisation programme included a severe fiscal adjustment by the incoming government to increase budget revenues and reduce spending. The latter included costly Treasury guarantees in the power sector and agricultural subsidies. Atiyas, in his review of the privatisation experience has concluded that 'fiscal considerations [. . .] have always dominated considerations regarding improvements in long-term productivity'.[28]

This had a negative impact on industry and associated services, such as energy and telecoms. In order to maximise privatisation revenues and increase the attractiveness of the asset, the government downplayed the objectives of increasing competition and improved productivity. In telecoms and electricity privatisations, this was evident in leaving open the possibility of monopoly rents for the bidders. Moreover, in addition to the decline in state investment due to fiscal constraints, there was a virtual abandonment of an active – transformative – industrial policy as privatisations took place.

Instead, the AKP government's efforts seemed to focus on fostering a loyal private sector, as seen in the energy privatisations discussed below. While industrial policy in terms of a transformative programme receded, the AKP-allied business continued to benefit from state largesse especially after the 2004 local elections. As these firms transformed into larger corporate entities, as Özcan and Turunç have noted, 'unlike their efforts to avoid the state in the 1990s, since the formation of the first AKP government in 2002, they [. . .] conducted most of their business with formal state institutions'.[29] This section of the business elite also benefited from 'soft' incentives, such as those structured around regional development which were part of the 'horizontal' and 'sector-neutral' industrial policy incentives that still continued. Hence, the privatisation process helped consolidate a new business circle around the AKP, while not alienating the established business elites who also expanded their activities into the fast-growing energy and financial services sectors. Meanwhile, an opportunity was lost to move Turkish industry into higher-technology production. With exception of the defence-related electronics sector (see Chapter 5), little support was given to the nascent technology-intensive 'new economy' sectors that were emerging in the late 1990s.

Governance Issues Cloud Power Sector Privatisations

The energy sector was seen as one of the biggest prizes in the privatisation portfolio, expected to bring in foreign and domestic private investment. Turkish energy demand was forecast to grow at 6–7 percent per year in the 2000s, with electricity growing 8–9 percent per year, which required an annual investment of around USD 4–5 billion.[30] At the time of privatisation, the electricity sector had a hybrid private/public structure built around the state monopoly, TEK. This had emerged, in the absence of a comprehensive legal framework, with piece-meal measures based on a 1984 legislation that granted licences to private investors to build-operate-transfer (BOT) schemes in electricity generation, and transfer of operating rights (in distribution). These reforms and the completion of big hydroelectric projects had helped overcome the persistent power cut-offs of the 1970s. But these arrangements still fell short of attracting the needed investment. During the Sixth (1990–95) and Seventh (1996–2000) Five-Year Plans, investment targets were only 60–70 percent met.[31] Moreover, these schemes involved costly Treasury guarantees with the off-take price of electricity (applied if the level of demand would not match contracted demand) guaranteed at double average market prices, resulting in a major build-up of inter-enterprise arrears. The large number of government entities involved and the weak transparency had prompted President Sezer to initiate corruption investigations into the activities of the Ministry of Energy and Natural Resources.

Legislative solutions began in the midst of the 2000–1 crisis. A constitutional amendment of January 2000 (Law No. 4501) allowing recourse to international arbitration by foreign firms lifted the main obstacle to foreign investment. This was followed by the Electricity Market Law in February 2001, which was hailed to reduce the 'state role in the electricity market to zero'. Many questioned whether this was appropriate for a country with high energy demand growth and, with 70 percent import dependence, security of supply a major issue; others thought that the existing public/private hybrid model should have been retained and built upon.[32] But in the midst of a financial and payments crisis, the imperatives of having to comply with multilateral conditions to release emergency funding and to secure energy supply overrode these qualms and prevented a slower experimental – and incremental – approach that could build on the strengths of existing structures and better fit domestic conditions.

The Electricity Market Law, set to go into effect by 2003, unbundled the vertically integrated state monopoly and proposed the privatisation of generation and distribution assets, while keeping transmission and hydroelectric plants in public ownership. The law established an Energy Market Regulatory Authority (EMRA) designed to be independent of the ministry. The original proposals envisaged the board members of the EMRA to be nominated by a wide range of interests, including the Union of Chambers (TOBB) and regulatory bodies such as the Competition Board and the Council of State (Danıştay), in addition to the Ministry of Energy and Natural Resources. However, in the final version of the law, the members of the board were all to be nominated by the Council of Ministers. This enabled the government to maintain influence in the sector almost from the start and to dilute the independence of the regulator. A later amendment in 2011 gave the ministry the authority to supervise all activities of the EMRA, which would completely reverse its original mandate.[33]

Despite improvements during the initial years of the institutional reforms, the privatisation process of the energy sector soon reverted to the weak governance that had previously prevailed. By 2007, for instance, a major cycle of gas privatisations saw 'politically connected persons' winning fifteen out of nineteen metropolitan centres and serving 76 percent of the population.[34] Investors not in AKP circles also won tenders – mostly in the bigger privatisations that required foreign partners and greater transparency. This included Sabancı Holding's Enerjisa winning the distribution network Başkent in Ankara, in a joint venture with Austria's Verbund, with a bid value of USD 1.2 billion.[35] However, foreign investment interest was limited by the weak governance in the sector.

Nor would the role of the state in the electricity market be 'reduced to zero', with increased government control over the regulator, some 15–20 percent of generation capacity remaining in state hands and the state monopoly over gas imports retained by Botaş. These factors gave the government wide powers to influence electricity pricing in the wholesale market – for example, by frequently holding down electricity prices in the lead up to elections. This increased profitability pressures on the private producers struggling with the burden of repaying foreign currency debts. Public entities in the sector also suffered. With their financial positions reverting to the build-up of inter-enterprise arrears last seen in the 1990s: energy arrears were estimated to have risen to 3.2 percent of GDP at the end of 2009.[36]

Türk Telekom Privatisation: The 'Biggest Default in Turkish Banking'

There was much early investor interest in the Turkish telecom sector, which was seen as one of the biggest telecom markets in the emerging world. In

2000, Türk Telekom (TT) had been given a market valuation of around USD 20 billion. Turkish holdings, mostly linked to European telecom firms, showing interest included a consortium of Sabancı, Doğan, Doğuş Holdings and Spain's Telefonica; İş Bank and Telecom Italia; and a consortium of Fiba Holding, Enka, Süzer Group, Finansbank and France Telecom. However, as in the energy sector, interest waned as it became apparent that the process was riddled with irregularities. Metin Münir reported for the *Financial Times* on the travails of the Telecom Italia and İş Bank joint venture which won the third cellular licence in 2001, with a bid of USD 2.52 billion: Telekom Italia almost walked away when the Ministry of Communications demanded last-minute changes on the terms of the deal, prompting veteran industrialist, Erol Sabancı, to remark: 'Every morning when I get up, I thank God that we did not win the contract'.[37] Telecom Italia would sell its 40.6-percent share in Avea in 2006.

These telecom privatisations were part of several in those years in emerging markets, including Moscow-based Mobile Tele-Systems (MTS) and Egypt Telecom. The sale of the latter would be delayed, as early marketing to London fund managers (in which this author participated) indicated that investors were reluctant to commit funds until there was a reform of the Egyptian Pound currency peg. Similarly, the sale of Türk Telekom in the Turkish case first needed the new Telecom Law to be passed in May 2001. Other issues to be resolved included the military insisting that Türksat satellites should not be sold and disagreements on the share of foreign ownership. By then the US Dot-com stock market bubble had burst, collapsing the valuations of IT and telecom firms. One of the conditions set by the Turkish parliament was that no sale should take place below a valuation of USD 10 billion for Türk Telekom, which further postponed the sale.

In the end, Türk Telekom was sold in December 2005 at almost half precrisis valuations to the Lebanese-Saudi Oger and Telecom Italia joint venture, in what would become one of the least successful privatisations. Despite having a seat on the board, the government failed to prevent the company – one of the most profitable firms in the country – from defaulting on its USD 4.5 billion loan, nor could it stop the management from engaging in illicit activities.[38] In 2018, the 55 percent of Türk Telekom shares owned by Oger were transferred to its main bank creditors, Akbank, Garanti and İşbank. The financing crisis of Türk Telekom – the 'biggest default in Turkish banking history' – was not simply due to bad management and weak supervisory capacity of the government and the telecom regulator. It was also a sign of the successive Turkish governments' lack of attention to the telecom, information technology and other high-tech sectors that needed ambitious industrial policies to develop in the 2000s.

Increased Private Sector Focus on Energy and Financial Services

The privatisation of major state-owned enterprises and the growth spurt of the 2000s brought two important changes to the Turkish private sector. First, it helped establish new holdings around AKP circles, widening the business elite. Second, it transformed the industrial profile of older conglomerates with their acquisitions in the energy and services sectors. But while this period saw sectoral, regional and business elite diversification, with an increase in medium-technology exports such as automotive, it was not into the 'new' industries with high-tech exports which had emerged in the 1990s and were generally overlooked in the early 2000s.

The nascent 'new economy' sector had been a focus of attention for the big holdings which, starting in the mid-1990s, had begun to establish or acquire Internet Service Providers (ISPs).[39] The top five holdings with ISPs included (in declining order of market size) were Çukurova Holding with Superonline, Vestel/Zorlu Holding with Vestel.net, Sabancı with Turk.net, Doğuş Holding with Garanti.net and İhlas Holding with Ihlas.net, having around 77 percent of the market share by the end of the 1990s.[40] For Turkey's biggest holding groups, the liberalisation of the telecom market had brought high expectations for their internet services firms. The Sabancı group, with plans to bid for a GSM licence, was expecting to reduce its share of revenues from industrials that accounted for 37 percent of the total in 1998. Similarly, Koç Holding, Turkey's premier automotive and consumer goods producer, was targeting telecoms and energy. A restructuring process in the late 1990s had seen Koç Holding divest its old-economy activities in textiles; it had entered a joint venture with Comsat and Sumitomo in satellite communications; and it was hoping to acquire a strategic stake in Türk Telekom and to bid for the third mobile licence.[41] There were also plans to develop the group's internet services through Koc.net, providing online shopping.

Two decades later, only part of these plans would be realised. In the Koç Holding, revenues from energy and refinery activities – that is, Aygaz, Tüpraş and Opet – had increased to around a third of the total. The group had also acquired one of Turkey's biggest banks, Yapı Kredi. However, Koc.net was sold to Vodafone Turkey in 2011, although there was still a presence in IT services, with Koç Sistem. Sabancı Holding revenues from energy had also risen to around a third of the total in 2019, with the biggest entity being Enerjisa.[42] The Sabancı group maintained a presence in the IT and telecom sectors with Teknosa and SabanciDx. However, Turk.net was sold in 2008, leaving banking and insurance – the destination of major FDI (see Figure 4.2) – as well as energy as the main revenue earners. These conglomerates remained successful diversified entities in those sectors where Turkey had a competitive advantage. For the Koç group, this included industrials such as the rapidly growing automotive and consumer durables sectors. However, as one of the more flexible conglomerates, the evolving structure of the Sabancı group, with its increased focus on energy and financial services, highlighted the structural changes in the Turkish economy.[43] During these years, the contribution of manufacturing to GDP declined, while that of services rose, in what came to be called 'premature de-industrialisation' (see Chapter 5, Table 5.1).

It seemed that, in the 2000s, telecoms and IT were rarely among the sectors where private wealth was being created in Turkey. According to the *Forbes* billionaire wealth list, newcomers on the Turkish list were involved in energy, construction, media, mining and consumer goods. The newcomers also tended to have close relationships with the AKP and included businessmen such as Murat Ülker of Yıldız Holding and Turgay Ciner, the owner of Ciner Media. Çukurova's Mehmet Emin Karamehmet, owner of Turkey's premier 'new economy' group and listed on the *Forbes* billionaire list with USD 8 billion of assets in 2000, would drop off the list by 2016. By 2021, Murat Ülker topped the list with USD 6.2 billion of assets.

Automotive Leads Growth in Medium-tech Exports, but the
'New Economy' is Neglected

In retrospect, a partial international revival of interest in industrial policies in response to the emergence of the 'new economy' sectors in the 1990s had little impact on Turkey. Drawing on 'endogenous growth theory', with its emphasis on human capital and innovation, this approach promoted public investment in education and scientific research to support the 'new economy' sectors.[44] This had been noted in a Scientific and Technological Research Council of Turkey (TÜBİTAK) report, entitled 'Turkish Science and Technology Policy: 1993–2003', commissioned by Prime Minister Demirel and proposing increased public investment in education and the technological upgrade of industry. But it was mostly ignored by the incoming AKP government. As a result, firms active in the high-tech information and communications technology sector in the late 1990s were left to fend for themselves under the harsh conditions that saw the bursting of the US Dot-com investment bubble in 2000.

It was already common knowledge by the end of the 1980s that, for 'the long-term economic development prospects of developing countries, telecommunications is [. . .] one of the most critical elements of industrial infrastructure'.[45] In Turkey, however, investment in telecom infrastructure fell over the 1990s.[46] As explained in the previous chapters, neither the Turkish state's capacity to guide market actors, nor state–business relations were sufficiently long-term-oriented to direct the Turkish industry towards high-tech sectors. For instance, Internet use was mostly an academic activity, with the first internet structure established at Middle East Technical University in 1993, with funds from TÜBİTAK. It was not until 1999 that Türk Telecom, working with Alcatel, set up TT.net, which began to provide national internet coverage. But TT.net was beset with technical problems and, by then, unable to compete with private-sector competitors which had already taken the initiative to establish internet service providers (ISPs) to tap into the potential of e-commerce. Although still in its infancy, there was rapid growth in the Turkish information, communication and technology sector. The number of internet users had been doubling every year in the five years up to 2000, and mobile phone users increased from 800,000 in 1996 to an estimated 13 million.[47] In May 2000, the first initial public offering in Turkey's IT sector came with the leading software producer Logo Business Solutions floating 15 percent of its capital.[48]

But private entrepreneurs active in the Turkish mobile phone, satellite TV and internet sectors had a troubled existence. In early 2000, the biggest were Turkcell and Telsim, which had recently won the mobile phone licences. Initially set up by Murat Vargı and Scandinavian investors, by the late 1990s the majority shares of Turkcell were mostly held by Mehmet Emin Karamehmet's Çukurova Holding and Telecom Finland. The Çukurova Holding that also owned Digiturk (the satellite network provider) and Superonline (Turkey's biggest internet provider) was the one diversified conglomerate during the 2000s that seemed set for being the premier telecom and IT services firm of Turkey.

Çukurova was badly damaged by the 2001 crisis and, from 2005 onwards, involved in long-running legal disputes with international shareholders. Two of its most valuable assets, Yapı Kredi Bank and Pamukbank, were taken over by the SDIF during the financial crisis. This left the group straddled with high debt, including USD 455 million to the SDIF and USD 1.6 billion borrowed from the state bank (Ziraat) to settle its dispute with the Stockholm-based Telia-Sonera and the Moscow-based Alfa Group over Turkcell. Failure to repay these debts culminated in more assets being taken over by the SDIF in 2013. These included its media assets in television and Digiturk. Digiturk would be subsequently sold in 2015, to the media group beIN Media Group based in Qatar – AKP's major regional ally. By 2018, the Turkey Wealth Fund (the sovereign wealth fund established in 2016, see Chapter 5) would take over 26.2 percent of the share in Turkcell. Similarly, the 2001 crisis was disastrous for Telsim, which held 25 percent of the mobile phone market. Telsim was owned by the Uzan family, who also was caught by the 2001 crisis unable to pay its foreign currency debts of USD 2.6 billion to Motorola and Nokia. Long-running legal disputes and alleged corruption investigations culminated in the seizure of Uzan family assets by the SDIF in March 2004. This was followed by the sale of Telsim to Vodafone for USD 4.5 billion in 2005, with the Doğan Holding acquiring its media assets.

The shrinking policy space for the government in industrialisation and the lack of a sector-specific industrial policy to support the 'new economy' sectors was a major lost opportunity in the 2000s. The Dot-com and the Turkish financial crises devastated the investments of the few entrepreneurs, such as Karamehmet, who ventured into these risky sectors in the late 1990s and early 2000s. More diversified entities, such as the Koç and Sabancı Holdings, were able to absorb such shocks, but they too had sold their ISP activities by the end of the decade. Others, such as the media giant Doğan Holding, declined once relations with the AKP deteriorated. Only Zorlu Holding with its Vestel consumer electronics, personal computer manufacturing arm and Vestel.net managed to navigate and grow under these treacherous macroeconomic and political conditions.

It was not only macroeconomic shocks and elite political divisions that held these activities back. Sufficient funding, R&D and educational requirements to establish and grow the information and communication sector that could have been provided by a tailored industrial policy at the time were missing. Belated awareness of this problem came at the end of the decade in a Tüsiad study, published in 2008, warning that the competitive position captured by the Turkish industry in the 1980s and 1990s was being lost, because there were insufficient resources allocated to providing the IT and telecom infrastructure – including education and R&D – needed to increase production in high-technology sectors.[49] This was illustrated by the rise and decline of the high-technology consumer electronics sector in these years. Growth of consumer electronics was led by the export of television screens, which by 2005 was supplying 65 percent of the EU market.[50] But Turkish exporters, relying on low-wage, low-cost imported inputs (mostly from Asia), failed to develop a domestic supplier base which could keep up with new technologies. This, and the appreciation of the Turkish Lira, proved fatal and led to the loss of markets as demand fell for cathode-ray tubes in favour of newer liquid-crystal display technology. Over this period, the share of 'high-technology' products in total manufactured exports peaked at 6.3 percent in 2004 – having grown at over 20 percent per year between 1997 and 2005 – but would then fall to 2.2 percent by 2010.[51]

This period did see strong growth in the medium-technology sectors, however. İzmen and Yılmaz have shown that 'upper middle' technology manufacturing industries grew by 17.5 percent per annum in 2001–5, only mildly slowing to 10.8 percent per annum in 2005–7, with strong productivity and export growth being maintained.[52] The combined medium- and high-technology exports grew from 32 percent of total manufactured exports in 2000 to 43.4 percent in 2007. This was led by break-out sectors such as automotive. In contrast to consumer electronics, the automotive sector benefited from an extensive domestic supplier base that had been built up in the 1990s and from integration with EU supply chains. The automotive sector was one of the rare sectors whose import dependence (ratio of imports to production) had declined somewhat, from 58 percent in 2000 to 52 percent by 2007.[53]

The success of the break-through sectors – such as automotive, consumer durables and iron and steel – eased but could not overcome the challenges facing the manufacturing sector during these years. Turkish manufacturing as a whole became increasingly import-dependent: imports to production ratio had doubled from 33 percent in 1997 to 65 percent by 2007.[54] This was mostly driven by the rise in imports in intermediate goods products and also reflected Turkey's mounting oil import bill, due to the rise in international oil prices. Increased competition from Asian producers was another international factor shaping Turkey's trade performance. Even textiles – where Turkey was among the top six exporters in the world – struggled to maintain competitiveness due to high raw material prices and growing competition from East Asian producers. Combined with the impact of the appreciating Lira, this reduced the traditional trade surplus generated by the textiles and clothing sector that had helped contain the trade deficit in previous years.[55] These structural trends would increase Turkish economy's vulnerability in the years following the global financial crisis.

The Global Financial Crisis and the Changing Institutional Context

The growth spurt during 2002–7 was based on the structural reforms enacted before the 2002 election and the discipline and coherence provided by the IMF stand-by programme on AKP policies, once in government. The start of privatisations of big public enterprises in turn attracted foreign direct investment inflows and also strengthened the domestic currency. The latter, combined with central bank independence and fiscal discipline, reduced inflation and interest rates and brought macroeconomic stability in the context of a favourable global environment. Moreover, the democratisation reforms associated with the EU membership process and the rise of new strata of business, including export-oriented Anatolian small and medium-sized enterprises (see Chapter 3), benefiting from globalisation and the emergence of supply chains 'opened a virtuous cycle whereby political and economic democratisation reforms moved in tandem'.[56] This political and policy stability resulted in a steady period of growth. During 2002–7, real GDP grew by an average of 7.2 percent per year – slightly over the critical 7-percent-per-year growth that doubles GDP over a decade. Meanwhile, nominal per capita income more than doubled in this period, from USD 4,315 to USD 9,871.

The global financial crisis interrupted this positive trajectory. In fact, growth had already begun to slow in 2007, with a slowdown in fixed investment by the now heavily indebted private sector facing increased uncertainty with the upcoming 2007 general election. There were also signs of problems in the foreign balances where imports were outstripping export growth. By 2006–7, the current account deficit had widened to over 5 percent of GDP, increasingly funded by foreign currency borrowing by Turkish corporates. The continued curbs on state-spending, including on public investment, contained public deficits and debt. But improved public sector balances came at the expense of rising private sector imbalances. While in 2002 the share of the private sector in total foreign debt had been around a third, by 2007 it was almost 60 percent. High foreign direct investment inflows masked these problems for a while. But from 2009 onwards and since the 2013 'taper tantrum', when direct and portfolio inflows to all emerging markets fell as the US Federal Reserve signalled monetary policy tightening, Turkey's foreign payments gap and economic vulnerabilities were exposed. This corresponded to the end of the IMF policy-anchor in May 2008, as the stand-by agreement was terminated and the AKP made the controversial decision not to renew.

Political factors that had anchored the AKP to Turkey's secular democracy also seemed to be weakening towards the end of its first term in office. This was the case with the role of the Turkish military. In its first term, in a bid to widen its support base, but also wary of possible military interventions that had shut down its former versions, the AKP leadership had moved to the political centre. But the EU democratisation reforms had reduced the political influence of the military – evident in the AKP's ability to brush off a warning from the chief of general staff, Yaşar Büyükanıt, in April 2007, of threats to Turkish secularism. The year 2007 also corresponded to the end of the term of President Sezer who, as a staunch secularist and former member of the Turkish Constitutional Court, had been a restraining force on the AKP's political influence over state institutions.

The EU anchor was also waning, as relations became strained over Cyprus, which had been allowed to join the EU in 2004, before a solution was found to the division of the island. Turkey's refusal to implement the Additional Protocol and open its ports and airspace to the vessels and aircraft from the 'Republic of Cyprus' had resulted in the suspension of negotiations of eight chapters by the EU Council in 2006. In addition, new political leadership in Germany and France was turning against Turkish EU membership, with France, led by President Sarkozy, blocking talks on economic and monetary policy chapters in 2007. Turkey had become a 'scapegoat and victim' of the EU's constitutional crisis and 'enlargement fatigue' that had set in after eight East European countries had joined in 2005.[57] As the AKP became more confident of its domestic political support, with the share of the popular vote up from 34.3 percent in 2002 to 46.6 percent in the July 2007 general election, the 'anchors' that had framed its first term were mostly on the decline and seemed no longer needed.

The Loss of Autonomy of the 'Independent' Regulatory Agencies

This included the autonomy of the independent regulatory agencies (IRAs) that began what Acemoğlu and Üçer have called an 'institutional slide'.[58] Compared to their counterparts in several other emerging markets, the IRAs in Turkey were judged to have had high levels of formal independence when they were established in the early 2000s. Yet, a major problem facing the regulatory reforms was the Turkish constitutional constraint that required all administrative agencies to be attached to ministries to provide 'integral unity of the administration'.[59] This restriction was by-passed by 'affiliating' the IRAs with the respective ministries, which left many legal ambiguities.[60] This led to persistent criticism of these agencies as being unconstitutional. There were also concerns about democratic accountability raised from wider political circles, including former Prime Minister Bülent Ecevit.

These ambiguities and criticisms were used by the AKP to chip away at their independence. Soon, despite their formal independence, their *de facto* operation began to suffer from 'high levels of government intervention'.[61] An early signal of the problems in the functioning of the IRAs was the 2003 resignation of Engin Akçakoca, veteran head of the banking regulator BRSA, complaining of interference by AKP members of parliament. Major curbs on the independence of the IRAs came in 2005 with Law No. 5018, which began to limit their financial independence and increase the authority of the minister of the affiliated ministry for approving expenses; these then culminated in the 2011 Decree-law No. 643 and 649, giving respective ministers full authority over the decisions of the IRAs.[62] The latter step, taken after the global financial crisis of 2008, was also justified in terms of giving the government more policy flexibility to respond to the crisis.

Democratic accountability is a legitimate concern regarding non-elected independent authorities in any country. However, the weakness of public scrutiny and transparency in Turkey, along with a tendency towards authoritarian trends by the AKP especially in the 2010s, has meant that curbs on the autonomy of the IRAs resulted in predictable negative outcomes. This was clearly evident in the telecom sector. Liberalisation had the ostensible aim of establishing a competitive market regulated by the Information and Communications Technologies Authority (ICTA). However, this did not prevent the continued monopoly of Türk Telekom in the fixed line segment, nor did it stop its owners from reaping monopoly profits while at the same time seemingly unable to repay its debts. This seemed to confirm the general view that (a) the Ministry of Communication and Transport had maintained significant discretionary power over the ICTA, and (b) the privatised Türk Telekom had undue influence – or political capture – of the ministry, which slowed the process of liberalisation.[63]

These curbs on regulatory authorities were replicated in other spheres of government activity, which reduced transparency. A 2010 OECD report noted the increasing scope of 'quasi-fiscal' activities that were not sufficiently recorded in fiscal reports which had been the source of the problems leading up to the 2001 crisis.[64] TOKİ was given a unique legal status, with a special law excluding it from the application of the Public Finance and Debt Management Law in 2005, as well as exemptions from the Public Procurement Law. In 2010, a law was passed that annulled the authority of the Sayıştay (State Audit Authority) to audit several state entities, including TOKİ. There was the re-drafting and repeated amendments of the Public Procurement Law to suit various outcomes in the bidding process at the local authority or central government level, which privileged loyal business partners. This involved 150 amendments between 2003 and 2015, progressively expanding exemptions from the law and replacing open tender auctions with less transparent tender procedures.[65]

The Persistence of Weak 'Embeddedness' in State–Business Relations

Underlying the establishment of the new institutional structures following the 2001 crisis was the remaking of the state–business alliance in Turkey. The traditional military–bureaucracy–business alliance had fragmented with the liberalisation reforms begun in the 1980s. As described in Chapter 3, this saw the bureaucracy weaken, the state role in the economy recede and divisions deepen among the business elite. The latter took a political form with the newly emerging Anatolian business supporting the conservative political movements.

However, the depth of the 2001 crisis brought, as Özel has noted, 'an unprecedented consensus [. . .] regarding stances towards market liberalisation accompanied by regulation and stabilisation'.[66] This consensus included the Islamist parties and allied business associations, such as Müsiad. The 2001 crisis also paved the way for the elimination of private corporations that were extensively exposed to rent-seeking and competitiveness problems. By the time of the 2002 general election, the AKP led by Recep Tayyip Erdoğan supported the reforms of the IMF package, as well as those associated with the EU accession process. Given the general political disillusion with the fractious parties in the 1990s coalitions, this provided a wide public and business support (secularist and Islamist) for the first AKP government. In its first term, the AKP enthusiastically pursued the democratisation reforms that came with the EU membership negotiations, including those curbing the power of the military which saw itself as the guarantor of Turkey's secularism. This first term of the AKP was what many observers called its reformist years, when political liberalisation accompanied economic reforms, strong growth and institutional transformation.[67]

This governing alliance began to weaken during the second term of the AKP. The improved economic performance that gave the AKP a second term in the 2007 general election also reduced its reliance on external anchors. This included cooling relations with the EU and a slowdown of the democratisation reforms that began to alienate urban middle-class liberals. At the same time, wider secular political opposition to the AKP began to grow, including an unconventional warning from the military on 27 April 2007, later dubbed 'e-memorandum' and 'e-*coup*', in a statement by the military published on the official website of the Turkish Armed Forces at midnight. This was followed by a legal attempt to ban the AKP in 2008, which was overturned by the Constitutional Court. Relations with the military deteriorated further, as a series of investigations directed by AKP allies, the influential Gülen movement (a religious sect), led to arrests of leading generals for allegedly 'plotting coups'.[68]

The growing ideological rifts between conservative and secular segments on the political scene also affected state–business relations. The government began to direct harsh criticisms at the established big business groups – known as 'İstanbul capital' – with a strong secular outlook. As a result, another opportunity was missed to consolidate 'embedded' institutional relations between state and big business, which could facilitate information flows, overcome collective action problems and design long-term industrial policies. As GDP contracted by 4.8 percent in 2009 during the global financial crisis and consequently growth became more volatile, the AKP adopted an increasingly defensive stance, narrowing the focus of its policies towards consolidating the support of its core constituencies.[69] The 'selective inclusion' of allied businesses in the distribution of resources further deepened divisions among the business elite, fragmenting the earlier, wider political alliance. There was also a reversion to a stridently anti-IMF stance, refusing to renew the stand-by agreement in 2008, in the midst of the global financial crisis. Freed from the policy discipline imposed by the IMF and the EU, the AKP shifted towards populist policies and *ad hoc* legislation that expanded the scope of political discretion, combined with authoritarian overtones (see Chapter 5).

Conclusion: The Return of the 'Crisis of Governance'

Şerif Mardin, eminent Turkish social scientist, had stated at a rare business briefing in İstanbul in the midst of the 2001 crisis that 'in Turkey you *don't have politics, you have patronage*'; he then advised increased education on 'individual rights and citizenship' to bring a new understanding of 'public interest', suggesting that there would be no easy solutions to these problems. Indeed, after a promising start, the end of the AKP's 'virtuous growth cycle' era with the 2008 global financial crisis set the incremental return of the 'crisis of governance' in motion.

Ten years on since their introduction, the authority of the independent regulatory agencies, established to reset the relations between the ministries and business, had been eroded. The country has reverted to what Devlet Bahçeli has described as 'the customary Turkish *way of doing politics*'. This was combined with a political shift towards the centralisation of power and increased state intervention in the economy. As in the crisis years of the 1990s, this growing state role in the economy had a reactive, discretionary and *ad hoc* character. But unlike the random populist measures of the 1990s or 'competitive populism', government intervention in the economy under the AKP had one consistent aim: to create and strengthen a politically loyal business elite around the AKP. This was the case when the state retreated from industrial production with the sale of state assets to favoured firms. It was also the case when – with the end of the major privatisations – the state role in the economy began to expand once again through reconstituted entities such as TOKİ and the KGF, as well as other instruments of 'market capture' (see Chapter 5).

It seemed, in some way, that the role of the state had reverted to the early years of the Republic, when state intervention had aimed at creating a 'Turkish' home-grown private sector to develop the Turkish economy (see Chapter 2). But this time around, the aim was to ensure the survival of the AKP in power, deepen-ing the cleavages in the business elite and increasing political polarisation.[70] These trends would accelerate after the challenge to the AKP rule by the Gezi Park pro-tests, the economic volatility following the 'taper tantrum' in 2013 and the grow-ing clash with the former Gülenist allies culminating in the failed military coup of 2016. Thereafter, stronger entities – such as the Central Bank, BRSA and the judiciary that had managed to maintain their autonomy in the 2000s – would also be weakened. The next chapter deals with these trends and examines the construc-tion of a new interventionist, centralised political authority where state–business relations would increasingly tend towards state capitalist forms. It will also criti-cally examine the return of industrial policy that has been heralded as part of 'new developmentalist' policies providing the solutions to existing problems.

Notes

1. Dani Rodrik, 'Institutions for High-Quality Growth: What They Are and How to Acquire Them', NBER Working Paper Series, Working Paper 7540, 2000. For a critical analysis of the post-Washington Consensus, see Ziya Öniş and Fikret Şenses, 'Rethinking the Emerging Post-Washington Consensus,' *Development and Change*, Vol. 36, No. 2 (2005), pp. 263–90.

2. On the emergence of the 'regulatory state' in Turkey, see Caner Bakır and Ziya Öniş, 'The Regulatory State and Turkish Banking Reforms in the Age of Post-Washington Consensus', *Development and Change*, Vol. 41, No. 1 (2010), pp. 77–106.

3. Ziya Öniş, 'Turkey under the Challenge of State Capitalism: The Political Econ-omy of the Late AKP Era', *Southeast European and Black Sea Studies*, Vol. 19, No. 2 (2019), pp. 201–25.

4. Izak Atiyas and Ozan Bakış, 'Structural Change and Industrial Policy in Turkey', *Emerging Markets Finance and Trade*, Vol. 51, No. 6 (2015), pp. 1209–29.

5. John Weiss, 'Neoclassical Economic Perspectives on Industrial Policy', in Arkebe Oqubay, Christopher Cramer, Ha-Joon Chang and Richard Kozul-Wright, eds,

The Oxford Handbook of Industrial Policy (Oxford: Oxford University Press, 2021), p. 130.

6. This was a big risk for Turkey, which had liberalised its capital account and had chronic current account deficits. Exchange rate-based stabilisation programmes could end in balance of payments and banking crises, as previously seen in Brazil. The problem was the difficulty of sustaining the intermediate (pegged) exchange rate regime, as opposed to a floating currency, in a global environment with liberalised capital flows.

7. Strict monitoring and inspections by the recently established Banking Regulation and Supervision Agency (BRSA) was creating alarm in some banking circles, not accustomed to this level of scrutiny (author's personal communication conducted in İstanbul, December 2001). The then head of the BRSA, Zekeriya Temizel – a member of Ecevit's DSP and a long-serving Ministry of Finance official – would resign from his position in March 2001, shortly following the appointment of Kemal Derviş in charge of the Transition Programme.

8. For an extensive political economy analysis of Turkey's 2001 crisis, see Ziya Öniş and Barry Rubin, eds, *The Turkish Economy in Crisis: Critical Perspectives on the 2000–1 Crises* (London: Routledge, 2003). See also Yılmaz Akyüz and Korkut Boratav, 'The Making of the Turkish Financial Crisis', *World Development*, Vol. 31, No. 9 (2003), pp. 1549–66.

9. 'Kicking and Screaming all the Way', EBA Agency Press, Ankara, Briefing, Issue No 1342, 14 May 2001.

10. On the fortuitous alignment of domestic and external factors that enabled these deep reforms to be implemented in a short period of time, see Mustafa Kutlay, *The Political Economies of Turkey and Greece: Crisis and Change* (London: Palgrave Macmillan, 2019), pp. 74–99.

11. There are many definitions of public debt. These data are Gross Turkish Treasury debt cited in the OECD Economics Department Working Paper No. 528, by Anne-Marie Brook, 'Policies to Improve Turkey's Resilience to Financial Market Shocks', 29 November 2006, Table 1, p. 10.

12. Kemal Derviş, Daniel Gros, Michael Emerson and Sinan Ülgen, 'The European Transformation of Modern Turkey,' Centre for European Policy Studies (Brussels) & Economics and Foreign Policy Forum (Istanbul), 2004, p. 14.

13. OECD *Economic Surveys, Turkey 2001–2002*, OECD, 2002.

14. 'Merkez Bankası Bağımsızlığını Nasıl Kazandı?' *Dünya*, 23 March 2021.

15. There were also regulatory agencies established in what Özel and Atiyas have called the 'unusual sectors' of sugar, tobacco and alcohol, which were set up to

reduce state intervention (and high subsidies through price support) in the sugar and tobacco industries. In the end, the opposite happened, especially with the Sugar Agency where new forms of rent arose from the process of quota distribution by its highly politicised board. See Işık Özel and İzak Atiyas, 'Regulatory Diffusion in Turkey: A Cross-Sectoral Assessment', in Tamer Çetin and Fuat Oğuz, eds, *The Political Economy of Regulation in Turkey* (New York: Springer, 2011), p. 68–69.

16. Işık Özel, 'Reverting Structural Reforms in Turkey: Towards an Illiberal Economic Governance?' *Global Turkey in Europe Policy Brief*, May 2015, p. 4. See also Işık Özel, *State-Business Alliances and Economic Development* (London: Routledge, 2015), pp. 118–21.

17. Güzin Gülsün Akın, Ahmet Faruk Aysan and Levent Yıldıran, 'Transformation of the Turkish Financial Sector in the Aftermath of the 2001 Crisis', in Ziya Öniş and Fikret Şenses, eds, *Turkey and the Global Economy* (London: Routledge, 2009), pp. 73–100.

18. Ibid., p. 96, Table 5.10, which shows that this compares with a much higher 50–80 percent in transition economies of Eastern Europe.

19. Thomas Marois, 'The Lost Logic of State-Owned Banks: Mexico, Turkey, and Neoliberalism', paper presented at 79th Annual Conference of Canadian Political Science Association, University of Saskatchewan, 31 May 2007.

20. Tülin Aygüneş, 'Turkey Prepares for Private Pension System', *Reuters*, 12 May 2000.

21. Mina Toksöz, 'Turkey: Pension Funds in the Pipeline', *AbnAmro Flashnote*, 14 June 2000.

22. World Bank, 'Turkey-Country Economic Memorandum: Sustaining High Growth – The Role of Domestic Savings', Report No. 66301-TR, 23 December 2011, pp. 39–40.

23. World Bank, 'Turkey Public Finance Review,' Report No. 85104-TR, 20 May 2014, p. 25.

24. Işıl Erol, 'Financial Transformation and Housing Finance in Turkey', in Galip Yalman, Thomas Marois and Ali Rıza Güngen, eds, *The Political Economy of Financial Transformation in Turkey* (London: Routledge, 2019), p. 254.

25. Aylin Topal, 'The State, Crisis and Transformation of Small and Medium-Sized Enterprise Finance in Turkey', in Galip Yalman, Thomas Marois and Ali Rıza Güngen, eds, *The Political Economy of Financial Transformation in Turkey* (London: Routledge, 2019), p. 229.

26. Ibid., p. 230.

27. Özelleştirme İdaresi Başkanlığı, 'Türkiye'de Özelleştirme', 2008, oib.gov.tr.

28. İzak Atiyas, 'Recent Privatisation Experience of Turkey', in Ziya Öniş and Fikret Şenses, eds, *Turkey and the Global Economy* (London: Routledge, 2009), pp. 101–22.

29. Gül Berna Özcan and Hasan Turunç, 'Economic Liberalisation and Class Dynamics in Turkey: New Business Groups and Islamic Mobilisation', *Insight Turkey*, Vol. 13, No. 3 (2011), p. 77.

30. Mina Toksöz, 'Turkey's Energy Market: Issues in Reform', *Journal of Southern Europe and the Balkans*, Vol. 4, No. 1 (2002), p. 47.

31. Ibid., p. 50.

32. Ibid., pp. 54–55.

33. Mesut Kılıç, 'Politics of Institutional Change in State-Business Relations: A Case Study in Turkey's Electricity Sector', PhD Thesis, Bilkent University, August 2018.

34. Ibid.

35. Ibid.

36. *OECD Economic Surveys: Turkey 2010*, OECD, 2010, p. 106.

37. Metin Munir, 'Travesty of Communication', in *Turkey: Industry & Inward Investment, Financial Times Survey*, 18 April 2001.

38. Türk Telekom had no debt and USD 2 billion cash reserve in its accounts when it was privatised in 2005. 'Türk Telekom'un Satışını ve Hariri Ailesini Unutmadık, Unutturmayacağız', *Cumhuriyet*, 3 May 2021.

39. Mina Toksöz, 'Turkish Holdings Reinvent Themselves', *Turkish Area Studies Review*, Spring 2000.

40. Data for this section are from Salomon Smith Barney, *The Internet in Turkey*, Industry Report, 8 February 2000. See also estimates by Ata Invest and IBS Research in *E-Business in Turkey*, Sector Report, published by AtaInvest, May 2000.

41. Koç Holding, *Plenty of Room to Grow: Caspian Securities*, 18 June 1998.

42. Sabancı Holding Investor Presentation, sabanci.com, February 2020.

43. Greater investment in R&D and technology and the 'new economy' sectors built around renewable energy and digitalisation was highlighted by the Sabancı Holding in its 2021 Financial Results: the sale of Philsa and PMSA – the 'old economy' tobacco business – and the acquisition of a minority stake in Esarj, Turkey's first electric vehicle charging station network. Sabancı Holding, *Q4 2021 Financial Results Earnings Release*, 24 February 2022.

44. Ricardo Hausman and Dani Rodrik, 'Economic Development as Self-Discovery', *Journal of Development Economics*, Vol. 72, No. 2 (2003), pp. 603–33.

45. UNIDO, *New Technologies and Global Industrialisation, Prospects for Developing Countries*, PPD.141, 13 November 1989, p. 30.

46. *Turkey: Country Commerce*, Economist Intelligence Unit, December 2000.

47. One of the few early reports that tried to estimate the size of the market was *The Internet in Turkey* by Salomon Smith Barney, Industry Report, 8 February 2000. According to this report, in 1999, internet usage per 1,000 persons in Turkey was 8, ahead of 5 in Mexico, but below 16 in Brazil, 66 in France and 330 in the US.

48. Logo has survived and grown to become a leading Turkish software producer focusing on the small and medium-sized enterprise sector, with a subsidiary in Romania.

49. TUSIAD, *A Sectoral View of Turkish Industry*, 2008, pp. 331–36.

50. Erol Taymaz and Ebru Voyvoda, 'Industrial Restructuring and Technological Capabilities in Turkey', in Ziya Öniş and Fikret Şenses, eds, *Turkey and the Global Economy* (London: Routledge, 2009), pp. 145–72.

51. Ümit İzmen and Kamil Yılmaz, 'Turkey's Recent Trade and Foreign Direct Investment Performance', in Ziya Öniş and Fikret Şenses, eds, *Turkey and the Global Economy* (London: Routledge, 2009), Table 9.2, p. 193.

52. Ibid., p. 193.

53. Zafer Yükseler and Ercan Türkan, 'Türkiye'nin Üretim ve Dış Ticaret Yapısında Dönüşüm', Tüsiad Publications No. 453, February 2008.

54. Ibid., p. 40.

55. Ibid., p. 48.

56. Abdurrahman Babacan, 'Political Economy of Transformation of Capital Structure in Turkey: A Historical and Comparative View', in Hatice Karahan et al., eds, *Turkish Economy Between Middle Income Trap and High Income Status* (London: Palgrave Macmillan, 2018), p. 56.

57. In 2005, former French President Giscard d'Estaing blamed President Chirac and EU leaders for leaving open the possibility of Turkey's full membership as the reason why the new EU Constitution was not approved in a popular vote in France. 'EU Leader Lays Blame on Chirac', *New York Times*, 16 June 2005. A decade later, although Turkish EU membership had become increasingly unlikely, this argument was to resurface during the 2016 Brexit referendum in the UK. The 'threat' of Turkish EU membership was a major slogan of the campaign for Brexit.

58. Daron Acemoğlu and Murat Üçer, 'The Ups and Downs of Turkish Growth, 2002–2015: Political Dynamics, the European Union and the Institutional Slide', NBER Working Paper Series No. w21608, October 2015.

59. Işık Özel, 'The Politics of De-Delegation: Regulatory (In)Dependence in Turkey', *Regulation and Governance*, Vol. 6, No. 1 (2012), pp. 119–29.

60. Ümit Sönmez, *Piyasanın İdaresi: Neoliberalizm ve Türkiye'de Bağımsız Düzenleyici Kurumların Anatomisi* (İstanbul: İletişim Yayınları, 2011), pp. 200–17.

61. Işık Özel and İzak Atiyas, 'Regulatory Diffusion in Turkey: A Cross-Sectoral Assessment', in Tamer Çetin and Fuat Oğuz, eds, *The Political Economy of Regulation in Turkey* (New York: Springer, 2011), p. 58.

62. Ibid.

63. Ibid.

64. Ibid., p. 105. This was also the case in agriculture. The Agricultural Purchasing Agency (TMO) resumed 'support purchases' since 2007 to support hazelnut producers, which was widened to other agricultural sectors such as wheat in later years. But various definitional factors recorded the direct borrowing by the TMO as debt only in the public sector debt figures that covered all state enterprises (commercially run and responsible for their own debt management). The OECD thought that it should be included in general government debt, because it was financially dependent on the general government.

65. Daron Acemoğlu and Murat Üçer, 'The Ups and Downs of Turkish Growth, 2002–2015: Political Dynamics, the European Union and the Institutional Slide', NBER Working Paper Series No. w21608, October 2015.

66. Işık Özel, *State-Business Alliances and Economic Development: Turkey, Mexico and North Africa* (London: Routledge, 2015), p. 123.

67. For a comprehensive account on this, see Ziya Öniş, 'The Triumph of Conservative Globalism: The Political Economy of the AKP Era,' *Turkish Studies*, Vol. 13, No. 2 (2012), pp. 135–52.

68. For the evolution of the AKP-Gülen alliance, see Ahmet Şık, *Parallel Yürüdük Biz Bu Yollarda: AKP-Cemaat İttifakı Nasıl Dağıldı?* (İstanbul: Postacı Yayınevi, 2014).

69. Ayşe Buğra and Osman Savaşkan have described the new mechanisms of government intervention in the economy introduced during AKP rule in *New Capitalism in Turkey: The Relationship Between Politics, Religion, and Business* (Cheltenham: Edward Elgar, 2014), pp. 77–101.

70. Ayşe Buğra and Osman Savaşkan have argued that this transformation was different from the early Republican period, in that 'the networks that brought business actors together with the government and operated according to a logic that extended beyond economic concerns and, in certain cases, even conflicted with efforts to maximize short-term private economic interests'. In *New Capitalism in Turkey: The Relationship Between Politics, Religion, and Business* (Cheltenham: Edward Elgar, 2014), p. 77.

5

THE RETURN OF INDUSTRIAL POLICY AFTER THE GLOBAL FINANCIAL CRISIS

This chapter covers developments in the Turkish economy and industrial policies in the decade following the global financial crisis, until the early 2020s. The global financial crisis revealed a number of structural issues and vulnerabilities of the Turkish economy, which led to increased state intervention in response to the more difficult global conditions. In line with global trends, a series of industrial policies were introduced by the AKP to address the issues of import-dependence and signs of premature de-industrialisation, proposing a technological upgrade of Turkish industry.

This decade can be divided into two sub-periods. The first half of the decade includes the strong recovery from the global financial crisis, when some progress was made with industrial policies. The second sub-period, spanning the late AKP era, begins around 2016 with the failed military *coup* and the consolidation of 'electoral autocracy' following the establishment of the presidential system with the 2017 constitutional referendum.[1] These events accelerated the pace of institutional weakening and the loss of policy coherence. The growing executive control over the central bank and other economic institutions also increased macro-instability.

In the 2010s, in line with shifts in the global development paradigm, state intervention in the economy became more pronounced and frequent – with Turkey showing some features of 'state capitalism'. However, the AKP still adhered to certain aspects of neoliberal policies.[2] The government, in this period, resisted direct controls on international capital flows, aimed at export growth and encouraged non-selective foreign direct investment inflows and integration with global value chains. The return of industrial policy also took different forms when compared with the 1960s and 1970s. This time around, the focus was on a tech-upgrade involving greater participation by the private sector, with a major expansion of investment incentives schemes. These features made 'new' industrial policy measures more complex and difficult to manage and implement, but also more likely to be abused and turned into instruments of patronage. Also, unlike in the 1960s, these initiatives have taken place in a period of heightened global and domestic macroeconomic instability and uncertainty, with policies becoming exceptionally erratic and short-termist dominated by electoral imperatives.

This chapter reconfirms the basic thesis of this study: that it is not so much the extent of state intervention in the economy, but the global conditions, the institutional capacity of the state and macro-policy (in)stability that determine the effectiveness of industrial policies. The chapter will begin with a brief overview of the global political economy context in the aftermath of the global financial crisis. This section will also trace the deterioration in the AKP policy mix that delivered 'low-quality growth' and responded to the regional and domestic conflicts with increased authoritarianism. This will be followed by an analysis of the revived industrial policies in this decade, focusing on some achievements as well as the domestic institutional context undermining their effectiveness towards the end of the decade.

In many key respects, the industrial policy challenges that Turkey faced in this period should be considered as part of a general trend in late developers. For instance, ambitious industrial policy initiatives encountered significant problems in Brazil, too, as discussed in Box 5.1 at the end of this chapter to place Turkish case into a comparative context.

From the 5-Percent-Growth Club to the Security Alliance

The Turkish economy recovered quickly from the shock of the global financial crisis, bouncing back with an 8.4-percent GDP growth in 2010, after falling 4.8 percent in 2009. The reforms of the previous decade – including the declines in inflation, fiscal deficits and public debt burden – provided the government with room for a fiscal stimulus to cushion the shock and restore growth. The financial sector restructuring and tighter regulation put in place after the 2001 crisis also provided resilience. Meanwhile, although Turkish industry had missed the 'new economy' transition to information and communication technology in the early 2000s, by 2011 it had managed to establish a position in 'escalator' industries such as automotive, on the back of foreign investment inflows following the Turkey-EU customs union deal.[3] In addition, paradoxically, the relatively underdeveloped capital markets limited Turkey's exposure to toxic mortgage and other complex derivatives products at the core of the US sub-prime mortgage crisis. The Turkish economy was also benefiting from a revival of south-south trade and investment at the time.

The rapid economic recovery of Turkey and other emerging markets suggested to some observers that they had 'decoupled' from the crisis-struck advanced economies. The strong economic performance of BRICS (Brazil, Russia, India, China, South Africa) were praised by several commentators, and there were optimistic theses that the global economy was in a new trade 'super-cycle' led by the industrialisation and urbanisation of emerging markets. Beyond BRICS, new acronyms were introduced, such as the '5-Percent-Growth Club', 'Next-11', 'MIKTA' and 'CIVETS', all of which included Turkey. These views and the search for higher yields brought a resurgence of capital flows from international financial centres to emerging markets. Also, Turkey's inclusion in the G-20, a platform that replaced G-7 in international economic governance in the aftermath of the global financial crisis, elevated its geopolitical position. These developments – as well as rising per-capita incomes and improved health and other social services – returned the AKP to power, with a strong mandate in the 2011 election. The AKP received 50 percent of total votes, making it the only political party in Turkish political history that ruled three subsequent terms with increasing vote shares.

Yet, the negative repercussions of the global financial crisis continued to affect the Turkish economy, including the Eurozone sovereign debt crisis. The geopolitical crisis – the Arab uprisings – that broke out in North Africa and spread to Syria resulted in the collapse of state structures in Turkey's immediate neighbourhood. The regional geopolitical turmoil and loss of competitiveness from the appreciating Lira due to the capital inflows weakened exports. Combined with the pre-election stimulus to domestic demand that boosted imports, this took the Turkish current account deficit to an unprecedented

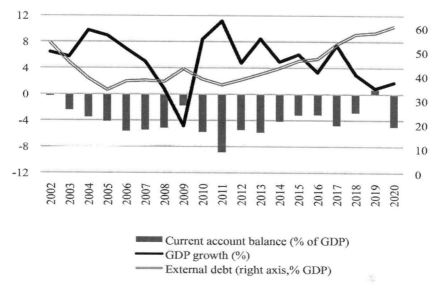

Figure 5.1 Macroeconomic trends after the 2008 global crisis
Source: World Bank, World Governance Indicators.

8.9 percent of GDP in 2011. In addition, there was the 'taper tantrum' in 2013, when the US Federal Reserve signalled a tightening of monetary policy, prompting a major capital flight from emerging markets. Turkey's stock market fell 28 percent (in USD terms), as its market capitalisation halved to 20 percent of GDP when compared with 2007. Having peaked at USD 12,500 in 2012, per capita income began its descent.

The domestic political setting also took a new turn in the second decade of the AKP government, with a series of political developments. The year 2013 was a turning point for the political fortunes of the AKP, as it faced two shocks in a row: first, there was the popular resistance against the AKP government with the Gezi Park protests; second, corruption allegations and the AKP's break-up with its long-time political ally, an Islamic sect known as the Gülenists, affected the domestic political contests in the coming years. Facing a weak parliamentary opposition after its 2011 election victory, the AKP drifted into a majoritarian stance that sharpened the political divisions in the country. The resulting social tensions that erupted in the 2013 Gezi protests led by mostly urban youth and, in the context of the Syrian crisis, the escalation of the Kurdish conflict became pretexts for the expansion of the security state.

As covered in Chapter 4, relations between the AKP and big business (and its secular representatives in Tüsiad) also deteriorated in the 2010s, with adverse consequences on the effectiveness of industrial policy.

Following the June 2015 general election, when the AKP failed to win a majority, a *de facto* partnership between the AKP and the MHP – a 'security alliance', was formed.[4] This alliance was consolidated with an emergency rule that followed the 2016 coup attempt and formalised following the establishment of the presidential system with the April 2017 constitutional referendum. The AKP government marshalled significant resources to engineer social changes, by reshaping the education system and religious affairs, centralised bureaucratic control and increased limits on democratic space with curbs on media, independence of the judicial system and freedom of speech.[5] As relations with the Western alliance (the US and the EU) as well as the Gulf States came under increasing strain, Turkey's geostrategic axis also shifted towards Russia and China.[6] It was in this international and domestic context that the ambitious 'new' industrial policies were launched and implemented. The following sections analyse this transformation and its impact on the evolution of industrial policy in Turkey.

The Global Revival of Industrial Policies

The global development paradigm underwent another important change after the global financial crisis of 2009. To be clear, there was greater interest by mainstream economists in a more 'active' state role and in industrial policies. For instance, Rodrik, Stiglitz and Lin, among others, widened the neoclassical role of government intervention to include financial support, resolving coordination problems and assistance in overcoming the 'discovery costs' of new scientific and technological advances (see Chapter 1).[7]

Industrial policies were not only of interest to developing economies, but also to advanced countries to overcome the stagnating productivity in the years following the global financial crisis. The experience of DARPA (Defence Advanced Research Projects Agency) was revisited in the US and the EU. Building on the 2009 'Strategy for American Innovation', President Obama introduced the 'Advanced Manufacturing Partnership' in 2011, which increased federal funding for R&D and brought together industry, universities and the federal government to invest in frontier technologies.[8] In the EU, an 'Integrated Industrial Policy for the Globalisation Era' was launched in

2010, with a focus on the radical changes in the global economy for industry – including global value chains, the increased competition from emerging markets and the transition towards a low-carbon economy.[9] The EU also drew up a list of 'Important Projects of Common European Interest', including government support to initiate twenty-five battery plants to service the green transformation of the automotive sector. In the UK, and despite a reluctant Treasury, the Conservative government of Teresa May adopted the Industrial Strategy in 2017 (building on earlier proposals by Vince Cable, the Liberal Democrat Business Secretary under the Cameron-Clegg coalition), targeting the development of high-technology sectors such as aerospace, life sciences and artificial intelligence.[10]

The loss of manufacturing capacity to China and other big emerging markets was a growing concern for policy-makers in the West, which was further amplified with geopolitical rivalries and complex supply chain issues. On the other hand, emerging powers continued to invest in industrial policy. For instance, China's 'Made in China 2025' strategy launched in 2015 and aiming for self-sufficiency in supply chains in high-tech sectors was making rapid progress. India had also launched its 'Made in India' programme in 2014. These 'new' industrial policies adopted by advanced and developing countries differed from previous versions. Unlike the 'old' – or classical – industrial policies of the 1960s and 1970s, as discussed in Chapter 1, they were export-oriented and advocated global integration via global supply chains, with a renewed focus on technology and innovation.[11] This was belatedly even endorsed by the IMF, with proposals for a 'Technology and Innovation Policy' or a 'True Industrial Policy (TIP)'.[12] The new policies also differed from the framework of the liberalisation era of the 1980s in that the old dichotomies of 'horizontal' versus 'vertical' measures were mostly dropped; the new industrial policies included sector-targeting strategies, as well as wider horizontal measures such as skills development and environmental sustainability. There was a regained legitimacy for national development strategies, exemplified by the French plans to revive its *Commissariat du Plan*. By 2018, the World Investment Report noted that eighty-four countries accounting for around 90 percent of the global GDP had adopted industrial policies over the past five years.[13]

The added urgency to address the COVID-19 pandemic as well as climate change reinforced these trends, prompting a further global shift away from the small state paradigm of the neoliberal framework.[14] Mariana Mazzucato, an advisor to the G7 Panel advising the 2021 G7 meeting in Cornwall, advocated a new 'Cornwall Consensus' with a revitalised economic role for the state and for government policies that move from *reactively fixing* market failures to *proactively shaping* and making the kinds of markets we need'.[15] The disruption to supply chains and travel triggered by the COVID-19-associated lockdowns reinforced these trends, with 'strategic' sectors such as airlines and automotive firms receiving state support in the UK, Germany and France. By 2022, the global shortage of microchips prompted the passage of the 'Chips Act', involving a USD 49-billion public–private support fund, with state subsidies for 'mega-fabs in the EU and, in the US, the CHIPS and Science Act allocating USD 52 billion to finance private sector investment in "fabs"'.[16]

The current industrial policy framework seems to include even modification of the restrictions on policy space embodied in international commitments. On the positive side, this reflects the debate over the relaxation of state-aid policies such as on EU subsidies to combat climate change and the reform of WTO and EU rules to 'exempt' various sectors and industrial policy instruments to facilitate COVID-19 related health and environmental measures. There was also a break with the old dichotomy of export-led versus import-substitution policies, tacitly accepting that late industrialisers and advanced economies positioning for the 'new industrial revolution' should take a pragmatic approach, with 'a blend of measures that mix import substitution with export promotion'.[17] However, the adoption of such measures by global powers also brings many risks, as seen since the US-China trade wars initiated by President Trump in 2017 and the sanctions and supply chain disruptions following the Russian invasion of the Ukraine.[18] These developments have entrenched the protectionist trend and fragmentation of world trade that has emerged since the global financial crisis and the 'weaponisation of economic interdependence' in the current context of increasing strategic tensions between global powers.

The Return of Turkish Industrial Policy: An Answer to All Problems?

The Turkish government's focus on industrial policies also began a few years after the global financial crisis, in relation to the search for a new growth model. During the AKP's second term, total factor productivity in the economy had slowed, as low-productivity construction and services sectors became the main drivers of growth.[19] This credit- and construction-driven 'low-quality' growth had seen the rise of the non-tradeable (services) sectors that were more amenable to domestic policy directives. With the exception of a few break-out industries – such as motor vehicles, basic metals and textiles – productivity in manufacturing had stagnated. As the contribution to growth from industry began to wane, and as consumption and investment became increasingly reliant on imports, worries about premature de-industrialisation emerged.[20]

Meanwhile, with the Turkish Lira appreciating, export-led growth had faltered, with Turkish goods unable to compete with China and other East Asian exporters as globalisation progressed in the 2000s. Although some services sectors (such as tourism, health, transport and contractors' services) had an export element – and some had backward linkages for the manufacture of equipment for these services, as a source of foreign currency revenues – these proved volatile and unable to offset the growing trade deficit. With domestic savings low relative to investment needs, this led to increased reliance on international capital inflows and foreign debt to fund the current account deficits. The decline of capital inflows following the 'taper tantrum' of 2013 exposed these structural problems.

Many of these issues had already been highlighted by a report from the Ministry of Science, Industry and Technology in 2010, which re-emphasised the 'industrial sector' as the main driver of the Turkish economy. These themes were further developed by the Tenth and Eleventh Development Plans covering 2014–23, proposing a 'tech-driven' upgrade of Turkish industry and, related to that, a reduction of its import dependence and an increase in high-technology exports. Since 2020, the need to respond to the COVID-19 pandemic and to adopt a green transition agenda have added more dimensions to Turkey's revitalised industrial policy agenda. In October 2021, after ratifying the Paris Agreement, the AKP government began to define a 'green agenda' for the Turkish economy, which, combined with the 'tech-driven' industrial policy, is to shape a 'new growth model'. This represented a big challenge but also an opportunity for the Turkish economy: the combination of high-tech and green transition could, if effectively pursued, also help 'solve' its foreign payments problem by reducing the hydrocarbon import bill.

Tech- and Environmental Upgrade of Turkish Industry

The 2010 document from the Ministry of Science, Industry and Technology, titled *Industrial Strategy for Turkey 2011–2014: Towards EU Membership*, proposed reshaping Turkish industry to become 'a medium-and-high technology production base for Eurasia'.[21] This return of industrial policy at first was not an ambitious attempt, as in China, at placing Turkish industry on the cutting edge of technology, but mostly based on Turkey's comparative advantage in sectors such as chemicals, automotive, white goods, machinery and electronics. The 2012 Incentives Law that provided the legislative framework brought back the idea of 'strategic investments' in those sectors with 'positive externalities' for the rest of the economy, of reducing import dependence and increasing value-added production. There were 'horizontal' measures that defined the general criteria of eligibility for incentives, such as sectors where dependence on imports is greater than 50 percent and investment projects that involve at least 40 percent domestic value added. Regional incentives were maintained with all industries eligible for support in the lowest income per capita regions; projects with larger economies of scale were also encouraged. This approach was integrated into the Tenth Five-Year Plan for 2014–18, with an increased focus on more transformative sectors producing high-technology products in pharmaceuticals, dual-use defence technology, medical equipment and increasing the domestic content of renewable energy equipment.[22]

By 2019, the secular trend towards de-industrialisation seemed to be turning (see Figure 5.2), albeit still below 1980s levels.[23] However, the problems of productivity and import dependence were still there. Import penetration of net domestic consumption had risen from around 20 percent in the 2000s to around 30 to 35 percent by the late 2010s.[24] The Eleventh Five-Year Plan published in 2019 proposed an industrial technological upgrade to raise the share of exports of medium- and high-tech products from 39 percent to 50 percent, with high-tech exports rising from 3.2 percent of manufactured exports in 2018 to 5.8 percent by 2023.[25] The plans were in line with 'mainstream' and IMF recommendations of project-based incentives for high-technology and export-oriented investments, within a framework to attract FDI and increase integration with global value chains.[26] The projects selected included bio-technology pharmaceutical production, a petrochemical hub in the Ceyhan Industrial Zone (already initiated), and further support for the extensive web of techno-parks across

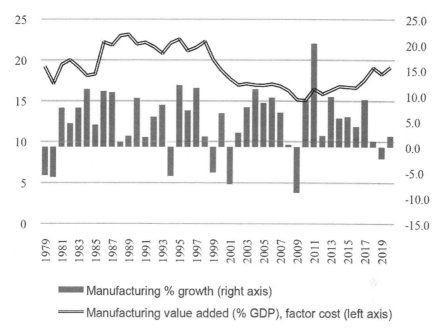

Figure 5.2 Manufacturing growth and share of GDP

Source: 'Manufacturing growth' from State Planning Organisation, % change in constant prices; 'manufacturing value added', share of GDP factor cost from the World Bank.

the country. In 2020, the support schemes for SMEs administered through KOSGEB (Small and Medium-Sized Enterprises Development Organisation) were expanded to also cope with the COVID-19 pandemic, by including a programme for health and hygiene products.

The Eleventh Five-Year Plan was complemented by an industrial policy package by the Ministry of Industry and Technology, which was called the 'Tech-Driven Industry Initiative' for 'end-to-end localisation'. It has a greater focus on high-tech sectors such as computer, electronics, optics and transportation vehicles and aims to cut the current account deficit by USD 30 billion, by reducing high import dependence in medium-high technology intermediate goods. In 2020, measures (designed in accordance with EU rules) to encourage domestic content in public procurement projects were also added. As seen everywhere since the onset of the COVID-19 pandemic, also included were incentives for 'reshoring' and increasing the share of domestic production in critical sectors such as health and defence industries. This focus on reducing 'import dependence' is combined with export orientation, drawing on the lessons from East Asia, and in line with the pragmatic new industrial policies of today.[27] Nevertheless, it looks set to be a difficult process, with the measures to incentivise domestic pharmaceutical production already being challenged by the EU and the US at the WTO.[28]

A Green Deal Action Plan released in July 2021 by the Turkish Ministry of Trade added an environmental dimension to the above. This followed Turkey's belated ratification of the Paris Agreement in October 2021, having held out for international financial assistance as a late-industrialising, urbanising economy with its per capita energy consumption a fraction of those in the advanced economies.[29] The Action Plan aims to establish compliance with the EU Green Deal in those sectors and exports that could be disrupted by the EU carbon tax. The government has had to respond to the EU carbon tax, proposed as part of the EU's 'Fit for 55' green agenda, on imports of highly polluting sectors such as cement, aluminium, fertilisers, electricity, iron and steel, and electricity. Turkey is in third place after Russia and China in terms of the vulnerability of its exports to the EU in these sectors.[30] There are also plans for a national 'emission trading system' that is compliant with the EU.

With a USD 40 billion per year energy import bill (risen to an estimated USD 70 billion in 2022), the switch to clean energy meets many objectives in Turkey. Turkey's share of renewables – hydro, solar, wind and geothermal – in electricity production has risen in the past decade, with a major potential for further growth. Wind has been supported with state subsidies under a feed-in tariff system via the YEKDEM (Renewable Energy Sources Support Mechanism) since 2011, with Turkey ranking fifth in Europe in wind turbine equipment production.[31] At around 44 percent, the share of renewables in power generation capacity in 2019 ranked Turkey between Finland and Germany. However, the share of renewable energy in the total final energy consumption was 11.9 percent in 2018, indicating more needs to be done in transport, housing and industry.[32]

Some sectors are already implementing their own 'green transitions'. Demand from major US and EU brands for 'sustainable' fashion has prompted Turkish textile and clothing suppliers to increase the recycling of materials and water use efficiency and to end the use of coal-powered energy.[33] But time is short for the green transformation required to avoid the EU carbon tax that could come into operation in 2026, after a transition period starting in 2023. Costing an estimated USD 50 billion, this will require a major restructuring of the Turkish industry that had a global niche as producer and exporter of heavy (polluting) industries, as advanced economies de-industrialised and moved into light industry and high-tech sectors.[34]

Project-based Policies, Start-ups and 'Pockets of Efficiency' in Defence

There were also certain high-tech initiatives that came from unexpected quarters of the Turkish economy. Indicators of digital preparedness for a technological leap compiled by a Digital Evolution Index in 2017 put Turkey in the border of a 'Stand-Out' crowd of countries, along with Poland and Malaysia.[35] As seen around the world, the COVID-19 lockdowns since 2020 also led to the rapid growth of e-commerce and other information and communications technologies (ICT) activities in Turkey, which has seen its first 'unicorns' emerge. The share of online retail in total has more than doubled to 15 percent in mid-2021, from 6.2 percent at the end of 2019, according to the Turkish Informatics Industry Association (TÜBİSAD). In the first half of 2021, USD 1.3 billion of investments went into start-ups, surpassing the USD 736 million of investment over the past ten years.[36] This has come not so much from government support, but mostly from a wide range of foreign and domestic 'angel' investors. Most important has been funding from the investment arms of established Turkish conglomerates, such as the Oyak Group, Vestel Ventures of Vestel Group, Inventram of Koç Holding and Yıldız Ventures of Ülker Group.

Government assistance has come from TÜBİTAK and the KOSGEB funds for SMEs, with additional funds provided by the state-owned Development and Investment Bank of Turkey, with a TL 350 million 'Technology and Innovation Fund' and another TL 150–200 million 'High Technology Fund'. There are also investment incentives in techno-parks that have grown from only two in 2001 to eighty-eight, housing 6,680 companies and employing some 60,000 people, with 45 percent focused on ICT. The techno-parks include ODTÜ-Teknokent at the Middle East Technical University in Ankara, which has participation by Turkey's major private sector firms. Set up in the late 1980s, it now houses 470 firms, including the R&D arms of Aselsan, Havelsan, Tusaş and Siemens in defence, electronics and aerospace; Türk Telekom and Netaş in telecoms; and Arçelik, Vestel and Samsung in consumer goods.[37] However, this remains exceptional, with many techno-parks struggling to overcome the problem of lack of cooperation between the private sector and research institutions (see below).[38]

Government assistance has mostly been effective when it comes to well-defined project-based schemes in line with industrial policy aims such as the objective of reducing import dependence in intermediate goods sectors with more than 40 percent import requirement. In 2012, these included (in descending order) coke and refined products, computers and electronics, basic metals, motor vehicles and electrical equipment.[39] The highest sector with 70 percent import requirement was coke and refined petroleum, which had a simple answer: the Turkish economy needed another major refinery in addition to the ones operated by Tüpraş. This has since been duly supplied with a Turkish-Azeri (Socar) joint venture, Star refinery in Aliağa, which came into operation in 2018.

Another state initiative relates to the reduction of carbon emissions in transport. Transition to electric vehicles (EVs) will be essential for Turkey to maintain its global position in 2020, as the third-largest commercial vehicle producer in Europe (with an 85-percent export rate).[40] Hence, a state-sponsored project is ongoing for a domestic electric vehicle production consortium TOGG, (Turkey's Automobile Joint Venture Group) as well as a lithium-ion battery production joint venture of Turkish and Chinese (Farasis) investors, provided with tax exemptions, investment site allocation and public purchase guarantees.[41] The government investment incentives for EV battery production are also attracting growing interest from Turkish automotive firms, including Koç Holding and Kalyon Holding.

In addition, the defence industries sector has become, as elsewhere, a significant conduit for high-tech production. Given Turkey's volatile geostrategic location and defence spending of 2.5 percent of GDP, governments have sought to increase defence self-sufficiency since the 1980s. The growing regional crises have reinforced this focus, with defence-related projects attracting high levels of investment incentives. One of the biggest incentive allocations in 2019 was to Aselsan Konya – a public–private defence industry project.[42] Aselsan, a corporation of the Turkish Armed Forces Foundation which produces defence electronics products, had increased its domestic content to around 70 percent by 2020, by fostering a wide network of domestic suppliers. With four Turkish firms listed in the top-100 global defence manufacturers and exporters and the highest R&D spending among Turkish manufacturing industries, the defence sector has the potential to produce what can be called a 'Turkish-DARPA' effect.[43] The defence industry stands out as one of the more resilient sectors continuing to grow under the current unstable macroeconomic conditions. With its extensive domestic SME supplier base and long-term, reliable investment support through various army funds, in addition to access to investment incentives, the sector is more cushioned against the market uncertainty facing most others (see the discussion on 'pockets of efficiency' in the Conclusion).

Heading for a Middle-of-the-road Innovator Trap?

The challenge for industrial policies in the coming period will be not only to sustain these trends in the high-tech sectors, but also to widen their use in industry, services and agriculture to generate an economy-wide productivity boost. Twenty years ago, there was another burst of activity in the ICT sector. Several internet service providers were set up by established holding groups in the late 1990s, and high-tech exports were growing fast. But the bursting of the US Dot-com bubble and the Turkish financial crisis of 2000–1 devastated many entities (see Chapter 4). Although there were strong growth and productivity increases in medium-technology exports such as automotives, high-tech exports such as computer, electronic and optical goods as a share of the total peaked in 2004–5. Despite a rapid economic recovery, the neglect of industrial policies by the incoming AKP government meant that the opportunity was missed to encourage a wider transformation of Turkish industry into a higher technology structure.

In contrast, the past decade has had a progressive focus on tech-oriented industrial policies offering major investment incentives.[44] As discussed above and as Table 5.1 suggests, although there has been some progress in Turkey, the pace of improvement has faltered in recent years. This is illustrated by the trends in gross expenditure in research and development (GERD) as a share of GDP, with the gap with comparable economies such as Poland widening after 2016 (also see Figure 5.4). GERD has risen from 0.8 percent in 2011 to 1.06 percent in 2019, but the government target of 1.8 percent by 2023 is looking hard to meet, as is the aim of raising the share of high-tech exports to 5.8 percent by 2023, an aim set by the Eleventh Five-Year Plan.

These trends are in line with the 2021 UNESCO *Science Report* that noted that Turkey could be heading for a 'middle-of-the-road-innovator trap', in

Table 5.1 ICT and R&D indicators in Turkey

	2000	2010	2020
Mobile phone subs (per 100 people)	12.5	85.4	96.8
vs Poland	17.5	122.5	127.7
Internet users (% of population)	3.8	39.8	74.0
vs Poland	7.3	62.3	84.5
High-tech exports (% of manufactured exports)	4.0	2.2	3.2
vs Poland	3.0	8.0	10.1
GERD (R&D spending, % GDP)	0.47	0.79	1.06*
vs Poland	0.64	0.75	1.32*

Source: Authors' own compilation from DEİK; World Bank; UNESCO, OECD. (*) 2019.

contrast to the earlier report's positive tone in 2015 that Turkey in economic and technological terms was catching up with advanced economies.[45] The problem identified was that the increased government incentives for R&D was not translating into overall productivity growth or high-tech exports, because business was not '*grasping the government's helping hand* in support of technological development and innovation' (italics added).[46] This point was repeated by the CEO of the Logo Group (one of the few software firms that survived the Dot-com and Turkish 2001 crises), Buğra Koyuncu, who lamented that Turkish firms are not investing sufficiently in ICT products when compared to peers such as Poland and South Africa.[47] Turkish firms lag behind their European counterparts when it comes to training their employees to 'develop ICT skills'. According to the Eurostat data, the shares of both large companies and small and medium-sized enterprises (over the total number of enterprises in each category) providing ICT training to their employees are below the EU-27 average – and that of the several comparable states (see Figure 5.3).

Small and medium-sized enterprises (SMEs) dominate the Turkish business environment. According to 2021 data, they constitute 99.7 percent of all enterprises; 71 percent of total employment; and 35.5 percent of value added at factor costs.[48] Almost 56 percent of all SMEs in the manufacturing sector rely on low technology in the production process. This ratio is almost 30 percent for large firms employing more than 250 persons. The share of high-tech for large-scale firms in the manufacturing industry is just 2.8 percent; medium-low

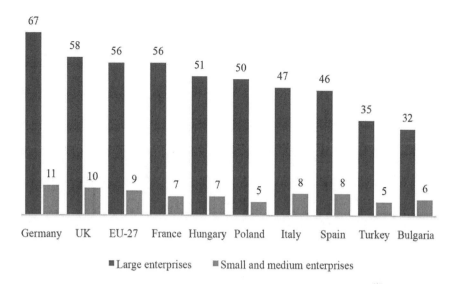

Figure 5.3 Enterprises training their employees to improve their ICT skills (% of all enterprises)

Source: Eurostat. According to Eurostat, large enterprises refer to '250 employees and self-employed persons or more, without financial sector'. Also, small and medium-sized enterprises refer to '10–249 employees and self-employed persons or more, without financial sector'. Data from 2019; EU-27 from 2020.

technology products constitute 46 percent, and medium-high technology constitute almost 23 percent for large-scale firms.[49] The share of R&D carried out by business only began to surpass government-funded R&D after 2017. It is closer to around two-thirds (versus 78 percent in South Korea) as of 2019, with the major contributors being the defence industries and multi-national corporations. The UNESCO report also noted that Turkish researchers' involvement in international research networks were limited and that there was a decline in research output between 2016 and 2018, due to the loss of academic research staff in the aftermath of the attempted coup in 2016.

A major barrier to 'business grasping the government's helping hand' has been problems with the implementation of industrial policies. The management of implementing a tech-upgrade is more difficult than the earlier industrialisation stages achieved in the 1960s. Greater institutional coherence and state-business cooperation is needed to manage the 'technical processes' involved with the digital technologies. Experience of industrial policies in Southeast Asia highlight other factors that are relevant to the Turkish conditions, which will be discussed below. In Malaysia, for example, the tech-upgrade policies adopted in 1991 lacked coherence and were undermined by their clientelist orientation to bumiputra circles.[50]

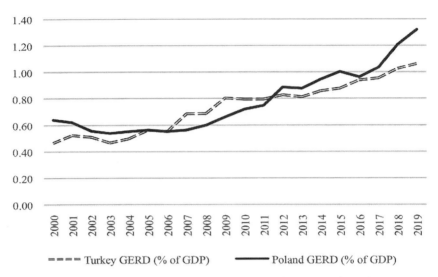

Figure 5.4 Gross expenditure in research and development (GERD, % of GDP)
Source: OECD.

Industrial Policy Funding Becomes More Complex

The funding for 'new' industrial policies in Turkey has involved greater participation by the private sector, while public investment as a share of the total has declined. However, there has been an increase in quasi-fiscal instruments, such as credit guarantees, and other sovereign guarantees on the extensive programme of public–private partnerships (PPPs); and the state banks' share of credit has risen. Meanwhile, state ownership in the form of majority or minority shares in strategic sectors has also increased through the newly established sovereign wealth fund (see below). This complex mix of funding instruments of industrial policies in the context of low availability and high cost of institutionalised long-term capital market finance, the lack of sufficient monitoring and declining transparency during the late AKP period have functioned in an investment environment that has increasingly blurred the public–private distinctions.

Unlike in many countries with industrial policies where development banks providing long-term funding are among the biggest banks in their countries, such as Brazil's BNDES or Germany's KfW, they play a marginal role in Turkey, with a small share of financial sector assets. The privately owned Industrial Development Bank of Turkey (TSKB), which once was a major driver of the industrialisation spurt of the 1950s, has been focusing on funding projects

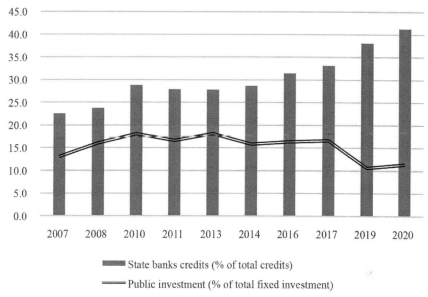

Figure 5.5 Increasing state bank loans since 2009
Source: Turkish Banking Association.

supporting the Green Agenda. The state-owned Development and Investment Bank of Turkey (TKYB), given the mission to lend to strategic sectors set by the Eleventh Five-Year Plan, has recently set aside two high-tech investment funds. The shallow capital markets have also not been a major source of long-term investment funding, although venture funds set up by established Turkish conglomerates have supported the recent increase in start-up activities.

In contrast, the activities of state commercial banks have risen, in line with the historical features of the bank-dominated Turkish financial sector (see Chapter 4 on financial reforms after the 2001 crisis). The share of total credit by the three state banks and their Islamic banking arms have risen from 24 percent of the total banking sector credits prior to the global financial crisis, to 41 percent by 2020. This includes lending to SMEs by Halk Bank, which has an element of interest rate support from the central government budget (as 'duty expenses', in Turkish *görevlendirme giderleri*) that allows for a higher risk appetite in lending to more risky start-ups and young firms which are major employers and seen as potential source of innovative consumer products. Although state bank financial metrics remain sound, they have had to be recapitalised in three separate rounds, totalling around USD 10 billion since

2019. The injection of funds for state bank recapitalisations came from the Turkey Wealth Fund.

There has also been a big expansion of quasi-fiscal measures, including Treasury guarantees on PPPs on mostly infrastructure projects and on loans to SMEs from the Credit Guarantee Fund. The number and value of PPP projects in Turkey rose rapidly after the global financial crisis, peaking in 2013. Turkey was ranked top country in Europe in 2015–19 by the European Investment Bank in the total value of PPPs, which included hospitals, energy and transport infrastructure projects. By 2020, it was estimated that the PPP portfolio had reached around 20 percent of GDP.[51]

Public guarantees on commercial credits through the KGF have also risen rapidly. The KGF is jointly owned by the Turkish Chambers of Commerce (TOBB), KOSGEB and commercial banks, with the Turkish Treasury providing counter-guarantees. It has been supporting loans to SMEs since 1994, with around half directed to manufacturing by backing commercial bank loans to SMEs. The level of loans shot up in 2017, in the aftermath of the failed *coup* in 2016, when the economy slowed sharply. Policy response to the COVID-19 pandemic also included a major increase of KGF-supported loans, expanded to include consumer credit and amounting to around 8.5 percent of total credits in 2020.

These interventions with increased lending by state banks, KGF credits and the large programme of PPPs have brought a number of problems. A survey by the EBRD of Turkish state bank lending patterns has shown that lending rose prior to local elections and in regions that were government strongholds – what is known as 'tactical redistribution', suggesting that available credit was 'not always allocated to the most deserving companies'.[52] Concerns about the loan purpose and quality in the KGF portfolio arose in the aftermath of the 2016 failed coup, when KGF credits expanded ten-fold in four months in 2017; the aim was to support investment, but it was found that 90 percent of the credits were used for working capital rather than new investment in machinery and equipment.[53] In early 2018, the government hastily issued new instructions to try to correct this and to ensure that KGF credits were directed to capital investment and exporters. There is also the fiscal implications of the contingent liabilities of PPPs, KGF and state bank credit guarantees.[54] Although the 2021 annual report of the KGF shows that the ratio of non-performing loans stood at a moderate 2.4 percent, the rules for the recognition of non-performing loans are thought to be lax when compared with international standards.[55] The rapid depreciation of the Turkish Lira in recent years has increased fiscal risks in PPPs, some of which have treasury guarantees based on foreign currency and lack transparency and standardisation of the complex public–private partnership contracts.

State interventionism in the late AKP era became more discernible with the establishment of new institutions such as the new sovereign wealth fund in Turkey – that is, the *Türkiye Varlık Fonu* or Turkey Wealth Fund (TWF). The TWF has been playing a growing role in the economy. It was established in 2016 with the transfer of assets of existing public enterprises, mostly in the financial, transport and energy sectors. Since then, more public assets have been added, with the market value of assets under management put at USD 245 billion in September 2020 by the Fitch ratings agency. This has resulted in the state becoming a minority or majority shareholder of some of Turkey's biggest corporates and banks.[56] Among the several stated aims of the TWF are the deepening of Turkish financial markets and the provision of equity for investments in the strategic sectors of petrochemicals, energy and mining, in line with the national goals of reducing import dependence in those sectors. However, the wide remit of its activities suggests a lack of clarity about its objectives.[57] In recent years, these have included funding the recapitalisation of state banks and the consolidation of state-owned insurance firms. As in many countries, it has also been used to take over failed firms such as Turkcell, Turkey's biggest mobile phone operator, in 2021 and, in 2022, the acquisition of 55 percent of shares of Türk Telekom for USD 1.7 billion from its creditor banks (see Chapter 4). With Turkey's satellite provider Türksat already in the TWF, these transactions put key assets in the telecom sector back in public hands since Türk Telekom's privatisation in 2005. The TWF's role as a holding fund for ailing firms partly overlaps with the SDIF (Savings Deposit Insurance Fund), which had a highly politicised role when hundreds of firms were taken over by the government after the 2016 attempted coup.[58]

Navigating Institutional Weakening, Uncertainty and Macro-instability

If growing state interventionism is one conspicuous aspect of the Turkish political economy in the 2010s, declining state capacity is the other. This is one of the key factors that explain the limited success of the industrial policy initiatives during the late AKP era. We stated in the conceptual chapter that 'new' industrial policy is as much about process and institutional coordination as it is about the content of the policy set. Seen this way, Turkey's new political orientation in the 2010s accelerated the erosion of much-needed 'embedded autonomy'.[59]

In terms of bureaucratic autonomy, the AKP gradually chipped away at the capacity of the 'independent' regulatory institutions which had been seen as not appropriate to 'the customary Turkish way of doing politics' (see Chapter 4). This process gained momentum after the passage of the 2011 Decree Law giving the respective ministries full authority over regulatory institutions. The 'top-down' decision-making practices began to dominate all aspects of political and economic life, reaching its zenith following the establishment of executive presidentialism with a referendum in 2017, which took place under repressive 'state of emergency' conditions.[60] The establishment of the presidential system, backed by a series of electoral victories, made President Erdoğan the most powerful political actor in Turkish politics. The resulting over-accumulation of political power in the hands of the incumbency – along with a weak political opposition – paved the way for the elimination of checks-and-balance mechanisms and the consolidation of an authoritarian rule. As a result, 'state power is personified by defining the leader as the state and loyalty to the leader as the loyalty to the state', and the centralisation of policy-making undermined the authority of the state bureaucracy, rendering bureaucratic expertise largely redundant.[61]

The growing problems associated with bureaucratic autonomy and the polarised nature of state–business relations came at a time when 'new' industrial policy measures became more complex and demanded closer coordination among economic actors and state bureaucracy. The main instrument of the revived industrial policies were credit support and other investment incentives, which have increased rapidly, with new ones rushed out following frequent crises or in the lead up to elections. The investment incentive regime began to be expanded from 2009 onwards (see Figure 5.6), with a legal framework provided by the new Incentives Law (Law No. 3305) in 2012. This framework provides four types of incentives: general incentives, regional scheme, priority investment scheme and strategic investment scheme.[62] The main form of support from the general scheme consists of exemptions from various taxes and customs duties. The regional, priority and large investment schemes widen the tax exemptions and provide other incentives, such as land allocation and interest rate support.

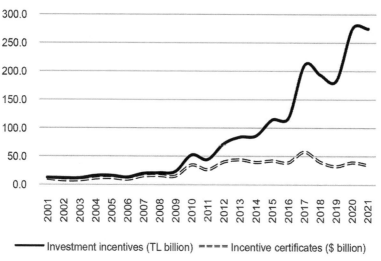

Figure 5.6 Rise of incentive certificates after 2009
Source: Ministry of Industry and Technology.

In 2016, a 'Super Incentive' scheme providing project-based incentives and, in 2019, investment incentives for new technologies were added.

With the outbreak of the COVID-19 epidemic in 2020, the investment incentives schemes were expanded to provide support for SMEs administered through KOSGEB.[63] Incentives from the general incentive schemes also rose rapidly, with the value of incentives up 30 percent in 2020 over the previous peak in 2017. In 2021, new schemes were introduced for sixteen high-tech health-related sectors such as biotechnology, immunology and robotics and covering 421 products with a generous five to ten years of new incentives, such as a 50-percent discount on energy costs.

However, even prior to the COVID-19 related expansion, the proliferation of incentives had reached '75 different incentive and subsidy schemes', according to an OECD report in 2018.[64] As the number of schemes grew, the effectiveness of targeting the incentives in line with industrial policy objectives declined. This became a cause of increasing concern, especially in the light of sluggish productivity trends. These issues had also been revealed in Kutlay and Karaoğuz's interviews with relevant state bureaucrats who had pointed out the many problems with monitoring the R&D funds as well as the lack of proper performance measurement criteria, which, in turn, constrained the developmental impact of the technological upgrading plans in Turkey.[65] A 2019 study comparing the effectiveness of the two state agencies tasked with accelerating R&D, innovation and total factor productivity growth – that is, TÜBİTAK and KOSGEB – found that, while support from both agencies increased employment, it was only the TÜBİTAK schemes that raised R&D and innovation.[66] The incentives also had unforeseen consequences: machinery manufacturers complained that investment incentives with customs duty exemption on imports of machinery and equipment brought a bias towards imports and away from domestic producers.[67] The fiscal cost of business subsidies have also risen, estimated at 30 percent of the corporate tax take due in 2019.

These problems with the management of incentive schemes were noted in a Ministry of Industry and Technology report in 2019, which proposed the incentives programmes and other measures to be simplified, made more transparent and targeted to increase their effectiveness.[68] There have also been suggestions to merge the relevant ministerial and incentive scheme and research entities into a Japanese-style MITI (which oversaw Japan's industrial transformation), in place of the disbanded SPO.[69] The SPO, shuffled around various ministries since 2017, had been finally closed down in 2018, and the responsibility for the Five-Year Plans had been placed under the Presidency of Strategy and Budget. Yet, the government has continued to approach these issues in a piecemeal way, with reactive measures and more extensions of the incentive schemes, creating more commissions and making frequent changes in the responsibilities of the ministries.

The incentive schemes have been expanded once more following Turkey signing the Paris Climate Agreement in 2021, so as to include 'green investments' while also adding measures to encourage the employment of women and youth. In addition, a new Climate Change Commission came into existence to prepare sectoral plans for the green transition, and the Ministry of Environment and Urbanisation has been renamed the Ministry of Environment, Urbanisation and Climate Change (MoEUCC). The new 'Green Agenda' adds yet another layer to the existing complex mix of industrial policy schemes. This increases the difficulty for business to navigate and utilise incentives and, by generating confusion and uncertainty, discourages private investment.

Déjà Vu *All Over Again: A Deteriorating Macroeconomic Environment*

The 'de-institutionalisation' of economic governance has had major negative consequences for macroeconomic policy. In fact, macroeconomic policies had already begun to lose coherence in the lead up to the global financial crisis, as the external anchors of the IMF and the EU membership process weakened.[70] In addition, the appreciation of domestic currency had undermined export growth, increased import dependence and widened the current account deficit. The global financial crisis of 2008–9 exposed these vulnerabilities. The government policy response was a construction- and credit-led 'low-quality growth', backed up by fiscal stimulus in the lead up to the 2011 elections. One of the pivotal moments was in 2010 when – despite its passage by the all-party Parliamentary Budget Committee and support by the Minister for the Economy, Ali Babacan – the government rejected the adoption of a fiscal rule at the last minute, because they did not want to 'create an internal IMF'.[71]

This policy mix became more difficult to sustain after 2013, as international portfolio flows reflected a more erratic trend and foreign direct investment started to slow. Economic policy-making reverted to a reactive mode, with more frequent *ad hoc* measures and administrative interventions reminiscent of the Özal years. Industrial productivity (total factor productivity, TFP) growth rates in 2013–18 also returned to the sluggish performance of the 1990s.[72]

Domestic funding struggled to replace the decline in external funds, as policies introduced after the 2001 crisis had not managed to mobilise domestic savings into capital markets or private pension funds established in 2003, to the scale that was required. With a target of raising the national savings ratio from around 25 percent of GDP to 30 percent by 2023, a major step to develop the private pension system (BES, *Bireysel Emeklilik Sistemi*) was taken in 2012. A 25-percent (later raised to a 30-percent) government contribution was introduced, and in 2017 automatic registration for those under forty-five years of age, which from 2018 onwards also included small enterprises employing more than five people. By then, the BES still had only 11.6 million enrolled, with a savings of TL 96.3 billion – a miniscule 2.6 percent of GDP.[73] The automatic enrolment did boost the participation rate to 13.4 million by 2021 and the savings ratio to rise towards its 2023 target; paradoxically, the natural disasters of fires and flooding due to climate change in recent years have supported the development of the insurance sector, which is also a potential source of long-term funds for capital markets. Even so, these funds have some way to go to meet the needs of the Turkish economy.[74] The macroeconomic volatility

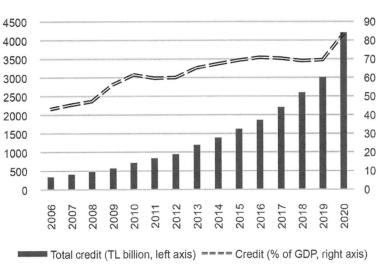

Figure 5.7 Rapid credit growth since 2009
Source: TÜİK.

and uncertainty in the Turkish economy has made the Turkish public wary of financial market products. Other structural factors affecting private savings have been the high levels of informal employment, as well as low labour force participation by women.[75]

To meet their investment needs, corporates increasingly turned to foreign currency loans that rose to 38 percent of GDP in 2018 – almost double its pre-global crisis levels. Domestic credit also grew with a major increase in mortgage loans and consumer credit, as shopping centres (AVM, *alışveriş merkezi*) became a common sight in rapidly urbanising Anatolia. Construction (including loans to construction, real estate and mortgage credits) as a share of total credits doubled its levels from a decade ago, to 20–25 percent, while also bringing a sharp rise in non-performing loans from 2018. The loss of central bank independence has eroded policy credibility and added a new erratic component to this credit- and construction-led growth. Negative real interest rates and repeated sharp depreciation of the currency since 2018, which accelerated inflation, have been given ex-post justification as a strategy to maintain a weak currency so as to boost exports while also appearing to support the industrial policy aims of reducing import dependence. This focus on the weak currency has been accompanied by talk of a 'Beijing model', as Turkey has become more engaged with China and Russia, in the context of declining prospects for EU membership.[76]

These conditions and increased authoritarianism have taken institutional weakening in Turkey to a new threshold. Rising uncertainty and macro-insta-bility in the business environment have undermined the traditional role of industrial policies as a framework for meeting long-term developmental objec-tives. Industrial policy has become more than a strategy for the technologi-cal upgrade of Turkish industry. Measures to reduce import dependence have gained a foreign policy dimension to provide policy autonomy for the AKP in the context of increased tensions in international relations. Meanwhile, industrial policy measures such as investment incentives are increasingly used as political instruments of patronage to sustain domestic support in this late AKP era. Hence, the earlier progress with high-tech-oriented industrial poli-cies has faltered and become more uneven in recent years, although some major project-based schemes have proceeded, such as the completion of the Star refinery in 2018 and the ongoing electric vehicle and battery production plans.

Conclusion: Industrial Policy Reduced to a Counter-cyclical Policy

The decade of industrial policies supporting high-technology investments has succeeded in establishing a threshold in Turkey in terms of 'learning by doing', human capital and infrastructure. Some major project-based schemes were also successfully delivered. However, supportive industrial policy is not sufficient to ensure that these developments are sustained and translate into economy-wide productivity gains as well as meet the government's 'zero-carbon' pledge by 2053. Industrial policies in Turkey have struggled with recurring problems of management due to weak institutions and state capacity, inadequate long-term investment funding and high levels of macroeconomic instability and uncer-tainty.[77] Many of these problems had been seen before under previous govern-ments. However, the longer rule of the AKP and the progressive changes made to the legal and constitutional framework have meant that the 'political and economic institutions in Turkey have declined further during the latter years of AKP rule' than seen before.[78] These multiple problems have reduced the role of industrial policy from a transformative initiative to yet another counter-cyclical policy under the current conditions.

The expansion of incentive schemes over the past decade in an attempt to direct investments into the strategic and high-tech sectors, while at the same time cushioning business against the volatile macroeconomic trends, as well as boosting AKP electoral prospects, have created a dependent 'private sector that is heavily involved and benefits from the state engineered rent-distribution process'.[79] Mechanisms such as repeated revisions to the public procurement law exempting some 44 percent of all public contracts have increased the risk of entrenchment of politically-connected firms.[80] Transparency has been further undermined by the informal government connections with religious networks and charities, the extent and cost of which were revealed during the collapse of the AKP-Gülen alliance.[81] Meanwhile, industrial policy has become an instrument of patronage undermining its limited achievements towards its transformative objectives.

These conditions and the centralisation of authority with the establishment of the presidential regime after the 2017 referendum have further weakened bureaucratic autonomy and public sector transparency and accountability. Administrative reforms enacted in 2018 also reinforced the decline of economic policy coherence and its effectiveness. These included the abolishment of the 'under-secretariats' in ministries, which had provided continuity and accumulated policy experience in contrast to the frequently changing ministers and the numerous presidential commissions that replaced them.[82]

This loss of bureaucratic autonomy was compounded by the erosion of the Central Bank's independence, resulting in *ad hoc* and erratic policy-making that has increased macro-volatility and market uncertainty. The centralisation of economic policy under the presidency and the demotion of the ministries had been partly justified to enable better coordination and effectiveness of policy implementation. But the general trajectory of the Turkish economy has been mostly negative since 2017. Despite the centralisation of power and an established loyal business circle, the AKP's management of the economy generated a complex crisis of governance that posed major barriers to long-term investments.[83]

This policy mix of maintaining negative real interest rates despite the persistent currency depreciation and accelerating inflation is driven by the AKP's electoral strategy, wrapped up in a moral objection to interest earnings. It is also a hurried attempt to reduce Turkey's external vulnerabilities, as geopolitical crises and competition among world powers increase protectionist trends and impose an extensive array of international sanctions in the region.[84] Business pleas for a 'stable' currency and alarm at its collapse have been dismissed as a price worth paying to increase exports and reduce import dependence and the current account deficit. This appeared to be a return to a version of the 'import-substituting industrialisation' paradigm, but with monetary policy 'shock-therapy' now replacing import tariffs.[85]

But the problem with the AKP macro-policy is not only that it is erratic and creates macro-instability; it also runs counter to Turkey's long-term developmental aim to overcome the middle-income trap. The oft-repeated aims of a technological upgrade of industry and the reduction of import dependence and the current account deficit are objectives that well-designed industrial policies can achieve over the longer term. Yet, export growth relying on a weak currency tends to increase exports of the *existing* technological base. The share of high-tech exports has been stuck at around 3 percent of total manufactured exports, and high-tech trade deficit continued to rise even though the Turkish Lira real exchange rate has been declining for a decade. A measure of progress made in reducing the core trade deficit (non-energy and non-gold) since 2013 has been on the basis of increased net exports of medium technology products. More recently, Turkey has been a beneficiary of the shift in supply chains during the COVID-19 pandemic, away from Asia to locations closer to EU markets. But these were largely in traditional low-to-medium technology sectors such as textiles and clothing, where low wages are a major factor in investment decisions; there were no microchip plants relocating to Turkey. Hence the current low interest rate and weak currency policy mix contributes little to the industrial policy objectives of raising the technological level and incomes in Turkey in order to overcome the middle-income trap.

This raises another old dichotomy in industrial policy debates as to whether it was sound macroeconomic policies or industrial policies that were responsible for the transformation of Asian economies.[86] The Turkish and many other countries' experiences suggest that both are needed – along with many other pre-conditions discussed in this study. The macro-instability of recent years has resulted in industrial policies increasingly playing a counter-cyclical role, rather than a transformative one in Turkey, similar to the many other emerging markets (see Box 5.1 below). A recent OECD report on Turkey noted not only the 'high entrepreneurial spirit' and the growth in 'young start-ups' that cluster around techno-parks, but also the slowdown in business dynamism since 2015.[87] Contributing to the slowdown was the low quality of investment (focused on construction), 'overly complex' investment incentives and the low availability and high cost of equity capital. Another important factor, not discussed in this study, consists of educational levels and digital skills, which were lower in Turkey than the OECD average. And last but not least, compared with those in peer countries, Turkish firms were having to operate in a 'less predictable' macroeconomic policy environment.

These points are also evident in other late developers. For instance, Brazil followed patterns similar to Turkey, with ISI policies until the 1980s, but industrial policies were revived earlier in 2003 under the Lula regime with a 'new developmentalist' mission. Of the three iterations in 2003–16, the first had a clear sectoral focus prioritising those sectors with a growing trade deficit, such as capital goods, semi-conductors and software. But during the global financial crisis, industrial policies mostly took on a counter-cyclical role. By the time of the Rousseff administration, the transformative role of industrial policies was overcome by political crises and institutional weakening, including widespread corruption. Thereafter, despite the rhetoric of support for higher-value-added, innovative firms, policies were increasingly focused on defending local industrial production. Many of these trends also feature in the current Turkish context. In addition, the global conditions of increased competition and demand from China that fed the commodity super-cycle resulted in a major de-industrialisation of the resource-rich Brazilian economy. In this latter sense, and in contrast to Brazil and many commodity-exporting emerging markets, Turkey's relatively poor resource endowment further underlines the centrality of the industrial sector in the economy and the importance of industrial policies. Box 5.1 offers a succinct analysis of the evolution of industrial policy in Brazil, which also provides a useful comparative context for the Turkish case.

Box 5.1 From Old to New Industrial Policies in Brazil

Judit Ricz (Associate Professor in the Department of World Economy, Corvinus University of Budapest, and Research Fellow at the Institute of World Economics, Centre for Economic and Regional Science, Hungary)

Looking at the role of the state in the economy in general and focusing on industrial policies especially, we can distinguish four phases in the short last century of modern Brazilian economic history (starting after the Great Depression of 1929–31; see Table 5.2) import substitution industrialisation (1930–85); 2) state-led governance by the market (1985–2002); 3) new industrial policies (2003–16); 4) the most recent illiberal turn (2016–current) side-lining industrial policies (again) and aiming at reducing the role of the state in the Brazilian economy.

During the era of import-substituting industrialisation Brazil has been transformed from a mainly agrarian economy based on primary exports to a modern, industrialised economy (and urban society) – along with an outstanding economic performance of close to 6 percent GDP growth rates on average.[88] These general trends, however, hide important variations within this period, which can be divided into three different stages (reflecting also changes in the external and domestic circumstances): primary, unstructured import substitution (IS), structured import substitution industrialisation (ISI) and extended ISI with export promotion (Table 1).

During the Getúlio Vargas administrations (1930s–50s), as a response to the changing external context and in the name of striving for economic independence, some *ad hoc* measures were enacted, and state-owned enterprises were established to support national strategic industries (such as mining, oil and steel). The spontaneous process of (restricted) import substitution started but became a conscious and systematic development strategy following World War II. In the 1950s, lack of foreign currency to import essential intermediate goods was the major constraint for industrial development. Consequently, conscious interventions (the import licensing system and multiple exchange rate regimes, along with wide-ranging subsidies and regulations) aimed at pushing resource allocation towards the national industrial sector, with emphasis on heavy industry and consumer durables. High growth rates of this period were however made possible by specific *internal factors* (authoritarian political regime, general belief in and support for developmentalism) and maybe even more important by *external conditions* (abundant cheap credit in the world market).

The role of the state was further strengthened under the era of Juscelino Kubitschek, the so-called 'golden age' of developmentalism, as shown by the slogan 'fifty years progress in five'. The two key initiatives were the Plan of Goals (*Plano de Metas*), which was the first comprehensive ISI plan (1956–61) and the transferring of the nation's capital to the interior of the country by building Brasilia city. The Plan of Goals focused primarily on energy and transport infrastructures, considered to be major bottlenecks for development. With the main overarching aim being to modernise and diversify the Brazilian economy, the plan also included sectoral plans for development of a wide range of industries, including intermediate and capital goods. The implementation of the Plan of Goals was financially not feasible (in spite of generous support from the US government). It resulted in rising fiscal deficit and inflation, on the one hand, and led to increasing foreign debt and seeded the roots of dependence on external finance, on the other hand.

The economic crisis culminated in political crises, leading to a military coup in 1964. The military dictatorship thereafter *continued* and even *strengthened* state interventionism. After an initial period of economic stabilisation, economic growth rates were resumed at even higher rates, and Brazil entered to the so-called *economic miracle* period from 1968 to the mid-1970s (with average annual growth rates of GDP above 11 percent between 1968 and 1973). The Brazilian government launched the first national development plan in Brazil (I. Plano National de Desenvolvimento—I. PND, 1972–74), focusing on transportation, telecommunications and the energy infrastructure. While the international economic context deteriorated heavily after the first oil crisis in 1973, the military government maintained the growth-*cum*-debt strategy, also dubbed 'forced march' (*marcha forçada*),[89] and institutionalised its priorities under the second national development plan (II. PND). This was enabled by cheap external borrowing (via the abundant supply of petro-dollars) and the overall optimist expectations regarding global economic recovery.

Table 5.2 Variations on economic policies in Brazil

Period	Political cycle	Applied economic policies
1930–1985	The old developmental state (Estado Desenvolvimentista)	Old Industrial Policies (IPs) – import substitution industrialization
1930–37	*Authoritarian regime*	*Restricted industrialization*
1937–45	*Open dictatorship (Estado Novo)*	
1944–64	*Populist state (restricted democracy)*	*Structured, heavy import substitution industrialization (ISI), developmentalism*
1964–1985	*Military developmentalist state*	*Extended ISI, export-promotion, towards EOI*
1985–2002	Democratization, political stabilization	End of old IPs, economic stabilization, market-oriented reforms – state-led governance by the market
	The Cardoso era (1995–2002)	
2003–2016	New developmentalism (the PT governments – Lula and Rousseff)	New industrial policies
		PITCE, PDP, PBM
2016–	Illiberal turn (Temer, Bolsonaro)	End of new IPs, market and pro-business turn: *With some programs redesigned (Rota2030, new ICT Law in 2019)*

Source: Author.

By the early 1980s, Brazil had substantially diversified its industrial production (and export) base, and industrial policies (even though unsustainable) have played a central role in this structural transformation.[90] Nevertheless, due to deteriorating international conditions and domestic imbalances, economic growth decreased gradually, and with the country's slide into the debt crisis at the beginning of 1980s, it turned into negative rates. During the first half of the 1980s, the stagnating economy and high unemployment rates inherently showed the *failures of the ISI model*: financial vulnerability and distributive shortcomings. The failure of the old development model also led to the loss of the military rule's political legitimacy, and the *democratisation process* in Brazil started with inherent changes, not only in the social and political, but also in the economic sphere.

Initially, most economic policy interventions aimed at *economic (and political) stabilisation*: chronic fiscal imbalances and hyperinflation were the two main challenges. Washington-Consensus-type economic reforms were nonetheless only half-heartedly implemented in Brazil, and despite privatisation, liberalisation and deregulation, the state remained a central actor in the economy (for example, via the national development bank, BNDES). This is why the Brazilian author Kerstenetzky has referred to this era as *state-led governance by the market*.[91] In terms of industrial policies, however, Brazil went along with the global tide and dismantled old industrial policies, to replace these with a horizontal type of interventions to attract FDI and promote a more business-friendly environment, while main keywords became technological capacity-building and forging competitiveness. In general, the government strove to become a 'neutral' coordinator in a bottom-up approach to modernise industries.

In the new millennium, amidst a more favourable international context (the start of the commodity boom and rising demand from China), industrial policy returned to the policy agenda starting with the presidency of Luis Inácio Lula da Silva (hereafter Lula) in 2003. In the following decade, three different IP documents were enacted: the Technological and Foreign Trade Policy (PITCE) from 2004 to 2007, the Productive Development Policy (PDP) from 2008 to 2010 and the Greater Brazil Plan (Plano Brasil Maior, PBM) from 2011 to 2014. Along these new Brazilian industrial policies there was some degree of continuity, as *promoting innovation and industrial competitiveness* were the clear priorities in each case. In reality, however, this was a rather flexible continuity, as the sectoral focus and the implementation in each case was tailored to tackle the different economic challenges at the time they were adopted.

The PITCE, as the first new attempt to bring back industrial policies, primarily aimed at strengthening the institutional framework by creating agencies[92] and modernising legislation.[93] It was organised along three rationales: 1) the macroeconomic dimension to remove external constraints; 2) the structural dimension focusing on strategic sectors; and 3) the innovative dimension for the development in scientific and technological systems. Accordingly, the PITCE had a clear sectoral focus, by prioritising those areas with large and growing trade deficits. Yet, admittedly, as no clear quantitative targets were set, this has made it difficult not only to implement, but also to evaluate the PITCE.

When the PDP was designed, the global growth was robust, and the country accumulated foreign currency reserves due to strong export performance. The Productive Development Policy aimed at leveraging innovation and investments to support economic growth, resulting in an increase in the number of benefiting sectors. (in fact, to twenty-five sectors, which in reality led to the dismantling of the strong sectoral focus of the PITCE). In the light of the global financial crisis of 2008–9, the implementation of the PDP achieved a counter-cyclical role rather than exercising a transformative function (even though it has improved its policy design by setting clear –industry-level – targets and enabling better coordination and monitoring).

Drawing a balance on Lula's industrial policies, it has to be highlighted that, even despite some initial positive results, 'low-tech' production driven by increasing demand mainly from China have led to unfavourable changes in the economic structure. De-industrialisation and reprimarisation became the name of the game, as revealed by the change in the composition of exports. In 2000, Brazilian exports mainly consisted of manufactured goods (mainly to the US); by 2010 it was dominated by agricultural products and commodities export, mainly to China (although high-tech export also grew but remained at very low levels).

Starting in 2011, when Dilma Rousseff replaced Lula, both domestic and external conditions started to provide a much less conducive environment for the Brazilian economy in general, and for industrial policies in particular. The industrial, technological and trade policy of the Rousseff administration was adopted in 2011, titled the Greater Brazil Plan (PBM).

This new plan focused mainly on relief measures related to investments and exports, so as to cope with the pressures of currency appreciation and credit constraints. The PBM was formulated in the context of the international crisis and fierce international competition, including the expansion of imports. Consequently, in spite of the rhetorical priority of increasing aggregate value-added through innovation, in reality its main aim became to defend local production. Other elements included expanding and creating new technological competence; developing energy supply chains; and promoting manufacturing products of intermediate technological level. Concrete measures to promote technological innovation and boost exports were set up to each of these directives. It is worth to mention that seven measures (including electronics, ICT and automobile sector) became highly controversial and led to a WTO dispute which Brazil lost. The best-known case was the Innovar-Auto, a subsidy scheme in the automotive sector, which had to be re-designed to comply with WTO prescriptions.

To sum up, there was some kind of 'flexible continuity' in the course of new IPs in Brazil, along with the 'refounding syndrome',[94] and to recall de Toni and Gaitán's insight, we can say that Brazilian industrial policies during these three programmes have represented a move 'from ideas without support to support without ideas'.[95]

With the new right-wing governments – first Michel Temer coming to power via the impeachment process in 2016, and then the presidential election with the clear victory of Jair Bolsonaro in autumn 2018 – an ideological turn has taken place, not only in high-level Brazilian politics (the illiberal turn), but also in terms of economic policies. Industrial policies were once again off the policy agenda, well signalled by Paulo Guedes, the new Brazilian Economy Minister's pro-market and pro-business economic stance. Still, some parts of the new industrial policies have remained in place and resulted in some degree of continuity overarching the policy cycles. A good example of the continuity of sectoral IP is the new ICT Law enacted in 2019, replacing the old one from 1991, containing fiscal subsidies for the electronics and ICT sectors.[96]

To conclude, industrial policies in Brazil show a certain degree of continuity and change over the past century; however, the overall results are mixed at best and are often shaped by external conditions. In general, it can be claimed that, despite some sectoral (or company-level) success stories, industrial policies in Brazil failed to promote the East-Asian type of economic upgrading and catching up. Among the main reasons, two major shortcomings stand out: first, the disregard of the reciprocity principle,[97] such as the reluctance of tying subsidies to company-level performance standards (which could have enabled policy learning by picking the losers); second, the failure to comply with the 'embedded autonomy' principle,[98] as despite some islands of excellence (such as the BNDES), the institutional framework for IP remained fragmented, and 'disembeddedness' from different interest groups dominated, leading to capture by sectors and lobbies and consequently to loosing sectoral focus of Brazil's industrial policies.

Notes

1. Turkey is considered one of the countries that experienced significant autocratisation in the 2010s. For details, see V-Dem Institute, *Autocratization Changing Nature? Democracy Report 2022* (Gothenburg: University of Gothenburg, V-Dem Institute, 2022), pp. 19, 25, 45. For an analysis of democratic breakdown in Turkey, see Murat Somer, 'Understanding Turkey's Democratic Breakdown: Old vs. New and Indigenous vs. Global Authoritarianism', *Journal of Southeast European and Black Sea*, Vol. 16, No. 4 (2016), pp. 481–503.

2. For more on growing state interventionism in the 2010s, see Ziya Öniş and Mustafa Kutlay, 'The Anatomy of Turkey's New Heterodox Crisis: The Interplay of Domestic Politics and Global Dynamics', *Turkish Studies*, Vol. 22, No. 4 (2021), pp. 499–529.

3. 'Escalator sectors' such as automotive provide an 'automatic escalator' to higher productivity activities in contrast to, for example, textiles. See Dani Rodrik, 'The Future of Economic Convergence', paper prepared for the 2011 Jackson Hole Symposium of the Federal Reserve Bank of Kansas City, 25–27 August 2011.

4. The failure of parliamentary parties to form a government led to the calling of a snap election on 1 November 2015, when the AKP government won the outright majority following a politically turbulent and violent period between June and November.

5. Mustafa Kutlay, *The Political Economies of Turkey and Greece: Crisis and Change* (London: Palgrave Macmillan, 2019), p. 105.

6. Bülent Gökay, *Turkey in the Global Economy: Neoliberalism, Global Shift and the Making of a Rising Power* (London: Agenda Publishing, 2021).

7. Dani Rodrik, Joseph Stiglitz and Justin Yifu Lin co-chaired a joint International Economic Association and World Bank conference on 'New Thinking in Industrial Policy' in Washington DC, 22–23 May 2012. For earlier papers, see Dani Rodrik, 'Normalizing Industrial Policy,' Commission on Growth and Development, Working Paper no. 3, 2008.

8. For more on this policy initiative, see www.Obamawhitehouse.archives.gov/inno-vation/strategy.

9. European Commission, *An Integrated Industrial Policy for the Global Era*, 2010.

10. Craig Berry, Julie Froud and Tom Barker, eds, *The Political Economy of Industrial Strategy in the UK* (London: Agenda Publishing, 2021), pp. 2–5. This was followed by the establishment of an 'Industrial Policy Council' in 2018, which was disbanded by the Johnson government in 2021.

11. Paul Cammack, 'The G20, the Crisis, and the Rise of Global Developmental Liberalism', *Third World Quarterly*, Vol. 33, No. 1 (2012), pp. 1–16.

12. Reda Cherif and Fuad Hasanov, 'The Return of the Policy That Shall Not Be Named: Principles of Industrial Policy', IMF Working Paper, WP 19/74, 2019.

13. UNCTAD, *World Investment Report: Investment and New Industrial Policies* (Geneva: United Nations Publications, 2018), p. 128.

14. G7, 'Panel on Economic Resilience', Cornwall, October 2021, https://www.mofa.go.jp/files/100200091.pdf.

15. Mariana Mazzucato, 'A New Global Economic Consensus', *Project Syndicate*, 13 October 2021.

16. The Economist, 'Chipmaking: Fabs with Benefits', 12 February 2022.

17. UNCTAD, *World Investment Report: Investment and New Industrial Policies* (Geneva: United Nations Publications, 2018), p. 144.

18. On the 'weaponisation' of global economic relations, see Filippo Fasulo, 'The EU, US and Asia: Economy as a Weapon', ISPI Policy Paper, September 2022.

19. World Bank, *Firm Productivity and Economic Growth in Turkey* (Washington DC: International Bank for Reconstruction and Development, 2019).

20. See İzak Atiyas and Ozan Bakış, 'Productivity, Reallocation, and Structural Change: An Assessment', in Asaf S. Akat and Seyfettin Gürsel, eds, *Turkish Economy at the Crossroads* (Singapore: World Scientific Publishing, 2021), pp. 91–122; Öner Günçavdı and Ayşe Aylin Bayar, 'Structural Transformation and Income Distribution in Turkey', in Asaf S. Akat and Seyfettin Gürsel, eds, *Turkish Economy at the Crossroads* (Singapore: World Scientific Publishing, 2021), pp. 153–209.

21. Republic of Turkey Ministry of Industry and Trade, *Turkish Industrial Strategy Document 2011–2014: Towards EU Membership*, https://www.ab.gov.tr/files/haberler/2011/turkish_industrial_strategy.pdf, 2010, pp. 13, 49.

22. State Planning Organisation, *10th Development Plan (2014–18)* (Ankara: State Planning Organisation, 2013), pp. 99–104.

23. The impact of COVID-19 is likely to reinforce this trend of a rising manufacturing share of GDP, given its negative impact on services.

24. Öner Günçavdı and Aylin Bayar, 'Structural Transformation and Income Distribution in Turkey', in Asaf S. Akat and Seyfettin Gürsel, eds, *Turkish Economy at the Crossroads* (Singapore: World Scientific Publishing, 2021), p. 208, Appendix A, Table A1.

25. This compares with 36 percent medium- and 18 percent high-tech in Poland. See Güven Sak, 'Türkiye Neden İçinden Değer Zinciri Geçen Bir Ülke Olamadı?' *Dünya*, 5 February 2018.

26. Reda Cherif and Fuad Hasanov, 'The Return of the Policy That Shall Not Be Named: Principles of Industrial Policy', IMF Working Paper, WP 19/74, 2019.

27. Robert Wade, 'The Role of the State in Escaping the Middle-Income Trap: The Case for Smart Industrial Policy', *METU Studies in Development*, 43 (2016), pp. 21–42.

28. The EU and the US argued that Turkish measures to incentivise public procurement of domestically manufactured pharmaceuticals and for EU firms to produce domestically undermined competition. The WTO ruled against Turkey, and the case was referred by Turkey to the Dispute Settlement process of the WTO in May 2022.

29. As a member of the OECD, Turkey is in the 'developed world' category in the Paris Accord (this differs from Turkey's UN categorisation as a 'developing country'), hence does not qualify for financial assistance.

30. Güven Sak, 'Sanayi Politikası Yoksa Yeşil Mutabakat Şoku Şiddetli Olur', *Dünya*, 30 August 2021.

31. 'Turkey's Installed Wind Capacity Reaches over 10GW', *Istanbul International Centre for Energy and Climate (IICEC) Newsletter*, November 2021. The feed in tariffs introduced in 2011 were changed from USD-based to TL-based in June 2021.

32. International Energy Agency (IEA), 'Turkey: Energy Policy Review', 2021, p. 74.

33. 'İşte Yeşil İçin Düğmeye Basan Şirketler', *Dünya*, 19 October 2021.

34. Cihat Köksal and Güldenur Çetin, 'The International Trade Analysis of Turkey's Polluting Industries', *Journal of Economic Policy Research*, Vol. 8, No. 2 (2021), pp. 257–75.

35. Bhaskar Chakravorti and Ravi S. Chaturvedi, 'Digital Planet 2017: How Competitiveness and Trust in Digital Economies Vary across the World,' The Fletcher School, Tufts University, July 2017.

36. Selenay Yağcı, 'Türkiye'de 10 Unicorn Yola Çıkmaya Hazırlanıyor', *Dünya*, 26 July 2021.

37. Hüseyin Gökçe, 'Devlerin Adresi: ODTÜ Teknokent', *Dünya*, 23 November 2021.

38. On the role of techno-parks and TÜBİTAK, see Mustafa Kutlay and Hüseyin Karaoğuz, 'Neo-Developmentalist Turn in the Global Political Economy? The Turkish Case', *Turkish Studies*, Vol. 19, No. 2 (2018), pp. 289–316; and Sabahattin İmer, Mustafa Öktem and Osman Kaskatı, 'Türkiye'nin Kalkınmasında Bir Adım Olarak Teknoparkların Etkin İşleyişi', *Sosyoekonomi*, Vol. 29, No. 48 (2021), pp. 407–26.

39. Yasemin Erduman, Okan Eren and Selçuk Gül, 'The Evolution of Import Content of Production and Exports in Turkey', Central Bank of Turkey, Working Paper No. 19/09, May 2019.

40. Data from the Automotive Manufacturers Association of Turkey.

41. *Is Bank Weekly Bulletin*, 30 December 2019.

42. 'Silah ve Mühimmat Yatırımları 11 Ayda 2 Milyar Liraya Ulaştı', *Dünya*, 7 January 2020.

43. DARPA – the US Defence Advanced Research Projects Agency – has been responsible for many pioneering R&D and innovations for defence technologies, which have been further developed into commercial use by the private sector.

44. For an extensive analysis of Turkish R&D policies, see Mustafa Kutlay and H. Emrah Karaoğuz, 'Neo-Developmentalist Turn in the Global Political Economy? The Turkish Case', *Turkish Studies*, Vol. 19, No. 2 (2018), pp. 289–316.

45. UNESCO, *UNESCO Science Report: The Race Against Time for Smarter Development* (Paris: The United Nations Educational, Scientific and Cultural Organization, 2021), p. 338.

46. Ibid.

47. Quoted in Selenay Yağcı, 'Yazılım İhracatında Hedef 5 Milyar Dolar', *Dünya*, 31 March 2022.

48. Turkish Statistical Institute, 'Small and Medium Sized Enterprises Statistics, 2021', Press Release, 26 December 2022. SMEs are defined as firms employing 'less than two hundred and fifty employees annually and whose annual net sales revenue or financial balance do not exceed 125 million Türkiye Liras'.

49. Ibid.

50. Rajah Rasiah, 'Industrial Policy and Industrialisation in South-East Asia', in Arkebe Oqubay, Christopher Cramer, Ha-Joon Chang and Richard Kozul-Wright, eds, *Oxford Handbook of Industrial Policy* (Oxford: Oxford University Press, 2020), p. 688.

51. M. Coşkun Cangöz, Uğur Emek and Nurhan Uyduranoğlu Karaca, *Türkiye'de Kamu-Özel İşbirliği Uygulaması: Etkin Risk Paylaşımına Yönelik Bir Model Önerisi* (Ankara: TEPAV Elektronik Yayınları, 2021).

52. EBRD, *Transition Report 2020–21: The State Strikes Back*, 2021, https://www.ebrd.com/news/publications/transition-report/transition-report-202021.html, pp. 82–84. See also Çağatay Bircan and Orkun Saka, 'Lending Cycles and Real Outcomes: Costs of Political Misalignment', *The Economic Journal*, Vol. 131, No. 639 (2021), pp. 2763–96.

53. IMF, *Article IV Consultation: Turkey*, April 2018.

54. IMF, *Fiscal Transparency Evaluation Report: Turkey*, 2016.

55. EBRD, 'Country Assessments: Turkey', in *Transition Report 2020–21: The State Strikes Back*, 2021, https://www.ebrd.com/news/publications/transition-report/transition-report-202021.html.

56. For an analysis of the 'state as a minority share-holder', see also Aldo Musaccio and Sergio Lazzarini, *Reinventing State Capitalism: Leviathan in Business, Brazil and Beyond* (Cambridge: Harvard University Press, 2014).

57. For an assessment of the TWF, see Tahsin Yamak and Emre Saygın, 'Turkey's Economic Power Potential: Turkiye Wealth Fund Practice as an Economic Diplomacy Instrument', *Fiscaoeconomia*, Vol. 3, No. 1 (2019), pp. 88–114.

58. By November 2016, there were 527 firms taken over by the SDIF valued around USD 13 billion. See Berk Esen and Şebnem Gümüşçü, 'Building a Competitive Authoritarian Regime: State-Business Relations in the AKP's Turkey', *Journal of Balkan and Near Eastern Studies*, Vol. 20, No. 4 (2018), p. 361.

59. Turkey's political transformation during the AKP era has been extensively analysed by researchers. For instance, see Bahar Baser and Ahmet Erdi Öztürk, eds, *Authoritarian Politics in Turkey: Elections, Resistance and the AKP* (London: I. B. Tauris, 2017); E. Fuat Keyman and Şebnem Gümüşçü, *Democracy, Identity and Foreign Policy in Turkey: Hegemony Through Transformation* (London: Palgrave Macmillan, 2014).

60. Ziya Öniş and Mustafa Kutlay, 'The Anatomy of Turkey's New Heterodox Crisis: The Interplay of Domestic Politics and Global Dynamics', *Turkish Studies*, Vol. 22, No. 4 (2021), pp. 512–15.

61. Berna Turnaoğlu and E. Fuat Keyman, 'Understanding the "New Turkey" through Max Weber's Category of Caesarism', *Max Weber Studies*, Vol. 22, No. 2 (2022), p. 83.

62. World Bank, *Turkey-Investment Policy and Regulatory Review*, 2019, pp. 19–25.

63. KOSGEB provides interest relief on loans, around half of which is allocated to manufacturing. See Aylin Topal, 'The State, Crisis and Transformation of Small and Medium-Sized Enterprise Finance in Turkey', in Galip Yalman, Thomas Marois and Ali Rıza Güngen, eds, *The Political Economy of Financial Transfers in Turkey* (London: Routledge, 2019), pp. 221–39.

64. OECD, *Economic Surveys: Turkey*, 2018, p. 41.

65. Mustafa Kutlay and H. Emrah Karaoğuz, 'Neo-Developmentalist Turn in the Global Political Economy? The Turkish Case', *Turkish Studies*, Vol. 19, No. 2 (2018), pp. 289–316.

66. World Bank, *Firm Productivity and Economic Growth in Turkey*, 2019, pp. 74–95.

67. Dünya, 'Incentivised Investments are Also Incentivising Imports of Machinery', 19 April 2021. By June, the government had passed a new measure that excluded 174 machinery and equipment imports from customs duty exemptions, on the basis that they were available in the domestic market.

68. Sanayi ve Teknoloji Bakanlığı, *2019 Yılı Faaliyet Raporu*, 2019, p. 47.

69. See Murat A. Yülek, 'Thinking about a New Industrial Policy Framework for Turkey', in Ahmet Faruk Aysan, Mehmet Babacan, Nurullah Gür and Hatice Karahan, eds, *Turkish Economy: Between Middle-Income Trap and High-Income Status* (London: Palgrave Macmillan, 2018), pp. 287–317.

70. On deteoriating ties between Turkey and the EU, see Senem Aydın-Düzgit and Alper Kaliber, 'Encounters with Europe in an Era of Domestic and International Turmoil: Is Turkey a De-Europeanising Candidate Country?' *South European Society and Politics*, Vol. 21, No. 1 (2016), pp. 1–14.

71. On a visit to Ankara in October 2010 by the author, we were told that this reversal was due to heavy lobbying of the government by 'investing' ministries such as the Ministry of Transport and Communications, as well as grassroots AKP organisers, with an eye on the June 2011 election. This reversal pushed Minister for the Economy Ali Babacan, who had worked hard on the fiscal rule, into a long sullen silence. He would resign from the AKP in 2019 and set up the DEVA Party (Demokrasi ve Atılım Partisi) in 2020.

72. Ozan Bakış, Uğurcan Acar and Gökhan Dilek, 'Total Factor Productivity in Agriculture, Manufacturing, Construction, and Services: 1980–2018', BETAM Research Brief 20/251, 14 May 2020.

73. Data from *11th Five Year Plan 2019–23*, p. 35. According to TUIK data, in 2021, the Turkish population fifteen years and older was 64 million, of which 34 million were in the labour force – a ratio of 52.5 percent; of the 30 million not in the labour force, 21 million were women.

74. The total size of these funds was still around 6 percent of GDP in 2021, according to the Turkish Insurance, Reinsurance and Pension Funds Association. See Capital, 'Türkiye Sigorta Sektörü 2021 Yılını Büyüme Rakamlarıyla Kapattı', July 2022.

75. Evren Ceritoğlu and Okan Eren, 'The Effects of Demographic and Social Changes on Household Savings in Turkey', *Central Bank Review*, September

2014, pp. 15–33. Female labour force participation rate in Turkey is the lowest in the OECD, at 32 percent in 2021.

76. Bülent Gökay, *Turkey in the Global Economy: Neoliberalism, Global Shift and the Making of a Rising Power* (London: Agenda Publishing, 2021).

77. See Estrin and Bruno who categorise countries according to institutional features that enable or hinder industrial policies. Saul Estrin and Randolph Bruno, 'Taxonomies and Typologies: Starting to Reframe Economic Systems', in Elodie Douarin and Oleh Havrylyshyn, eds, *Handbook of Comparative Economics* (London: Palgrave Macmillan, 2020).

78. Şevket Pamuk, 'Economic Policies, Institutional Change, and Economic Growth since 1980', in Asaf Savaş Akat and Seyfettin Gürsel, eds, *Turkish Economy at the Crossroads: Facing the Challenges Ahead* (Singapore: World Scientific Publishing, 2021), p. 31.

79. Ziya Öniş, 'Turkey under the Challenge of State Capitalism: The Political Economy of the Late AKP Era', *Southeast European and Black Sea Studies*, Vol. 19, No. 2 (2019), p. 207.

80. Daron Acemoğlu and Murat Üçer, 'High-Quality versus Low-quality Growth in Turkey: Causes and Consequences', in Asaf Savaş Akat and Seyfettin Gürsel, eds, *Turkish Economy at the Crossroads* (Singapore: World Scientific Publishing, 2021), p. 72.

81. *Hurriyet Daily News*, 14 September 2016. Following the 2016 attempted coup, even the Ministry of Religious Affairs had recognised that 'the solution is transparency' at a conference with religious orders where they were advised to stay out of politics. The advice was ignored.

82. Güven Sak, 'What Happened to the Turkish Lira?' *TEPAV Evaluation Note*, March 2022.

83. Even Müsiad, the business association loyal to the AKP, has reluctantly admitted that the currency volatility is negatively affecting its members. See 'Müsiad Başkanı Asmalı: Kurdan Etkilenmiyorum Diyen Sanayici Doğru Söylemiyor', *Dünya*, 8 December 2021.

84. This difficult balancing act is also taking place in international relations. See Mustafa Kutlay and Ziya Öniş, 'Turkish Foreign Policy in a Post-Western Order: Strategic Autonomy or New Forms of Dependence?' *International Affairs*, Vol. 97, No. 4 (2021), pp. 1085–1104.

85. Bloomberg, 'Kavcıoğlu: Current Account Surplus Would Mean Price Stability', *Bloomberg*, 28 October 2021. See Chapter 1, footnote 111.

86. Gary Hufbauer and Euijin Jung, 'Scoring 50 Years of US Industrial Policy', PIIE Briefing, November 2021.

87. Dennis Dlugosch, Yusuf Bağır, Rauf Gönenç, Hüzeyfe Torun and Eun Jung Kim, 'Unleashing the Full Potential of the Turkish Business Sector', OECD Economic Department Working Paper No. 1665, 2021.

88. Angus Maddison, *The World Economy: A Millennial Perspective* (Paris: OECD, 2001), p. 74. The analysis in Box 5.1 is based on author's earlier works: See, Judit Ricz, 'The Rise and Fall (?) of a New Developmental State in Brazil,' *Society and Economy*, Vol. 39, No. 1 (2017), pp. 85–108; Judit Ricz, 'Developmental State in Brazil: Past, Present and Future,' federalismi.it, n. 20/2014.

89. Castro, 2004, cited in Nobuaki Hamaguchi, 'Industrial Policy and Structural Transformation of Brazilian Economy', in Ohno Izumi, Amatsu Kuniaki and Hosono Akio, eds, *Policy Learning for Industrial Development and the Role of Development Cooperation* (Tokyo: JICA Ogata Sadako Research Institute for Peace and Development, 2022), pp. 101–49.

90. Industrial policies were more successful in some sectors (such as automobile, aircraft and petroleum) than in others (such as informatics and microelectronics); thus, it is very difficult to draw a general balance, as there is a need for sectoral analysis. See Heike Döring, Rodrigo Salles Pereira dos Santos and Eva Pocher, 'New Developmentalism in Brazil? The Need for Sectoral Analysis', *Review of International Political Economy*, Vol. 24, No. 2 (2017), pp. 332–62; Ben R. Schneider, 'The Developmental State in Brazil: Comparative and Historical Perspectives', *Revista de Economia Política*, Vol. 35, No. 1 (2015), pp. 114–32.

91. Celia Lessa Kerstenetzky, 'The Brazilian Social Developmental State: A Progressive Agenda in a (Still) Conservative Political Society', in Michelle Williams, ed., *The End of the Developmental State?* (New York: Routledge, 2014), p. 175.

92. Such as the Economic and Social Development Council (CDES), the Council for National Industrial Development (CNDI) and the Brazilian Industrial Development Agency (ABDI).

93. Such as the Innovation Act (Law 10.973), the Law of Good (Law 11.196), the Biosecurity Act (Law 8.974) and the Biotechnology Development Policy (Decree 6.041).

94. Robert Devlin and Graciela Moguillansky, 'What's New in the New Industrial Policy in Latin America?' The World Bank, Washington DC, Policy Research Working Paper 6191, 2012, p. 29.

95. Jackson de Toni and Flavio Gaitan, 'Ideas and Interests in the Trajectory of Industrial Policies in Brazil between 2003 and 2014', in Moisés Balestro and Flavio Gaitan, eds, *Untangling Industrial Policy: Ideas and Coordination between State and Business* (Brasília: Verbena Editora, 2019), p. 174.

96. According to estimations, informatics companies invested around USD 3 billion in R&D in Brazil between 2006 and 2017, mainly because of the favourable conditions under the old IT law from 1991.

97. Alice Amsden, *Asia's Next Giant: South Korea and Late Industrialization* (New York: Oxford University Press, 1989); Alice Amsden, *The Rise of 'The Rest': Challenges to the West from Late-Industrializing Economies* (New York: Oxford University Press, 2001).

98. Peter Evans, *Embedded Autonomy: States and Industrial Transformation* (Princeton: Princeton University Press, 1995).

CONCLUSION
RETHINKING INDUSTRIAL POLICY

The case *against* industrial policy is clear. Badly designed policies, weak institutional capacity, macroeconomic instability, 'state capture' by private interests or 'market capture' by overbearing government, as well as global economic conditions – these all can conspire against well-meaning industrial policy efforts. In addition, industrial policies adopted by global powers in the context of today's geopolitical rivalries and trade wars increase the risks of state intervention turning into international conflict. This adds a treacherous element that was mostly absent in the 'hey-day' of industrial policies in the 1960s, prompting *The Economist* to warn of an 'industrial policy arms race'.[1] These problems perpetuate the debate over market versus state in development, as discussed in Chapter 1.

But the case *for* industrial policy is also compelling, not least in the case of developing economies.[2] There are no historic precedents of advanced economies that have managed to industrialise without active state support. After thirty years of retreat, many governments have brought back active industrial policies to overcome stagnant productivity following the global financial crisis, as well as to address environmental concerns and the transition to Industry 4.0. However, today's 'new' industrial policies have been designed differently to avoid the pitfalls of the 'old' ones implemented in the 1960s and 1970s. In place of state-owned investment in strategic industries, the new policies mostly rely on private-sector funding and participation. They also prioritise exports and green growth and are focused on global supply chains, even though the latter is being re-shaped following the COVID-19 pandemic and 'friend-shoring' in the context of increasing geo-economic rivalries in a shifting international order. These 'new' industrial policies are also different because of their tech-focus on Industry 4.0, which requires higher educational and human resource skills. Also, economic networks – at the international and subnational levels – are more inter-connected and difficult to manage when compared to earlier stages of industrialisation.

It is in this contested framework and the current period of transition in the global economic paradigm that we have assessed industrial policies in Turkey – as a necessary but highly context-dependent strategy for economic development. We have argued that the basic issue with industrial policies in the Turkish economy is not fundamentally 'how much' state intervention is involved, but the *specific institutional context* in which industrial policies are pursued. This analysis also departs from the traditional dichotomies that have characterised debates over industrial policies – such as 'import-substitution' versus 'export-led industrialisation', or the use of 'horizontal' measures supporting a wide range of skills and technologies versus 'vertical' measures that support strategic industries. The historical experience of successful industrialisation shows that all these policies need to go together within the context of a robust state-business cooperation.

A Long-term View

Turkey is one of the late developers with a diversified economy and solid industrial base. The scope and content of the industrial policy measures, however, have changed considerably over the past decades. The main determinants of Turkish industrial policies that have been explored in this book are (1) global trends that define the nature of the industrial policy paradigm and the extent of 'policy-space' for late industrialisers to pursue transformative policies, (2) the domestic institutional framework for government policy effectiveness, and (3) macroeconomic (in)stability (including the supply of long-term investment funding) and associated political-economic uncertainty. The table below summarises the periodisation and changing form of global and Turkish industrial policies within this framework.

Table C.1 Periodisation of Turkish industrial policy

Period	Global trends and Turkish development paradigm	Industrial policy (IP) measures
1930s to late 1970s Import substitution industrialisation, with a brief period of liberalisation in 1950s, ending with 1960 coup.	**Old-style state-led development** Establishment of heavy and consumer goods industry and indigenous private sector; statism in 1930s and import substitution industrialisation (ISI) in 1960s.	**Classical (active) IP** Vertical industrial policies such as state-owned enterprises; import controls with tariffs, licences and quotas; directed state bank credits; targeted strategic sectors within national development plans.
1980s–90s Export-oriented industrialisation: Following single-party governments in the 1980s, multiple weak coalitions and unstable global environment in the 1990s.	**Washington consensus** Reduced state role; reorienting industry from ISI to EOI; state support for infrastructure and defence industries. Weak institutions to manage liberalised markets leading to ad hoc policies and corruption.	**Retreat of IP** Reduced controls on trade and capital flows; increased reliance on export incentives and off-budget funds; shift from vertical (sector-targeting) to horizontal incentives in line with WTO and EU Customs Union rules.
2001–7/8 Rise of the regulatory state: AKP elected in 2002; IMF and EU anchors support a rare period of macro-stability between 2002 and 2007.	**Post-Washington consensus** Institutional reforms for a regulatory state established in Turkey to reduce patronage and corruption; alignment with and access to EU market helps break-through sectors in automotive, white goods, chemicals, but neglect of 'new economy'.	**Neutral (horizontal) IP** Business environment reforms and comparative advantage-led passive industrial policy measures; privatisation of state enterprises; focus on regional development and SMEs, in line with support for AKP's political base.
2010–15 State-activism (yet again): AKP third term from 2011; dismantling of regulatory reforms begins; a series of domestic and regional political crises.	**Return of IP post-global financial crisis** Export-oriented, private sector participation. Parallel to shifts in international order and global development paradigm; Turkish industry seen as driver of growth and the 'medium and high-tech production base for Eurasia'. Some progress achieved in defence and project-based schemes.	**2010 Industrial Strategy for Turkey** Investment incentives for medium- (intermediate) and high-tech sectors to reduce import dependence and unemployment; targeted state bank funding; mix of private–public funding through PPPs, KGFs increasingly blurring political and business interests.
2016–still More state intervention, less policy coherence: Failed 2016 coup followed by emergency rule and authoritarian populist presidential system from 2018.	**New IP** Global acceptance of state role post-COVID-19 and environmental goals shed old dichotomies of IP. Turkish Eleventh Five-Year Plan increases focus on tech upgrade, but economy-wide productivity gains remain elusive as AKP electoral aims, patronage and geopolitical instability dominate incoherent/reactive economic policies.	**'Tech-driven Industry Initiative'** From 2019 targets strategic sectors. Environmental investment incentives added to align with EU Green Deal; growing focus on a transformative tech upgrade overwhelmed by macro-instability and de-institutionalisation that prevents effective implementation of increasingly complex IP measures.

Source: Authors' compilation.

This schematic presentation highlights the correspondence between global and Turkish industrial policies, with Turkey following the international development paradigms closely. Related to that is the close connection between global conditions and macro-stability in Turkey, where favourable external economic conditions such as low international interest rates and the rise in capital inflows would periodically ease foreign payments constraints and allow a semblance of macroeconomic stability. For instance, the effective state-led industrialisation in the 1960s took place when favourable national and global conditions combined to support rapid industrialisation. There was a national consensus and a relatively coherent framework for industrialisation established around five-year development plans which had international technical, managerial and financial support, as described in the text box in Chapter 2.

However, the import-substituting industrialisation in this era was mostly producing for the domestic market. There was little focus on export-orientation that could take advantage of economies of scale and provide the basis for a globally competitive industrial base, as it emerged in some East Asian economies at this time. Thus, the industrialisation that was achieved in Turkey came with a high level of import dependence on intermediate and capital goods in addition to its long-term dependence on energy imports – a problem that was starkly revealed with the oil price increases in the second half of the 1970s. This industrial structure formed the foundation for the global integration of the Turkish economy from the 1980s onwards, as a consumer-goods manufacturer based on its comparative advantage, when active or vertical industrial policies took a back seat to market forces.

The Turkish economy's vulnerability to global conditions once again became evident when a rare private-sector-led investment boom in 2002–7 came to an end with the global financial crisis. The early 2010s were critical for the Turkish political economy. The GDP per capita in current prices surpassed the USD 12,000 threshold in 2013. But policy-makers started to talk about a possible 'middle-income trap' if proper economic policies were not put in place. In this context, also with the growing visibility of the state-led development models in large non-Western economies such as China, Brazil and India, industrial policies were revived from 2011 onwards, in the search for a new growth model that could reduce the external vulnerability of the economy and overcome the middle-income trap. These policies reconfirmed the importance of the industrial sector and aimed to establish Turkish industry as the 'medium- and high-tech production base for Eurasia'. Some progress was achieved towards these aims in the initial years, supported by a renewed cycle of international capital flows to emerging markets and the diversification of Turkey's export markets. There were breakthrough sectors such as automotive, chemicals and iron and steel. However, progress stalled with the incremental de-institutionalisation, decline in capital flows following the 2013 'Taper Tantrum' and major regional crises that disrupted foreign trade and widened the foreign payments gap.

This book has also argued that macroeconomic stability is one of the necessary, but not sufficient conditions for an effective industrial policy. Turkey's dependence on volatile capital inflows to close the national savings-investment gap while pursuing a credit-led growth strategy remains a major source of macroeconomic instability and uncertainty for economic actors. These conditions create a dearth of long-term funding for industrial development. Attempts to overcome such constraints by encouraging the growth of private-pension funds and the development of institutional investors and capital markets since the 1980s have made only slow progress. Hence, financial support for industrial policy objectives has continued to rely on the usual sources of funding from foreign investment and government-guaranteed bank-lending, as well as an extensive range of investment incentives such as tax breaks to the private sector. The government guarantees on subsidised bank credits and public–private partnership infrastructure projects as well as the ever-widening tax breaks have increased the fiscal risks associated with industrial policies in recent years, as discussed in Chapter 5.

Macroeconomic instability not only discourages savings and investment, but also tends to overwhelm industrial policies when governments utilise them as part of counter-cyclical policy. This was the case, for example, in Brazil (see the text box 'Brazil, from Old to New Industrial Policies') where, to maintain growth, the investment incentives schemes of the Industrial, Technological and Foreign Trade Policy of the Lula administration became subsumed into generalised stimulus policies to counter the shock of the global financial crisis. In Turkey, this has become almost permanent after the centralisation of policy in the presidency and the loss of independence of the Central Bank, driven by electoral cycles and attempts to cushion the economy from frequent domestic political crises and external shocks. This policy mix, including a disproportionate monetary easing to sustain credit- and consumption-led growth in the early 2020s, has brought macroeconomic instability not seen since the 1990s (which has been further amplified by the Russian invasion of Ukraine in 2022).

Meanwhile, the global turn towards protectionism and tightening monetary conditions in advanced economies add to the volatility facing emerging markets. In the case of Turkey, this also includes geopolitical instability and political uncertainty. As relations with the EU, Turkey's biggest trading partner, have stalled, Middle East crises persist and the war in Ukraine continues, Turkish geostrategic orientation has undergone multiple shifts in an increasingly difficult balancing act. These trends interact with and destabilise Turkey's policy orientation, as seen with the AKP's 'New Economic Model' seeking to emulate a 'Beijing model'. This new programme, adopted in 2021, over-emphasises and elevates the role of a weak currency as a central driver of production and export performance, in a desperate attempt to reduce Turkey's trade deficit and to cushion the economy from global shocks. But the resulting acceleration of inflation further damages the credibility and coherence of economic policies (see Chapter 5).

We have argued in this context that industrial policy has become not so much an economic strategy for development, but a component of defence policy to cushion Turkey from regional security threats, as well as a political tool for the survival of the AKP rule. This has become more evident since the waning of political support for the AKP after the loss of its parliamentary majority in the 2015 elections and the 2016 failed coup, followed by emergency rule. Industrial policy measures such as investment incentives have multiplied, creating a complex web of support for electoral constituencies and to maintain clientelist networks. Patronage relations have been expanded through credit guarantees from the Credit Guarantee Fund (KGF), state bank lending, the operations of the Mass Housing Fund (TOKİ) and other measures highlighted in the previous chapters.

The institutional context within which industrial policy is designed and implemented constitutes the final pillar. As Evans has pointed out, 'sterile debates about "how much" states intervene have to be replaced with arguments about different kinds of involvement and their effects [. . .] The appropriate question is not "how much" but "what kind"'.[3] What distinguishes successful state intervention is the degree of a state's 'embedded autonomy'

– that is, the internal organisation of the state (to what extent the Weberian bureaucratic autonomy is ensured) and the state's external links with the society (to what extent state–society relations are embedded through dense reciprocal networks).[4] As discussed in Chapter 1, insulating state institutions might be necessary to avoid 'state capture', but this should not come at the expense of isolation from institutional economic actors in order to implement effective industrial policies.[5] Seen this way, a long-term view suggests that the Turkish state has been relatively autonomous, but not properly embedded into the society. However, at times, this weakness has been compensated for with a consensus around industrial policies. Different from most post-colonial states in the global South, the Turkish state with its relative autonomy has historically been able to exercise control over non-state actors and deliver core public goods. This was the case in the 1960s and partially in the initial years of the 2010s, before de-institutionalisation became entrenched from 2015–16 onwards.

Yet, compared to developmental states with high capacity, the Turkish state has not been able to fare well, as industrial transformation in coordination with key economic groups remained an incomplete long-term task. Comparing the technology adoption policies in Turkey with South Korea, for instance, reveals the importance of this point. The interventions of the state in South Korea and the institutional structure for state–business relations helped to reduce market uncertainty and transaction costs. This is in contrast to Turkey where state intervention, in the absence of a coherent institutional framework, has often tended to amplify risks for market actors. Another difference from South Korea is the ability of the state to impose reciprocity in offering incentives conditional on business meeting export or R&D targets. As discussed in the preceding empirical chapters, a reactive policy-making by Turkish governments with frequently changing *ad hoc* measures has often characterised state–business relations. In response, the latter have sought to reduce or manage this uncertainty by establishing personalised links with the political authorities, which increased the scope for inevitable favouritism and corruption. Yet, policy-makers usually conceived private business as an area to exercise patronage, especially when political power is overly accumulated in their hands.

What makes things more complicated is that – compared to the earlier stages of industrialisation in the 1960s, with its focus on basic consumer and heavy industries – the tech-upgrade for the middle-income industrial econo-mies requires a higher skill set and governance capacity to cope with the greater complexity of industrial policies required for digital transformation.[6] Yet, as we have shown, the Turkish state's transformative capacity has been weakened since the 1980s. Attempts to reverse this decline came after the 2001 crisis with comprehensive institutional reforms (see Chapters 3 and 4). These reforms established independent regulatory agencies to reduce corruption and clien-telism in Turkish politics. The regulatory capacity of the state was considerably enhanced during the first decade of the 2000s, although the AKP government chipped away at these policies in the 2010s. In contrast to this (albeit tempo-rary) improvement on the regulatory front, the transformative capacity of the state, strongly needed for active industrial policies, continued to weaken. The demotion of the authority of the State Planning Organisation, the widespread irregularities with the privatisation process of state-owned enterprises, the fis-cal constraints and open capital account that restricted financial policy space, as well as the strictures of the WTO and the EU against 'state aids' cumula-tively acted to restrict the scope for active industrial policies in the early 2000s. Furthermore, the late AKP era brought about the weakening of both regula-tory and transformative capacities of the state, as institutional erosion accel-erated with a new threshold being passed following the newly established presidential system.

On a positive note, despite the demotion of active industrial policy, the 2002–7 period also saw private-sector-led investment growth and productiv-ity gains. This was a unique phase when the political support for the start of the EU accession negotiations provided elite social cohesion and institutional reforms. Also, an IMF programme adopted after the 2001 crisis provided the fiscal and financial policy discipline to the newly elected AKP government. These factors reduced macro-instability and political uncertainty, which paved the way for a foreign and domestic private-sector-led investment boom. How-ever, this investment revival was focused on already established industrial sectors and neglected the infrastructure needed to support the nascent 'new economy' industries that had emerged in Turkey at the turn of the millennium, such as internet and mobile telephone service providers and firms producing high-tech exports such as computers, electronic and optical goods. Given the high sensitivity and vulnerability of such investments at start-up and new technology adoption stages to macroeconomic instability and uncertainty, these sectors were fatally damaged by the US dot-com crisis and the 2001 Turkish financial and banking crisis.

State capacity is crucial for industrial policies aiming at a tech-upgrade. This was seen, for example, in the Southeast Asian economies where, with the exception of Singapore, weak governance and institutional support, as well as insufficient funding undermined their science, technology and innovation plans to achieve technological upgrading.[7] Singapore began its tech-upgrade strategy early in 1979, while Indonesia, the Philippines and Thailand only launched their tech-upgrade policies in 2005. In a similar vein, in Turkey, despite an early emphasis on the importance of R&D, industrial policies were primarily focused on reducing import dependence and foreign payments constraints. It was not until 2017 that the share of R&D carried out by business surpassed government-funded R&D – with defence industries being the main contributors. The government focus on a technology upgrade belatedly became a central driver of industrial policies as late as 2019 with the 'Tech Driven Industry Initiative', and the 'Green Deal Agenda' was even later in 2021 – both of which, of course, also support the process of reducing import dependence.[8]

The long-term investments required by both the high-tech and the green transformation have become more difficult to fund with the current levels of macroeconomic and geopolitical instability, despite the ample incentives on offer and the creation of a number of venture capital funds by established holdings. Expensive equity financing, the fragmented structure of the Turkish business sector and regulatory barriers in digital services are among the other factors that limit the potential positive effect of technology diffusion brought by the recent growth of 'young start-ups'.[9]

However, one sector seems to stand out. There has been relatively successful industrial policy implementation in the indigenous defence industry, where the objectives of a technological upgrade and the reduction of import dependence have been largely met. The literature suggests that, even though it is highly difficult to build fully functional developmental states for a myriad reasons, it might still be possible for states to create 'pockets of efficiency' by decoupling 'a key set of organizations sufficiently from other parts of the state apparatus'.[10] The automobile industry in Iran[11] and the aircraft industry in Brazil[12] are just two examples where efficient industrial sectors emerged in otherwise non-developmental states.[13] This might also be the case for the indigenous defence industry in Turkey. Raising the domestic content of production in the Turkish defence industry has been a long-term aim that has become more urgent with the escalation of regional conflicts and Turkey's growing problems with traditional transatlantic allies, first and foremost the US. This long-term focus and an element of cushion from the macro-instability and uncertainty have resulted in one of the rare achievements of industrial policies in the 2010s. But this is yet to translate into an economy-wide productivity increase; only time will tell whether the indigenous defence industry, along with Turkey's attempts to mass-produce domestic EV passenger cars, would add as new cases to the existing global examples of 'pockets of efficiency' in the medium term.

Lessons Learned

Based on the analysis throughout this book, our conclusions are as follows: Turkey has been able to pursue relatively effective industrial policies in the past, when global conditions were favourable. In theory, it could do so again, despite the ongoing deterioration of the international environment. Working in its favour is the wide global acceptance of a greater state role in the economy in tackling the big issues of today: de-industrialisation, climate change, income and wealth inequality, as well as the technological upgrade to Industry 4.0. However, effective industrial policy for a tech-upgrade requires enhanced state capacity, political ownership and a responsive business sector. Given that state capacity in Turkey has deteriorated gradually but significantly over the last decade, there is a low probability that industrial policies can be effectively implemented under the current conditions. The combination of macroeconomic instability, deteriorating institutional environment and short-term-oriented political survival motives are likely to crowd out long-term goals that can deliver an economy-wide upgrade in productivity for Turkey, so as to move it beyond its middle-income position.

Despite these shortcomings, industrial policies are set to stay, as they have become part of the policy mix to achieve the political priorities of the AKP government to remain in power. This outlook could change if the post-election (May 2023) government, at a minimum, ensures the independence of the Central Bank that could begin to reduce macroeconomic instability. However, repairing state institutions will take more time. It is difficult to reverse long-standing slides in institutional quality and human capital that are already hampered by Turkey's historical legacy. This will continue to impair industrial policies, whichever government is in power. Nevertheless, given the threshold that has been reached in terms of skills, industrial base and technology, well-defined, project-based industrialisation objectives can still be successfully pursued. The recent growth of start-ups, the increased activity in the nation-wide techno-parks, as well as the proven flexibility and resilience of Turkish entrepreneurs show the potential that exists.

The Turkish case offers a number of lessons for other countries pursuing industrial policies. Based on our premise that industrial policy is essential for all economies, and especially so for late developers, the key question is not whether industrial policy should be implemented, but how it should be done. There is no simple answer to this fundamental question, but some key factors stand out for rethinking industrial policy in the twenty-first century.

First, one set of necessary but not sufficient conditions for attaining industrial policy objectives are favourable global conditions, macroeconomic stability and the availability of funding for science, technology and innovation programmes. During periods of high macro-instability, industrial policy measures and schemes tend to become subsumed into counter-cyclical stimulus policies – a pattern that has seen many industrial policy strategies dissipate. Industrial policies in economies dependent on capital inflows to close the savings-investment gap are more vulnerable to deteriorating global conditions. However, favourable global conditions do not always help. For instance, commodity exporters from Brazil to Indonesia, which grew rapidly during the long commodity boom until 2014, experienced rapid de-industrialisation in that period. As a result, the new developmentalist turn in the Brazilian political economy did not yield the expected results in the 2000s.[14]

Second, industrial policies on trade and investment should be formulated to utilise many combinations of tools and measures, avoiding the traditional dichotomies of 'vertical versus horizontal incentives' and 'import substitution versus export orientation'. The policy options should not be 'autarky' or 'full integration' into the global economy, but 'selective integration' based on the national economic conditions and institutional structures. Similarly, strictures against 'state-aid' in international commitments should be adjusted to allow for pursuing national objectives that have positive global externalities, such as decarbonisation and coping with epidemics. However, when implemented by global powers, these measures need to be designed to minimise their external negative impact.[15]

Third, strong institutions are crucial for effective industrial policies. A wide political consensus on the objectives of industrial policies is also critical. Turkey has become an extreme case in declining institutional quality in the 2010s, but this trend is not unique to Turkey, or even limited to late industrialisers. Some authors argue that there is a broader, global weakening of state capacity in advanced economies such as the US and UK since the 1980s, due to the combination of 'conservative anti-statism' and 'progressive proceduralism'.[16] This was amply illustrated by the lack of effective capacity to combat the COVID-19 epidemic in its early phases. This decline and the current global macroeconomic volatility, along with growing geopolitical uncertainty and multiple crises, will make it more difficult to pursue transformative policies and ensure equitable growth – even in advanced economies with relatively consolidated institutional structures.

This is especially the case with industrial policies that have broad multiple objectives, such as the 2016 UK industrial policy (ten priority sectors and the four 'grand challenges' of artificial intelligence, ageing society, clean growth and the future of mobility) or the European Green Deal. Well-defined, limited objectives and project-based schemes offering investment incentives to firms conditional on clear targets and performance criteria are more likely to be successful. It is important to think about industrial policy in a context-dependent manner, as there is no 'magic bullet' working across time and space. Formulas that worked in one country may not work in others. An example consists of the attempts by many countries to emulate the experience of the DARPA (Defence Advanced Research Projects Agency) in the US. For instance, plans by the French government in 2005 to establish a DARPA-like agency with a EUR 2-billion budget to support investment in disruptive technologies such as nanotechnology were disappointing.[17]

The conditions for an effective industrial policy are many and hard to achieve. But even in the midst of multiple challenges, as we have them today, there are always opportunities. We began this book with a discussion of the rise and decline of Turkey's domestic automotive project, 'Devrim arabaları', in the early 1960s. This project failed, but the Turkish automotive industry expanded significantly with a wide domestic supply chain, as well as established export markets (see Chapter 3). Turkey, this time, seems closer to producing its own national car brand, TOGG, an all-Turkish electric vehicle. Turkey meets many conditions for successful implementation, as there is a focused project with TOGG: it is private-sector led; it has wide government and public support; and there are established lines of communication between the government and business. Despite the deep problems of Turkey's industrial policies today and the difficult macroeconomic backdrop, there could be a chance that TOGG can succeed where 'Devrim arabaları' had failed. This, however, primarily depends on how domestic institutional structures will evolve in the coming years.

Notes

1. The Economist, 'The New Interventionism', 15 January 2022.
2. Although it has become increasingly challenged with attempts to narrow its scope, this special position of developing economies was embedded in the global international order established after World War II, with the Special and Differentiated Treatment (STD) exempting developing countries from various obligations under WTO rules. See UNCTAD, *Trade and Development Report Overview, 2022: Development Prospects in a Fractured World* (Geneva: United Nations Publications, 2023), p. 14. See also Mehmet Sait Akman, 'Helping the WTO Move Forward: The EU Role', in Lucia Tajiolu and Davide Tentori, eds, *Falling into Pieces: The EU in the Puzzle of the Global Economy*, ISPI Policy Paper, January 2023.
3. Peter Evans, *Embedded Autonomy: States and Industrial Transformation* (Princeton: Princeton University Press, 1995), p. 10.
4. Ibid., pp. 12, 17, 39–42.
5. Ibid., p. 41.
6. UNCTAD, *World Investment Report 2018* (Geneva: United Nations Publications, 2018), pp. 128–45.
7. Rajah Rasiah, 'Industrial Policy and Industrialisation in Southeast Asia', in Arkebe Oqubay, Christopher Cramer, Ha-Joon Chang and Richard Kozul-Wright, eds, *Oxford Handbook of Industrial Policy* (Oxford: Oxford University Press, 2021), pp. 705–11.
8. World Bank, *Türkiye: Country Climate and Development Report* (Washington: World Bank, 2022).
9. Dennis Dlugosch, Rauf Gönenç, Yusuf Kenan Bağır, Hüzeyfe Torun and Eun Jung Kim, 'Unleashing the Full Potential of the Turkish Business Sector', OECD, Economic Department Working Paper No. 1665, 2021.

10. Darius B. Mehri, 'Pockets of Efficiency and the Rise of Iran Auto: Implications for Theories of the Developmental State,' *Studies in Comparative International Development*, Vol. 50 (2015), p. 429.

11. Ibid.

12. For more on the concept of 'pockets of efficiency' and how it works in the Brazilian case, see Ben R. Schneider, 'The Developmental State in Brazil: Comparative and Historical Perspectives', *Revista de Economia Política*, Vol. 35, No. 1 (2015), pp. 114–32.

13. Non-developmental states can take 'intermediary' or 'predatory' forms, depending on how internal bureaucratic structures and state-society linkages are organised. For the concepts of 'predatory', 'intermediate' and 'developmental' states, see Peter B. Evans, 'Predatory, Developmental, and Other Apparatuses: A Comparative Political Economy Perspective on the Third World State', *Sociological Forum*, Vol. 4, No. 4 (1989), pp. 561–87. See also Chapter 1.

14. For an assessment of new developmentalism in the Brazilian context, see Judit Ricz, 'The Rise and Fall (?) of a New Developmental State in Brazil', *Society and Economy*, Vol. 39, No. 1 (2017), pp. 85–108.

15. For example, by coordinating with trade partners, phasing in the measures to allow time for adjustment and avoiding trade-war rhetoric. On the latter, see Adam Tooze on the EU response to the US Inflation Reduction Act: 'An Arms Race on Industrial Policy is the Last Thing Europe Needs', *Financial Times*, 24/25 December 2022.

16. Brink Lindsey, 'State Capacity: What is it, How We Lost it, and How to Get it Back,' Niskanen Centre, Washington DC, November 2021.

17. Simone Tagliapetra, 'New EU Industrial Policy Can Only Succeed with Focus on Completion of Single Market and Public Procurement', *Bruegel*, 18 March 2019.

BIBLIOGRAPHY

Acemoglu, Daron, and James A. Robinson, *Why Nations Fail* (London: Profile Books, 2013).

Acemoğlu, Daron, and Murat Üçer, 'High Quality versus Low-quality Growth in Turkey: Causes and Consequences', in Asaf Savaş Akat and Seyfettin Gürsel, eds, *Turkish Economy at the Crossroads* (Singapore: World Scientific Publishing, 2021), pp. 37–89.

Acemoğlu, Daron, and Murat Üçer, 'The Ups and Downs of Turkish Growth, 2002–2015: Political Dynamics, the European Union and the Institutional Slide', NBER Working Paper Series No. w21608, October 2015.

Ahmad, Feroz, *The Turkish Experiment in Democracy* (London: Hurst, for Royal Institute of International Affairs, 1977).

Akgün, Müge, 'Cemal Paşa Bile Devrim'e Sırtını Döndü', *Hürriyet*, 25 October, 2008.

Akın, Güzin Gülsün, Ahmet Faruk Aysan and Levent Yıldıran, 'Transformation of the Turkish Financial Sector in the Aftermath of the 2001 Crisis', in Ziya Öniş and Fikret Şenses, eds, *Turkey and the Global Economy* (London: Routledge, 2009), pp. 73–100.

Akman, Mehmet Sait, 'Helping the WTO Move Forward in post-MC12', in Lucia Tajioli and Davide Tentori, eds, *Falling into Pieces: The EU in the Puzzle of the Global Economy*, ISPI Policy Paper, January 2023.

Akyüz, Yılmaz, and Korkut Boratav, 'The Making of the Turkish Financial Crisis', *World Development*, Vol. 31, No. 9 (2003), pp. 1549–66.

Altug, Sumru, Alpay Filiztekin, and Şevket Pamuk, 'Sources of Long-Term Economic Growth for Turkey, 1880–2005', *European Review of Economic History*, Vol. 12, No. 3 (2008), pp. 393–430.

Amsden, Alice, *Asia's Next Giant: South Korea and Late Industrialization* (New York and Oxford: Oxford University Press, 1989).

Andreoni, Antonio, 'Varieties of Industrial Policy: Models, Packages, and Transformation Cycles', in Akbar Noman and Joseph E. Stiglitz, eds, *Efficiency, Finance, and Varieties of Industrial Policy* (New York: Columbia University Press, 2016), pp. 245–305.

Andreoni, Antonio, and Ha-Joon Chang, 'Industrial Policy and the Future of Manufacturing', *Economia e Politica Industriale*, Vol. 43, No. 4 (2016), pp. 491–502.

Andreoni, Antonio, and Ha-Joon Chang, 'The Political Economy of Industrial Policy: Structural Interdependencies, Policy Alignment and Conflict Management', *Structural Change and Economic Dynamics*, Vol. 48 (2019), pp. 136–50.

Ansal, Hacer, 'International Competitiveness and Industrial Policy: The Turkish Experience in the Textile and Truck Manufacturing Industries', in Fikret Şenses, ed., *Recent Industrialisation Experience of Turkey in a Global Context* (Westport: Greenwood Press, 1994), pp. 175–89.

Arıcanlı, Tosun, and Dani Rodrik, eds, *The Political Economy of Turkey: Debt, Adjustment and Sustainability* (Basingstoke: Palgrave Macmillan, 1990).

Arnold, Caroline E., 'In the Service of Industrialization: Etatism, Social Services and the Construction of Industrial Labour Forces in Turkey (1930–50)', *Middle Eastern Studies*, Vol. 48, No. 3 (2012), pp. 363–85.

Arthur, W. Brian, *Increasing Returns and Path Dependence in the Economy* (Ann Arbor: University of Michigan Press, 1994).

Aşık, Süleyman, *Devrim Arabaları* (İstanbul: Kopernik Kitap, 2020).

Ata Invest and IBS Research, *E-Business in Turkey, Sector Report* (Istanbul: AtaInvest, May 2000).

Atasoy, Yıldız, *Turkey, Islamists and Democracy: Transition and Globalization in a Muslim State* (London: I. B. Tauris, 2005).

Athanassopoulou, Ekavi, *Turkey-Anglo-American Security Interests* (London: Cass, 1999).

Atiyas, İzak, 'Recent Privatisation Experience of Turkey', in Ziya Öniş and Fikret Şenses, eds, *Turkey and the Global Economy* (London: Routledge, 2009), pp. 101–22.

Atiyas, İzak, 'The Private Sector's Response to Financial Liberalisation in Turkey: 1980–82', World Bank Working Papers No. WPS147, 1989.

Atiyas, İzak, and Ozan Bakış, 'Productivity, Reallocation, and Structural Change: An Assessment', in Asaf S. Akat and Seyfettin Gürsel, eds, *Turkish Economy at the Crossroads* (Singapore: World Scientific Publishing, 2021), pp. 91–122.

Atiyas, İzak, and Ozan Bakış, 'Structural Change and Industrial Policy in Turkey', *Emerging Markets Finance and Trade*, Vol. 51, No. 6 (2015), pp. 1209–29.

Aydın-Düzgit, Senem, and Alper Kaliber, 'Encounters with Europe in an Era of Domestic and International Turmoil: Is Turkey a De-Europeanising Candidate Country?' *South European Society and Politics,* Vol. 21, No. 1 (2016), pp. 1–14.

Aygüneş, Tülin, 'Turkey Prepares for Private Pension System', *Reuters,* 12 May 2000.

Babacan, Abdurrahman, 'Political Economy of Transformation of Capital Structure in Turkey: A Historical and Comparative View', in Ahmet Faruk Aysan, Mehmet Babacan, Nurullah Gur and Hatice Karahan, eds, *Turkish Economy Between Middle Income Trap and High-Income Status* (London: Palgrave Macmillan, 2018), pp. 39–58.

Babb, Sarah, 'The Washington Consensus as Transnational Policy Paradigm: Its Origins, Trajectory and likely Successor', *Review of International Political Economy*, Vol. 20, No. 2 (2013), pp. 268–97.

Bakır, Caner, and Ziya Öniş, 'The Regulatory State and Turkish Banking Reforms in the Age of Post-Washington Consensus', *Development and Change*, Vol. 41, No. 1 (2010), pp. 77–106.

Bakış, Ozan, Uğurcan Acar and Gökhan Dilek, 'Total Factor Productivity in Agriculture, Manufacturing, Construction, and Services: 1980–2018', BETAM Research Brief No. 20/251, 14 May 2020.

Barkey, Henri J., *The State and the Industrialization Crisis in Turkey* (Boulder: Westview Press, 1990).

Barney, Salomon Smith, *The Internet in Turkey*, Industry Report, 8 February 2000.

Baser, Bahar, and Ahmet Erdi Öztürk, eds, *Authoritarian Politics in Turkey Elections, Resistance and the AKP* (London: I. B. Tauris, 2017).

Beeley, Brian, ed., *Turkish Transformation: New Century, New Challenges* (Huntingdon: Eothen Press, 2002).

Berry, Craig, Julie Froud and Tom Baker, eds, *The Political Economy of Industrial Strategy in the UK* (London: Agenda Publishing, 2021).

Bianchi, Patrizio, and Sandrine Labory, 'European Industrial Policy: A Comparative Perspective', in Arkebe Oqubay, Christopher Cramer, Ha-Joon Chang and Richard Kozul-Wright, eds, *The Oxford Handbook of Industrial Policy* (Oxford University Press, 2020), pp. 594–620.

Birand, Mehmet Ali, *Türkiye'nin Ortak Pazar Macerası, 1959–1985* (İstanbul: Milliyet Yayınları, 1987).

Bircan, Çağatay, and Orkun Saka, 'Lending Cycles and Real Outcomes: Costs of Political Misalignment', *The Economic Journal*, Vol. 131, No. 639 (2021), pp. 2763–96.

Bloomberg, 'Kavcıoğlu: Current Account Surplus would mean Price Stability', *Bloomberg*, 28 October 2021.

Bolt, Jutta, and Jan Luiten van Zanden, 'Maddison Style Estimates of the Evolution of the World Economy: A New 2020 Update', Maddison-Project Working Paper No. WP-15, October 2020.

Boratav, Korkut, *Türkiye İktisat Tarihi 1908–2015* (Ankara: İmge Yayınevi, 2019).

Boratav, Korkut, *Türkiye'de Devletçilik* (Istanbul: Gerçek Yayınevi, 1974).

Brook, Anne-Marie, 'Policies to Improve Turkey's Resilience to Financial Market Shocks', *OECD Economics Department Working Paper No 528*, OECD, 29 November 2006.

Brown, John Murray, 'Promises of a Better Life', *FT Survey: Turkish Finance Investment & Industry*, 17 December 1991.

Buğra, Ayşe, 'Political Sources of Uncertainty in Business Life', in Metin Heper, ed., *Strong State and Economic Interest Groups: The Post-1980 Turkish Experience* (Berlin: De Gruyter, 1991), pp. 151–62.

Buğra, Ayşe, *State and Business in Modern Turkey: A Comparative Study* (Albany: SUNY Press, 1994).

Buğra, Ayşe, and Osman Savaşkan, *New Capitalism in Turkey: The Relationship Between Politics, Religion, and Business* (Cheltenham: Edward Elgar, 2014).

Bulfone, Fabio, 'Industrial Policy and Comparative Political Economy: A Literature Review and Research Agenda', *Competition & Change*, Vol. 27, No. 1 (2023), pp. 22–43.

Bulutay, Tuncer, Nuri Yıldırım and Yahya S. Tezel, *Türkiye Milli Geliri (1923–1948)* (Ankara: Ankara University, Political Science Faculty, 1974).

Butler, Creon, 'Today's Sanctions Change Everything', *World Today*, Chatham House, June/July 2022.

Cammack, Paul, 'The G20, the Crisis, and the Rise of Global Developmental Liberalism', *Third World Quarterly*, Vol. 33, No. 1 (2012), pp. 1–16.

Cangöz, M. Coşkun, Uğur Emek and Nurhan Uyduranoğlu Karaca, *Türkiye'de Kamu-Özel İşbirliği Uygulaması: Etkin Risk Paylaşımına Yönelik Bir Model Önerisi* (Ankara: TEPAV Elektronik Yayınları, 2021).

Cardoso, Fernando Henrique, and Enzo Faletto, *Dependency and Development in Latin America*, transl. Marjory Mattingly Urquidi (Berkeley: University of California Press, 1979).

Capital, 'Türkiye Sigorta Sektörü 2021 Yılını Büyüme Rakamlarıyla Kapattı', *Capital Dergi*, July 2022.

Capital Markets Board, *Turkish Capital Markets* (Istanbul: CMB, 1996).

Celasun, Merih, ed., *State Owned Enterprises in the Middle East and North Africa: Privatisation, Performance, and Reform* (London: Routledge, 2001).

Chakravorti, Bhaskar, and Ravi S. Chaturvedi, 'Digital Planet 2017: How Competitiveness and Trust in Digital Economies Vary Across the World', The Fletcher School, Tufts University, July 2017.

Chang, Ha-Joon, 'Breaking the Mould: An Institutionalist Political Economy Alternative to the Neo-liberal Theory of the Market and the State', *Cambridge Journal of Economics*, Vol. 26, No. 5 (2022), pp. 539–59.

Chang, Ha-Joon, *Bad Samaritans: The Guilty Secrets of Rich Nations and the Threat to Global Prosperity* (London: Random House Business Books, 2007).

Chang, Ha-joon, *Kicking Away the Ladder: Development Strategy in Historical Perspective* (London: Anthem Press, 2002).

Chang, Ha-Joon, 'The Political Economy of Industrial Policy in Korea', *Cambridge Journal of Economics*, Vol. 17, No. 2 (1993), pp. 131–57.

Chang, Ha-Joon, and Antonio Andreoni, 'Industrial Policy in the 21st Century', *Development and Change*, Vol. 51, No. 2 (2020), pp. 324–51.

Chang, Ha-Joon, and Antonio Andreoni, 'Industrial Policy in a Changing World: Basic Principles, Neglected Issues and New Challenges', *Cambridge Journal of Economics: 40th Year Conference*, https://cpes.org.uk/wp-content/uploads/2016/06/Chang_Andreoni_2016_Industrial-Policy.pdf, 2016.

Cherif, Reda, and Fuad Hasanov, 'The Return of the Policy That Shall Not Be Named: Principles of Industrial Policy', IMF Working Paper No. WP 19/74, 2019.

Cramer, Christopher, and Fiona Tregenna, 'Heterodox Approaches to Industrial Policy and the Implications for Industrial Hubs', in Arkebe Qqubay and Justin Yifu Lin, eds, *The Oxford Handbook of Industrial Hubs and Economic Development* (Oxford: Oxford University Press, 2020), pp. 40–63.

Ceritoğlu, Evren, and Okan Eren, 'The Effects of Demographic and Social Changes on Household Savings in Turkey', *Central Bank Review*, Vol. 14 (2014), pp. 15–33.

Cumhuriyet, 'Türk Telekom'un Satışını ve Hariri Ailesini Unutmadık, Unutturmayacağız', *Cumhuriyet*, 3 May 2021.

Dale, Reginald, 'Governments Fail at Picking Winners', *The New York Times*, 22 April 1994.

Deese, Brian, 'The Biden White House Plan for a New US Industrial Policy', speech delivered at the Atlantic Council, 23 June 2021, https://www.atlanticcouncil.org/commentary/transcript/the-biden-white-house-plan-for-a-new-us-industrial-policy/

Derviş, Kemal, Daniel Gros, Michael Emerson and Sinan Ülgen, 'The European Transformation of Modern Turkey', Centre for European Policy Studies (Brussels) & Economics and Foreign Policy Forum (Istanbul), 2004.

Devlin, Robert, and Graciela Moguillansky, 'What's New in the New Industrial Policy in Latin America?' The World Bank, Policy Research Working Paper No. 6191, 2012.

Divan, Ishac, Adeel Malik, and Izak Atiyas, editors, *Crony Capitalism in the Middle East* (Oxford: Oxford University Press, 2019).

Dlugosch, Dennis, Rauf Gönenç, Yusuf Kenan Bağır, Hüzeyfe Torun and Eun Jung Kim, 'Unleashing the Full Potential of the Turkish Business Sector', OECD, Economic Department Working Paper No. 1665, 2021.

Dodd, C. H., *Politics and Government in Turkey* (Manchester: Manchester University Press, 1969).

Döring, Heike, Rodrigo Salles Pereira dos Santos and Eva Pocher, 'New Developmentalism in Brazil? The Need for Sectoral Analysis', *Review of International Political Economy* Vol. 24, No. 2 (2017), pp. 332–62.

Durdağ, Mete, *Some Problems of Development Financing: A Case Study of the Turkish First Five Year Plan* (Dordrecht: D. Reidel Publishing Co., 1973).

Dünya, 'Fon Uygulamaları Ekonominin Makro Dengelerini Bozuyor', *Dünya*, 14 May 1987.

Dünya, 'Gümrük Birliği İçin Teşvik İstemiyoruz, Önlem Alınsın', 3 August 1993.

Dünya, 'İşte Yeşil İçin Düğmeye Basan Şirketler', *Dünya*, 19 October 2021.

Dünya, 'Merkez Bankası Bağımsızlığını Nasıl Kazandı?' *Dünya*, 23 March 2021.

Dünya, 'Müsiad Başkanı Asmalı: Kurdan Etkilenmiyorum Diyen Sanayici Doğru Söylemiyor', *Dünya*, 8 December 2021.

Dünya, 'Sanayiciden Birliğe "Şartlı Evet"', *Dünya*, 3 July 1993.

Dünya, 'Silah ve Mühimmat Yatırımları 11 Ayda 2 Milyar Liraya Ulaştı', 7 January 2020.

DW, 'Macron Unveils Massive "France 2030" Green Investment Plan', 12 October 2021, https://www.dw.com/en/macron-unveils-massive-france-2030-green-investment-plan/a-59478618

EBA Agency Press, 'Kicking and Screaming all the Way', Briefing, Issue No. 1342, Ankara, 14 May 2001.

EBRD, 'Transition Report 2020 21: The State Strikes Back', https://www.ebrd.com/news/publications/transition-report/transition-report-202021.html.

Economist Intelligence Unit, *Turkey: Country Commerce*, December 2000.

Erduman, Yasemin, Okan Eren and Selçuk Gül, 'The Evolution of Import Content of Production and Exports in Turkey', Central Bank of Turkey, Working Paper No. 19/09, May 2019.

Erol, Işıl, 'Financial Transformation and Housing Finance in Turkey', in Galip Yalman, Thomas Marois and Ali Rıza Güngen, eds, *The Political Economy of Financial Transformation in Turkey* (London: Routledge, 2019), pp. 243–68.

Esen, Berk, and Şebnem Gümüşçü, 'Building a Competitive Authoritarian Regime: State-Business Relations in the AKP's Turkey', *Journal of Balkan and Near Eastern Studies*, Vol. 20, No. 4 (2018), pp. 349–72.

Estrin, Saul, and Randolph Bruno, 'Taxonomies and Typologies: Starting to Reframe Economic Systems', in Elodie Douarin and Oleh Havrylyshyn, eds, *The Palgrave Handbook of Comparative Economics* (London: Palgrave Macmillan, 2020), pp. 871–96.

European Commission, 'For a European Industrial Renaissance', Brussels, Final Report, 22 January 2014 COM (2014) 14 final.

European Commission, 'Study of the EU-Turkey Bilateral Preferential Trade Framework Including the Customs Union, and an Assessment of its Possible Enhancement', Final Report, 26 October 2016.

European Stability Initiative, 'Islamic Calvinists, Change and Conservatism in Central Anatolia', 19 September 2005, https://www.esiweb.org/publications/islamic-calvinists-change-and-conservatism-central-anatolia.

Evans, Peter B., 'Predatory, Developmental, and Other Apparatuses: A Comparative Political Economy Perspective on the Third World State', *Sociological Forum*, Vol. 4, No. 4 (1989), pp. 561–87.

Evans, Peter B., 'Predatory, Developmental, and Other Apparatuses: A Comparative Political Economy Perspective on the Third World State', *Sociological Forum*, Vol. 4, No. 4 (1989), pp. 561–87.

Evans, Peter, 'In Search of the 21st Century Developmental State', University of Sussex, The Center for Global Political Economy, Working Paper No. 4, 2008.

Evans, Peter, 'The Eclipse of the State? Reflections on Stateness in an Era of Globalization', *World Politics*, Vol. 50, No. 1 (1997), pp. 62–87.

Evans, Peter, *Embedded Autonomy: States and Industrial Transformation* (Princeton: Princeton University Press, 1995).

Farrell, Henry, and Abraham L. Newman, 'Weaponized Interdependence: How Global Economic Networks Shape State Coercion', *International Security*, Vol. 44, No. 1 (2019), pp. 42–79.

Fasulo, Filippo, 'The EU, US and Asia: Economy as a Weapon', ISPI Policy Paper, September 2022.

Ferrannini, Andrea, Elisa Barbieri, Mario Biggeri and Marco R. di Tommaso, 'Industrial Policy for Sustainable Human Development in the post-Covid19 Era', *World Development*, Vol. 137 (2021), pp. 1–15.

Fioretos, Orfeo, Tulia G. Falleti, and Adam Sheingate, eds, *The Oxford Handbook of Historical Institutionalism* (Oxford: Oxford University Press, 2016).

Gazete Vatan, 'Babayiğit Arıyorum', 26 September 2011.

G7, 'Panel on Economic Resilience', Cornwall, October 2021, https://www.mofa.go.jp/files/100200091.pdf.

Gökay, Bülent, *Turkey in the Global Economy: Neoliberalism, Global Shift and the Making of a Rising Power* (London: Agenda Publishing, 2021).

Gökçe, Hüseyin, 'Devlerin Adresi: ODTÜ Teknokent', *Dünya*, 23 November 2021.

Greenwald, Bruce, and Joseph E. Stiglitz, 'Industrial Policies, the Creation of a Learning Society, and Economic Development', in Joseph E. Stiglitz and Justin Yifu Lin, eds, *The Industrial Policy Revolution I* (London: Palgrave Macmillan, 2013), pp. 43–71.

Günce, E., 'Early Planning Experiences in Turkey', in S. İlkin and E. İnanç, eds, *Planning in Turkey (Selected Papers)* (Ankara: Middle East Technical University, Faculty of Administrative Sciences, 1967), pp. 1–27.

Günçavdı, Öner, and Aylin Bayar, 'Structural Transformation and Income Distribution in Turkey', in Asaf S. Akat and Seyfettin Gürsel, eds, *Turkish Economy at the Crossroads* (Singapore: World Scientific Publishing, 2021), pp. 153–209.

Gürsoy, Özgür Burçak, 'Struggle over Regulation in the Turkish Tobacco Market: The Failure of Institutional Reform, 1936–1960', *Middle Eastern Studies*, Vol. 16, No. 4 (2015), pp. 588–607.

Hale, William, 'Democracy and the Party System in Turkey', in Brian Beeley, ed., *Turkish Transformation, New Century, New Challenges* (Huntingdon: Eothen Press, 2002).

Hale, William, 'Ideology and Economic Development in Turkey, 1930–1945', *British Society of Middle Eastern Studies Bulletin*, Vol. 7, No. 2 (1980), pp. 100–17.

Hale, William, 'Turkey and Britain in World War II: Origins and Results of the Triple Alliance, 1935–40', *Journal of Balkan and Near Eastern Studies*, Vol. 23, No. 6 (2021), pp. 824–44.

Hale, William, *The Political and Economic Development of Modern Turkey* (Beckenham: Croom Helm, 1981; repr. Abingdon: Routledge, 2014).

Hale, William, *Turkish Politics and the Military* (Abingdon: Routledge, 1994).

Hamaguchi, Nobuaki, 'Industrial Policy and Structural Transformation of Brazilian Economy', in Ohno Izumi, Amatsu Kuniaki and Hosono Akio, eds, *Policy Learning for Industrial Development and the Role of Development Cooperation* (Tokyo: JICA Ogata Sadako Research Institute for Peace and Development, 2022), pp. 101–49.

Hammaş, H., 'The Plan and the State Economic Enterprises', in S. İlkin and E. İnanç, eds, *Planning in Turkey (Selected Papers)* (Ankara: Middle East Technical University, Faculty of Administrative Sciences, 1967), pp. 134–49.

Hausman, Ricardo, and Dani Rodrik, 'Economic Development as Self-Discovery', *Journal of Development Economics*, Vol. 72, No. 2 (2003), pp. 603–33.

Hayek, F. A., *The Road to Serfdom* (London and Henley: Routledge and Kegan Paul, 1976 [1944]).

Helleiner, Eric, *States and the Reemergence of Global Finance: From Bretton Woods to the 1990s* (Ithaca and London: Cornell University Press, 1994).

Helleiner, Eric, *The Neomercantilists* (Ithaca: Cornell University Press, 2021).

Heper, Metin, and E. Fuat Keyman, 'Double-Faced State: Political Patronage and the Consolidation of Democracy in Turkey', *Middle Eastern Studies*, Vol. 34, No. 4 (1998), pp. 259–77.

Heper, Metin, 'The Strong State as a Problem for the Consolidation of Democracy: Turkey and Germany Compared', *Comparative Political Studies*, Vol. 25, No. 2 (1992), pp. 169–94.

Heper, Metin, ed., *Democracy and Local Government: Istanbul in the 1980s* (Huntingdon: Eothen Press, 1987).

Heper, Metin, *The State Tradition in Turkey* (North Humberside: Eothen Press, 1985).

Hershlag, Z. Y., *Turkey: An Economy in Transition* (The Hague: van Keulen, 1958).

Hiç, Mükerrem, 'Turkey's Customs Union with the EU', Stiftung Wissenschaft und Politik, September 1995.

Hirschman, Albert O., 'The Rise and Decline of Development Economics', in *Essays in Trespassing: Economics to Politics and Beyond* (Cambridge: Cambridge University Press, 1981), pp. 1–23.

Hufbauer, Gary, and Euijin Jung, 'Scoring 50 Years of US Industrial Policy', PIIE Briefing 21–5, November 2021.

İçduygu, Ahmet, Şule Toktaş and B. Ali Soner, 'The Politics of Population in a Nation-Building Process: Emigration of Non-Muslims from Turkey', *Ethnic and Racial Studies*, Vol. 31, No.2 (2008), pp. 358–69.

İmer, Sabahattin, Mustafa Öktem and Osman Kaskatı, 'Türkiye'nin Kalkınmasında Bir Adım Olarak Teknoparkların Etkin İşleyişi', *Sosyoekonomi*, Vol. 29, No. 48 (2021), pp. 407–26.

IMF, 'IMF Approves Stand-By Credit for Turkey', IMF Press Release No 94/48, 8 July 1994.

IMF, 'Turkey: Recent Economic Developments and Selected Issues', IMF Staff Country Report No 97/110, November 1997.

International Bank for Reconstruction and Development [IBRD], *The Economy of Turkey: An Analysis and Recommendations for a Development Program* (Baltimore: Johns Hopkins Press, for IBRD, 1951).

International Energy Agency (IEA), *Turkey 2021: Energy Policy Review* (Paris: IEA, 2021).

İnan, Afet, *Devletçilik İlkesi ve Türkiye Cumhuriyetinin Birinci Sanayi Planı, 1933* (Ankara: Türk Tarih Kurumu, 1972).

İnan, Afet, *Türkiye Cumhuriyetinin İkinci Sanayi Planı* (Ankara: Türk Tarih Kurumu, 1973).

İzmen, Ümit, and Kamil Yılmaz, 'Turkey's Recent Trade and Foreign Direct Investment Performance', in Ziya Öniş and Fikret Şenses, eds, *Turkey and the Global Economy* (London: Routledge, 2009), pp. 145–72.

Johnson, Chalmers, *MITI and the Japanese Miracle: The Growth of Industrial Policy, 1925–1975* (Palo Alto: Stanford University Press, 1982).

Juhász, Réka, Nathan Lane, Emily Oehlsen and Verónica C. Pérez, 'The Who, What, When, and How of Industrial Policy: A Text-Based Approach', *SocArXiv*, https://doi.org/10.31235/osf.io/uyxh9, 2022.

Kafaoğlu, Arslan Başer, *Bankerler ve Kastelli Olayı* (İstanbul: Alan Yayıncılık, 1982).

Kansu, Günal, *Planlı Yıllar: Anılarla DPT'nin Öyküsü* (İstanbul: İş Bankası Kültür Yayınları, 2004).

Karaca, Osman Cenk, '1950–1960 Arası Türkiye'de Uygulanan Sosyo-Ekonomik Politikalar', *Mustafa Kemal University Journal of Social Sciences Institute*, Vol. 9, No. 19 (2012), pp. 47–63.

Karaman, K. Kıvanç, and Şevket Pamuk, 'Different Paths to the Modern State in Europe: The Integration Between Warfare, Economic Structure, and Political Regime', *American Political Science Review*, Vol. 107, No. 3 (2013), pp. 603–26.

Karaman, K. Kıvanç, and Şevket Pamuk, 'Ottoman State Finances in European Perspective, 1500–1914', *The Journal of Economic History*, Vol. 70, No. 3 (2010), pp. 593–629.

Karaoğuz, Emrah Hüseyin, 'The Developmental State in the 21st Century: A Critical Analysis and a Suggested Way Forward', *Panoeconomicus*, Vol. 69, No. 1 (2022), pp. 55–72.

Karaoğuz, Hüseyin Emrah, 'The Political Dynamics of R&D Policy in Turkey: Party Differences and Executive Interference during the AKP Period', *Journal of Balkan and Near Eastern Studies*, Vol. 20, No. 4 (2018), pp. 388–404.

Kazgan, Gülten, *Ekonomide Dışa Açık Büyüme* (İstanbul: Altın Kitaplar Yayınevi, 1984).

Kazgan, Gülten, *Tanzimattan 21. Yüzyıla Türkiye Ekonomisi* (İstanbul: Bilgi Üniversitesi Yayınevi, 2021).

Kepenek, Yakup, *Gelişim, Üretim Yapısı ve Sorunlarıyla Türkiye Ekonomisi* (Ankara: Teori Yayınları, 1983).

Kepenek, Yakup, *Türkiye Ekonomisi* (Ankara: Remzi Kitabevi, 2019).

Kerstenetzky, Celia Lessa, 'The Brazilian Social Developmental State: A Progressive Agenda in a (Still) Conservative Political Society', in Michelle Williams, ed., *The End of the Developmental State?* (New York: Routledge, 2014), pp. 172–96.

Keyman, E. Fuat, and Şebnem Gümüşçü, *Democracy, Identity and Foreign Policy in Turkey: Hegemony Through Transformation* (London: Palgrave Macmillan, 2014).

Kher, Priyanka, et al., *Firm Productivity and Economic Growth in Turkey* (Washington DC: World Bank, 2019).

Kinross, Lord [Patrick], *Ataturk: The Rebirth of a Nation* (London: Weidenfeld and Nicolson, 1964).

Kılıç, Mesut, 'Politics of Institutional Change in State-Business Relations: A Case Study in Turkey's Electricity Sector' (PhD Thesis, Bilkent University, Ankara, 2018).

Kılıçkaya, Çiğdem, 'Tekstil Sektörünün Yapısı ve Türkiye'de Tekstil Sektörü', *Hazine ve Dış Ticaret Dergisi*, Vol. 16, No. 1 (1993), pp. 59–66.

Koç Holding, *Plenty of Room to Grow: Caspian Securities*, 18 June 1998.

Kohli, Atul, *Greed and Guns: Imperial Origins of the Developing World* (Cambridge: Cambridge University Press, 2022).

Kohli, Atul, *State-Directed Development: Political Power and Industrialization in the Global Periphery* (Cambridge: Cambridge University Press, 2004).

Korutürk, Murat, 'Karabük Demir-Çelik İşletmeleri', *Atatürk Ansiklopedisi* (www. ataturkansiklopedisi.gov.tr/bilgi/katrabuk-demir-celik-isletmeleri/).

Koyama, Mark, and Jared Rubin, *How the World Became Rich: The Historical Origins of Economic Growth* (Cambridge: Polity Press, 2022).

Köksal, Cihat, and Güldenur Çetin, 'The International Trade Analysis of Turkey's Polluting Industries', *Journal of Economic Policy Research*, Vol. 8, No. 2 (2021), pp. 257–75.

Krueger, Anne O., *Turkey, Foreign Trade Regimes and Economic Development Series* (London and New York: Columbia University Press, 1974).

Kruger, Anne O., and Baran Tuncer, 'Industrial Priorities in Turkey', in *Industrial Priorities in Developing Countries* (New York: UNIDO, 1979), pp. 129–80.

Kuruç, Bilsay, *Mustafa Kemal Döneminde Ekonomi: Büyük Devletler ve Türkiye*, 3rd ed. (İstanbul: Bilgi Üniversitesi Yayınları, 2018).

Kus, Basak, 'Weak States, Unruly Capitalists, and the Rise of Etatism in Late Developers: The Case of Turkey', *British Journal of Middle Eastern Studies*, Vol. 42, No. 3 (2015), pp. 358–74.

Kutlay, Mustafa, 'The Politics of State Capitalism in a Post-liberal International Order: The Case of Turkey', *Third World Quarterly*, Vol. 41, No. 4 (2020), pp. 683–706.

Kutlay, Mustafa, *The Political Economies of Turkey and Greece: Crisis and Change* (London: Palgrave Macmillan, 2019).

Kutlay, Mustafa, and Emrah Karaoğuz, 'Neo-Developmentalist Turn in the Global Political Economy? The Turkish Case', *Turkish Studies*, Vol. 19, No. 2 (2018), pp. 289–316.

Kutlay, Mustafa, and Ziya Öniş, 'Turkish Foreign Policy in a Post-Western Order: Strategic Autonomy or New Forms of Dependence?' *International Affairs*, Vol. 97, No. 4 (2021), pp. 1085–1104.

Küçük, Yalçın, 'The Macro-Model of the Plan', in S. İlkin and E. İnanç, eds, *Planning in Turkey (Selected Papers)* (Ankara: Middle East Technical University, Faculty of Administrative Sciences, 1967), pp. 78–95.

Lauridsen, Laurids S., 'New Economic Globalization, New Industrial Policy and Late Development in the 21st Century: A Critical Analytical Review', *Development Policy Review*, Vol. 36, No. 3 (2018), pp. 329–46.

Lefebre, T. 'La densité de la population en Turquie en 1914 et en 1927', *Annales de Géographie*, Vol. 37, No. 210 (1928), pp. 520–26.

Levi, Margaret, 'A Model, a Method, and a Map: Rational Choice in Comparative and Historical Analysis', in Mark I. Lichbach and Alan S. Zuckerman, eds, *Comparative Politics: Rationality, Culture, and Structure* (Cambridge: Cambridge University Press, 1997), pp. 19–41.

Lin, Justin Yifu, 'New Structural Economics: A Framework for Rethinking Development', *The World Bank Research Observer*, Vol. 26, No. 2 (2011), pp. 193–221.

Lindsey, Brink, 'State Capacity: What is it, How We Lost it, and How to Get it Back', Niskanen Centre, Washington DC, November 2021.

Lingeman, E. R., *Turkey: Economic and Commercial Conditions in Turkey* (London: HMSO, 1948).

Maddison, Angus, *Dynamic Forces in Capitalist Development* (Oxford: Oxford University Press, 1991).

Maddison, Angus, *The World Economy: A Millennial Perspective* (Paris: OECD, 2001).

di Maio, Michele, 'Industrial Policies in Developing Countries: History and Perspectives', in Mario Cimoli, Giovanni Dosi and Joseph E. Stiglitz, eds, *Industrial Policy and Development: The Political Economy of Capabilities Accumulation* (Oxford: Oxford University Press, 2009), pp. 107–43.

Mann, Michael, 'The Autonomous Power of the State: Its Origins, Mechanisms and Results', *European Journal of Sociology*, Vol. 25, No. 2 (1984), pp. 185–213.

Marois, Thomas, 'The Lost Logic of State-Owned Banks: Mexico, Turkey, and Neoliberalism', paper presented at 79th Annual Conference of Canadian Political Science Association, University of Saskatchewan, 31 May 2007.

Mazzucato, Mariana, 'A New Global Economic Consensus', *Project Syndicate*, 13 October 2021.

Mazzucato, Mariana, 'Mission-Oriented Innovation Policies: Challenges and Opportunities', *Industrial and Corporate Change*, Vol. 27, No. 5 (2018), pp. 803–15.

Mazzucato, Mariana, *The Entrepreneurial State: Debunking Public vs. Private Sector Myths* (London: Anthem Press, 2013).

Mehri, Darius B., 'Pockets of Efficiency and the Rise of Iran Auto: Implications for Theories of the Developmental State', *Studies in Comparative International Development*, Vol. 50 (2015), pp. 408–32.

Migdal, Joel S., *Strong Societies, Weak States: State-Society Relations and State Capabilities in the Third World* (Princeton: Princeton University Press, 1989).

Milor, Vedat, 'The Genesis of Planning in Turkey', *New Perspectives on Turkey*, Vol. 4, No. 2 (1990), pp. 1–30.

Milor, Vedat, *Devleti Geri Getirmek: Türkiye ve Fransa'da Planlama ve Ekonomik Kalkınma Üzerine Karşılaştırmalı bir Çalışma* (İstanbul: İletişim Yayınları, 2022).

Morris, James A., 'Recent Problems of Economic Development in Turkey', *Middle East Journal*, Vol. 14, No. 1 (1960), pp. 1–14.

Munir, Metin, 'Travesty of Communication', in *Turkey: Industry & Inward Investment, Financial Times Survey*, 18 April 2001.

Musaccio, Aldo, and Sergio Lazzarini, *Reinventing State Capitalism: Leviathan in Business, Brazil and Beyond* (Cambridge, MA: Harvard University Press, 2014).

Nacar, Can, '"Our Lives Were Not as Valuable as an Animal"': Workers in State-Run Industries in World War II Turkey', *International Review of Social History*, Vol. 54, Supplement S16 (2009), [n. p., online].

Naudé, Wim, 'Industrial Policy: Old and New Issues', UNU-WIDER Working Paper No. 2010/106, 2010.

Naudé, Wim, 'New Challenges for Industrial Policy', UNU-WIDER Working Paper No. 2010/107, 2010.

New York Times, 'EU Leader Lays Blame on Chirac', 16 June 2005.

North, Douglas C., *Institutions, Institutional Change and Economic Performance* (Cambridge: Cambridge University Press, 1990).

Ocak, Safa, 'General Outlook of the Turkish Industry and Competitiveness of the Private Sector', *Istanbul Stock Exchange Review*, Vol. l, No. 1 (1997), pp. 1–11.

OECD, *Economic Surveys: Turkey 1981*, 1981.

OECD, *Economic Surveys: Turkey 1989–90*, 1990.

OECD, *Economic Surveys: Turkey 1999*, 1999.

OECD, *Economic Surveys: Turkey 2001–2*, 2002.

OECD, *Economic Surveys: Turkey 2010*, 2010.

OECD, *The Mediterranean Regional Project: Turkey* (Paris: OECD, 1965).

Ongut, I., 'The Private Sector in the Five Year Plan', in S. İlkin and E. İnanç, eds, *Planning in Turkey (Selected Papers)* (Ankara: Middle East Technical University, Faculty of Administrative Sciences, 1967), pp. 150–65.

Oqubay, Arkebe, 'The Theory and Practice of Industrial Policy', in Arkebe Oqubay, Christopher Cramer, Ha-Joon Chang and Richard Kozul-Wright, eds, *The Oxford Handbook of Industrial Policy* (Oxford: Oxford University Press, 2020), pp. 17–60.

Oyan, Oğuz, 'An Overall Evaluation of the Causes of Use of Special Funds in Turkey and Their Place in the Economy', *Yapı Kredi Economic Review*, Vol. 1, No. 4 (1987), pp. 83–116.

Ökçün, Gündüz, *Türkiye İktisat Kongresi 1923: İzmir* (Ankara: Ankara University Political Science Faculty, 1968).

Öniş, Ziya, 'Crises and Transformations in Turkish Political Economy', *Turkish Policy Quarterly*, Vol. 9, No. 3 (2010), pp. 45–61.

Öniş, Ziya, 'Political Economy of Turkey in the 1980s: Anatomy of Unorthodox Liberalism', in Metin Heper, ed., *Strong State and Economic Interest Groups: The Post-1980 Turkish Experience* (Berlin: De Gruyter, 1991), pp. 27–39.

Öniş, Ziya, 'The Logic of the Developmental State', *Comparative Politics*, Vol. 24, No. 1 (1991), pp. 109–26.

Öniş, Ziya, 'The State and Economic Development in Contemporary Turkey: Etatism to Neoliberalism and Beyond', in Vojtech Mastny and Craig Nation, eds, *Turkey Between East and West* (Boulder: Westview Press, 1996), pp. 155–78.

Öniş, Ziya, 'The Triumph of Conservative Globalism: The Political Economy of the AKP Era', *Turkish Studies*, Vol. 13, No. 2 (2012), pp. 135–52.

Öniş, Ziya, 'Turkey under the Challenge of State Capitalism: The Political Economy of the Late AKP Era', *Southeast European and Black Sea Studies*, Vol. 19, No. 2 (2019), pp. 201–25.

Öniş, Ziya, *State and Market: The Political Economy of Turkey* (Istanbul: Boğaziçi University Press, 1998).

Öniş, Ziya, and Barry Rubin, eds., *The Turkish Economy in Crisis: Critical Perspectives on the 2000–1 Crises* (London: Routledge, 2003).

Öniş, Ziya, and Fikret Şenses, 'Global Dynamics, Domestic Coalitions and Reactive State', *METU Studies in Development*, Vol. 34, No. 2 (2007), pp. 251–86.

Öniş, Ziya, and Fikret Şenses, 'Rethinking the Emerging Post-Washington Consensus', *Development and Change*, Vol. 36, No. 2 (2005), pp. 263–90.

Öniş, Ziya, and Fikret Şenses, eds, *Turkey and the Global Economy: Neoliberal Restructuring and Integration in the Post-Crisis Era* (London: Routledge, 2009).

Öniş, Ziya, and Mustafa Kutlay, 'The Anatomy of Turkey's New Heterodox Crisis: The Interplay of Domestic Politics and Global Dynamics', *Turkish Studies*, Vol. 22, No. 4 (2021), pp. 499–529.

Öniş, Ziya, and Mustafa Kutlay, 'The New Age of Hybridity and Clash of Norms: China, BRICS, and Challenges of Global Governance in a Postliberal International Order', *Alternatives: Global, Local, Political*, Vol. 45, No. 3 (2020), pp. 123–42.

Öniş, Ziya, and Süleyman Özmucur, 'Supply Side Origins of Macroeconomic Crises in Turkey', Boğaziçi University Research Papers, 1988.

Özcan, Gül Berna, and Hasan Turunç, 'Economic Liberalisation and Class Dynamics in Turkey: New Business Groups and Islamic Mobilisation', *Insight Turkey*, Vol. 13, No. 3 (2011), pp. 63–86.

Özcan, Gül Berna, *Small Firms and Local Economic Development: Entrepreneurship in Southern Europe and Turkey* (Aldershot: Ashgate Publishing, 1995).

Özel, Işık, 'Reverting Structural Reforms in Turkey: Towards an Illiberal Economic Governance?' *Global Turkey in Europe Policy Brief*, May 2015.

Özel, Işık, 'The Politics of De-Delegation: Regulatory (In)Dependence in Turkey', *Regulation and Governance*, Vol. 6, No. 1 (2012), pp. 119–29.

Özel, Işık, *State-Business Alliances and Economic Development* (London: Routledge, 2015).

Özel, Işık, and İzak Atiyas, 'Regulatory Diffusion in Turkey: A Cross-Sectoral Assessment', in Tamer Çetin and Fuat Oğuz, eds, *The Political Economy of Regulation in Turkey* (New York: Springer, 2011), pp. 51–73.

Özelleştirme İdaresi Başkanlığı, *Türkiye'de Özelleştirme*, https://www.oib.gov.tr, 2008.

Özmucur, Süleyman, 'Productivity and Profitability in 500 Largest Firms of Turkey, 1980–1990', *Yapı Kredi Economic Review*, Vol. 5, No. 2 (1992), pp. 41–136.

Pack, Howard, 'Industrial Policy: Growth Elixir or Poison?' *The World Bank Research Observer*, Vol. 15, No. 1 (2000), pp. 47–67.

Pack, Howard, and Kamal Saggi, 'Is There a Case for Industrial Policy? A Critical Survey', *The World Bank Research Observer*, Vol. 21, No. 2 (2006), pp. 267–97.

Pamuk, Şevket, 'Economic Policies, Institutional Change, and Economic Growth since 1980', in Asaf Savaş Akat and Seyfettin Gürsel, eds, *Turkish Economy at the Crossroads: Facing the Challenges Ahead* (Singapore: World Scientific Publishing, 2021), pp. 1–36.

Pamuk, Şevket, 'Turkey's Response to the Great Depression in Comparative Perspective, 1929–1939', European University Institute, Florence, EUI Working Paper No. 2000/21, 2000.

Pamuk, Şevket, *Osmanlı Ekonomisinde Bağımlılık ve Büyüme (1820–1913)* (İstanbul: İş Bankası Kültür Yayınları, 2017).

Pamuk, Şevket, *Uneven Centuries: Economic Development of Turkey Since 1820* (Princeton: Princeton University Press, 2018).

Pierson, Paul, 'Increasing Returns, Path Dependence, and the Study of Politics', *American Political Science Review*, Vol. 94, No. 2 (2000), pp. 251–67.

Polanyi, Karl, *The Great Transformation: The Political and Economic Origins of Our Time*, 2nd ed. (Boston: Beacon Press, 2001).

Public Participation Administration, *Privatisation in Turkey* (Ankara: PPA, 1992).

Rasiah, Rajah, 'Industrial Policy and Industrialisation in South-East Asia', in Arkebe Oqubay, Christopher Cramer, Ha-Joon Chang and Richard Kozul-Wright, eds, *Oxford Handbook of Industrial Policy* (Oxford: Oxford University Press, 2020), pp. 681–715.

Ricz, Judit, 'The Rise and Fall (?) of a New Developmental State in Brazil', *Society and Economy*, Vol. 39, No. 1 (2017), pp. 85–108.

Republic of Turkey Ministry of Industry and Trade, *Turkish Industrial Strategy Document 2011–2014: Towards EU Membership*, https://www.ab.gov.tr/files/haberler/2011/turkish_industrial_strategy.pdf, 2010.

Rodrik, Dani, 'Industrial Policy for the Twenty-First Century', Harvard University, 2004, https://drodrik.scholar.harvard.edu/files/dani-rodrik/files/industrial-policy-twenty-first-century.pdf.

Rodrik, Dani, 'Institutions for High-Quality Growth: What They are and How to Acquire Them', NBER Working Paper Series no. 7540, 2000.

Rodrik, Dani, 'Normalizing Industrial Policy', Commission on Growth and Development, Working Paper No. 3, 2008.

Ruggie, John Gerard, 'International Regimes, Transactions, and Change: Embedded Liberalism in the Postwar Economic Order', *International Organization*, Vol. 36, No. 2 (1982), pp. 379–415.

Rumford, Chris, *State Aid to Industry: Turkey and the Customs Union* (Istanbul: Intermedia Publications, 1997).

Sabancı Holding, *Q4 2021 Financial Results Earnings Release*, 24 February 2022.

Sak, Güven, 'Sanayi Politikası Yoksa Yeşil Mutabakat Şoku Şiddetli Olur', *Dünya*, 30 August 2021.

Sak, Güven, 'Türkiye Neden İçinden Değer Zinciri Geçen Bir Ülke Olamadı?' *Dünya*, 5 February 2018.

Sak, Güven, 'What Happened to the Turkish Lira?' *TEPAV Evaluation Note*, March 2022.

Sami, Mehmet, *Developments in Turkish Capital Markets* (Istanbul: ATA Securities, 1996).

Sanayi ve Teknoloji Bakanlığı, *2019 Yılı Faaliyet Raporu*, https://www.sanayi.gov.tr/assets/pdf/plan-program/STB-2019YılıFaaliyetRaporu.pdf, 2019.

Sayarı, Sabri, 'Clientelism and Patronage in Turkish Politics and Society', in Faruk Birtek and Binnaz Toprak, eds, *The Post-Modern Abyss and the New Politics of Islam: Assabiyah Revisited – Essays in Honour of Şerif Mardin* (Istanbul: Istanbul Bilgi University Press, 2011), pp. 81–94.

Schneider, Ben R., 'The Developmental State in Brazil: Comparative and Historical Perspectives', *Revista de Economia Política*, Vol. 35, No. 1 (2015), pp. 114–32.

Schneider, Ben R., *Designing Industrial Policy in Latin America* (Basingstoke: Palgrave Macmillan, 2015).

Schumpeter, Joseph A., *Capitalism, Socialism, and Democracy* (London and New York: Routledge, [1942] 2010).

Scott, James C., *Seeing Like a State: How Certain Schemes to Improve the Human Condition Have Failed* (New Haven: Yale University Press, 1998).

Sen, Amartya, *Development as Freedom* (New York: Anchor Books, 2000).

Simpson, Dwight J., 'Development as a Process: The Menderes Phase in Turkey', *Middle East Journal*, Vol. 19, No. 2 (1965), pp. 141–52.

Singer, Morris, *The Economic Advance of Turkey, 1938–1960* (Ankara: Turkish Economic Society, 1977).

Somer, Murat, 'Understanding Turkey's Democratic Breakdown: Old vs. New and Indigenous vs. Global Authoritarianism', *Journal of Southeast European and Black Sea*, Vol. 16, No. 4 (2016), pp. 481–503.

Somuncuoğlu, Ünal, 'Atatürk'ün Vasiyeti, İş Bankası Hisse Senetleri ve Cumhuriyet Halk Partisi', http://www.unalsomuncuoglu.net/ataturkun-vasiyeti-is-bankasi-hisse-senetleri-ve-cumhuriyet-halk...

Sönmez, Attila, 'The Re-Emergence of the Idea of Planning and the Scope and Targets of the 1963–1967 Plan', in S. İlkin and E. İnanç, eds, *Planning in Turkey* (Ankara: Middle East Technical University, 1967), pp. 28–43.

Sönmez, Ümit, *Piyasanın İdaresi: Neoliberalizm ve Bağımsız Düzenleyici Kurumların Anatomisi* (İstanbul: İletişim Yayınları, 2011).

State Planning Organisation, *10th Development Plan (2014–18)* (Ankara: SPO, 2013).

State Planning Organisation, *7th Five Year Plan 1996–2000* (Ankara: SPO, 1995).

State Planning Organisation, *Kalkınma Planı, İkinci Beş Yıl, 1968–1972* (Ankara: SPO, 1967).

State Planning Organisation, *V. Beş Yıllık Kalkınma Planı Döneminde Sektörel Gelişmeler (1985–89)* (Ankara: SPO, 1985).

State Planning Organisation, *Yabancı Sermaye Raporu* (Ankara: SPO, June 1990).

State Planning Organisation, *First Five Year Development Plan, 1963–1967* (Ankara: Prime Ministry, 1962).

Stiglitz, Joseph, *Globalisation and Its Discontents* (New York: W. W. Norton, 2002).

Stiglitz, Joseph E., Justin Yifu Lin and Celestin Monga, 'Introduction: The Rejuvenation of Industrial Policy', in Joseph E. Stiglitz and Justin Yifu Lin, eds, *The Industrial Policy Revolution I* (London: Palgrave Macmillan, 2013), pp. 1–15.

Strange, Susan, *States and Markets* (London: Pinter Publishers, 1988).

Subacchi, Paola, 'From Bretton Woods Onwards: The Birth and Rebirth of the World's Hegemon', *Cambridge Review of International Affairs*, Vol. 21, No. 3 (2008), pp. 347–65.

Şenses, Fikret, 'The Stabilisation and Structural Adjustment Program and the Process of Turkish Industrialisation: Main Policies and their Impact', in Fikret Şenses, ed., *Recent Industrialisation Experience of Turkey in a Global Context* (Westport: Greenwood Press, 1994), pp. 51–73.

Şenses, Fikret, *1980 Sonrası Ekonomi Politikaları Işığında Türkiye'de Sanayileşme: Bugün ve Yarın* (Ankara: V Yayınları, 1989).

Şenses, Fikret, ed., *Recent Industrialization Experience of Turkey in a Global Context* (Westport: Greenwood Press, 1994).

Şenses, Fikret, *İktisada (Farklı Bir) Giriş* (İstanbul: İletişim Yayınları, 2021).

Şenses, Fikret, and Erol Taymaz, 'Unutulan Bir Toplumsal Amaç: Sanayileşme Ne Oluyor? Ne Olmalı?' ERC Working Papers in Economics No. 03/01, February 2003.

Şık, Ahmet, *Parallel Yürüdük Biz Bu Yollarda: AKP-Cemaat İttifakı Nasıl Dağıldı?* (İstanbul: Postacı Yayınevi, 2014).

Tagliapetra, Simone, 'New EU Industrial Policy Can Only Succeed with Focus on Completion of Single Market and Public Procurement', Bruegel, 18 March 2019.

Taymaz, Erol, and Ebru Voyvoda, 'Industrial Restructuring and Technological Capabilities in Turkey', in Ziya Öniş and Fikret Şenses, eds, *Turkey and the Global Economy* (London: Routledge, 2009), pp. 145–72.

Taymaz, Erol, and Kamil Yılmaz, *Political Economy of Industrial Policy in Turkey: The Case of the Automotive Industry*, Global Development Institute, The University of Manchester, ESID Working Paper No. 90, September 2017.

Tekeli, İlhan, 'Regional Planning in Turkey and Regional Policy in the First Five Year Development Plan', in Selim İlkin and E. İnanç, eds, *Planning in Turkey* (Ankara: Middle East Technical University, 1967), pp. 254–78.

Tekeli, İlhan, and Selim İlkin, *1929 Dünya Buhranında Türkiye İktisadi Politika Arayışları* (Ankara: Middle East Technical University, 1977).

Tekin, Ali, 'Turkey's Aborted Attempt at Export-Led Growth Strategy: Anatomy of the 1970 Economic Reform', *Middle Eastern Studies*, Vol. 42, No. 1 (2006), pp. 133–63.

The Economist, 'Beware of the Bossy State', 15–21 January 2022.

The Economist, 'Chipmaking: Fabs with Benefits', *The Economist*, 12 February 2022.

The Economist, 'The New Interventionism', 15 January 2022.

The Economist, 'Why Industrial Decline Has Been So Stark in Brazil', 5 March 2022.

Thornburg, Max Weston, Graham Spry and George Soule, *Turkey: An Economic Appraisal* (New York: The Twentieth Century Fund, 1949).

Tinbergen, J., 'Methodological Background of the Plan', in S. İlkin and E. İnanç, eds, *Planning in Turkey (Selected Papers)* (Ankara: Middle East Technical University, Faculty of Administrative Sciences, 1967), pp. 71–77.

Tiryakioğlu, Murad, ed., *Devletle Kalkınma* (İstanbul: İletişim Yayınları, 2020).

Tiryakioğlu, Murad, *Türkiye'nin Yerli Üretimi ve Politik Ekonomisi* (İstanbul: Bilgi Üniversitesi Yayınları, 2021).

Toksoz, Mina (with a contribution by David Barchard), 'Turkey to 1992: Missing Another Chance?' EIU Economic Prospects Series, Special Report No. 1136, September 1988.

Toksoz, Mina, 'The Return of Industrial Policy in Turkey', in Judit Ricz and Tamás Gerőcs, eds, *The Political Economy of Emerging Markets and Alternative Development Paths* (London: Palgrave Macmillan, 2023), pp. 203–28.

Toksöz, Mina, *The Economist Guide to Country Risk* (London: Profile Books, 2014).

Toksöz, Mina, 'Turkey: Pension Funds in the Pipeline', *AbnAmro Flashnote*, 14 June 2000.

Toksöz, Mina, 'Turkey's Energy Market: Issues in Reform', *Journal of Southern Europe and the Balkans*, Vol. 4, No. 1 (2002), pp. 47–55.

Toksöz, Mina, 'Turkish Holdings Reinvent Themselves', *Turkish Area Studies Review*, Vol. 50 (2000), pp. 24–27.

de Toni, Jackson, and Flavio Gaitan, 'Ideas and Interests in the Trajectory of Industrial Policies in Brazil between 2003 and 2014', in Moisés Balestro and Flavio Gaitan, eds, *Untangling Industrial Policy: Ideas and Coordination between State and Business* (Brasília: Verbena Editora, 2019), pp. 216–54.

Tooze, Adam, 'An Arms Race on Industrial Policy is the Last Thing Europe Needs', *Financial Times*, 24/25 December 2022.

Topal, Aylin, 'The State, Crisis and Transformation of Small and Medium-sized Enterprise Finance in Turkey', in Galip Yalman, Thomas Marois and Ali Rıza Güngen, eds, *The Political Economy of Financial Transformation in Turkey* (London: Routledge, 2019), pp. 221–42.

Torun, O. N., 'The Establishment and Structure of the State Planning Organisation', in S. İlkin and E. İnanç, eds, *Planning in Turkey (Selected Papers)* (Ankara: Middle East Technical University, Faculty of Administrative Sciences, 1967), pp. 44–70.

Treaty of Peace with Turkey and other Instruments signed at Lausanne on July 24, 1923: *Commercial Convention* (London, HMSO, 1923).

'Turkey's Installed Wind Capacity Reaches over 10GW', *Istanbul International Centre for Energy and Climate (IICEC) Newsletter*, November 2021.

Turnaoğlu, Berna, and E. Fuat Keyman, 'Understanding the 'New Turkey' through Max Weber's Category of Caesarism', *Max Weber Studies*, Vol. 22, No. 2 (2022), pp. 60–93.

TÜBİTAK, *Turkish Science and Technology Policy: 1993–2003* (Ankara: TÜBİTAK, 1993).

TÜSİAD, *A Sectoral View of Turkish Industry* (Istanbul: TÜSİAD, 2008).

TÜSİAD, *The Turkish Economy* (Istanbul: TÜSİAD, 1990).

UNCTAD, *Trade and Development Report Overview, 2022*: *Development Prospects in a Fractured World* (Geneva: United Nations Publications, 2023).

UNCTAD, *World Investment Report 2018* (Geneva: United Nations Publications, 2018).

UNCTAD, *World Investment Report: Investment and New Industrial Policies* (Geneva: United Nations Publication, 2018).

UNCTAD, *World Investment Report: Investment and New Industrial Policies* (Geneva: United Nations Publications, 2018).

UNESCO, *UNESCO Science Report: The Race against Time for Smarter Development* (Paris: The United Nations Educational, Scientific and Cultural Organization, 2021).

UNIDO, *New Technologies and Global Industrialisation: Prospects for Developing Countries* (Vienna: UNIDO, 1989).

Ünay, Sadık, *Neoliberal Globalization and Institutional Reform: The Political Economy of Development Planning in Turkey* (New York: Nova Science Publishers, 2006).

V-Dem Institute, *Autocratization Changing Nature?' Democracy Report 2022* (Gothenburg: University of Gothenburg V-Dem Institute, 2022).

Wade, Robert, 'Return of Industrial Policy?' *International Review of Applied Economics*, Vol. 26, No. 2 (2012), pp. 223–39.

Wade, Robert, 'The Role of the State in Escaping the Middle-Income Trap: The Case for Smart Industrial Policy', *METU Studies in Development*, Vol. 43 (2016), pp. 21–42.

Wallerstein, Immanuel, *World-Systems Analysis: An Introduction* (Durham, NC and London: Duke University Press, 2004).

Warwick, Ken, 'Beyond Industrial Policy: Emerging Issues and New Trends', OECD Science, Technology and Industry Policy Papers No. 2, 2013.

Weber, Isabella M., *How China Escaped Shock Therapy: The Market Reform Debate* (London: Routledge, 2021).

Weiss, John, 'Neoclassical Economic Perspectives on Industrial Policy', in Arkebe Oqubay, Christopher Cramer, Ha-Joon Chang and Richard Kosul-Wright, eds, *The Oxford Handbook of Industrial Policy* (Oxford: Oxford University Press, 2020), pp. 125–49.

Weiss, Linda, *The Myth of the Powerless State* (Ithaca: Cornell University Press, 1998).

Wolf, Martin, 'The "Elites" against the "People": The Crisis of Democratic Capitalism', in Luís Catão and Maurice Obstfeld, eds, *Meeting Globalization's Challenges: Policies to Make Trade Work for All* (Princeton and Oxford: Princeton University Press, 2019), pp. 237–60.

Woo-Cumings, Meredith, ed., *The Developmental State* (Ithaca and London: Cornell University Press, 1999).

World Bank, 'Turkey Public Finance Review', Report No 85104-TR, 20 May 2014.

World Bank, 'Turkey-Country Economic Memorandum: Sustaining High Growth-the Role of Domestic Savings', Report No: 66301-TR, 23 December 2011.

World Bank, 'Turkey: State Owned Enterprise Sector Review (in Two Volumes)', Report No 10014-TU, 3 March 1993.

World Bank, *China 2030: Building a Modern, Harmonious, and Creative High-Income Society* (Washington DC: World Bank, 2013).

World Bank, *East Asian Miracle: Economic Growth and Public Policy* (Oxford: Oxford University Press, for the World Bank, 1993).

World Bank, *Firm Productivity and Economic Growth in Turkey* (Washington DC: International Bank for Reconstruction and Development, 2019).

World Bank, 'Turkey Country Economic Memorandum: Structural Reforms for Sustainable Growth', Report No: 20657-TU, 15 September 2000.

World Bank, *Türkiye: Country Climate and Development Report* (Washington DC: World Bank, 2022).

Yağcı, Selenay, 'Türkiye'de 10 Unicorn Yola Çıkmaya Hazırlanıyor', *Dünya*, 26 July 2021.

Yağcı, Selenay, 'Yazılım İhracatında Hedef 5 Milyar Dolar', *Dünya*, 31 March 2022.

Yalman, Galip, 'The Neoliberal Transformation of State and Market in Turkey: An Overview of Financial Developments from 1980 to 2000', in Galip Yalman, Thomas Marois and Ali Rıza Güngen, eds, *The Political Economy of Financial Transformation in Turkey* (London: Routledge, 2019), pp. 51–87.

Yalman, Galip, *Transition to Neoliberalism: The Case of Turkey in the 1980s* (İstanbul: Bilgi Üniversitesi Yayınları, 2009).

Yamak, Tahsin, and Emre Saygın, 'Turkey's Economic Power Potential: Turkiye Wealth Fund Practice as an Economic Diplomacy Instrument', *Fiscaoeconomia*, Vol. 3, No. 1 (2019), pp. 88–14.

Yeldan, Erinç, 'The Economic Structure of Power under Turkish Structural Adjustment: Prices, Growth and Accumulation', in Fikret Şenses, ed., *Recent Industrialisation Experience of Turkey in a Global Context* (Westport: Greenwood Press, 1994), pp. 75–89.

Yılmaz, Kamil, 'Industry', in Metin Heper and Sabri Gultekin, eds, *The Routledge Handbook of Modern Turkey* (London: Routledge, 2012), pp. 352–63.

Yönezer, Nurhan, 'Demir Çelik Sektörü AT Üyeliğine Hazır Değil', *Dünya*, 11 July 1988.

Yükseler, Zafer, and Ercan Türkan, 'Türkiye'nin Üretim ve Dış Ticaret Yapısında Dönüşüm', Tüsiad Publications No. 453, February 2008.

Yülek, Murat A., Kwon Hyung Lee, Jungsuk Kim and Donghyun Park, 'State Capacity and the Role of Industrial Policy in Automobile Industry: A Comparative Analysis of Turkey and South Korea', *Journal of Industry, Competition, and Trade*, Vol. 20 (2020), pp. 307–31.

Yülek, Murat A., 'Thinking about a New Industrial Policy Framework for Turkey', in Ahmet Faruk Aysan, Mehmet Babacan, Nurullah Gür and Hatice Karahan, eds, *Turkish Economy: Between Middle-Income Trap and High-Income Status* (London: Palgrave Macmillan, 2018), pp. 287–317.

INDEX

EU Authorised Representative: Easy Access System Europe Mustamäe tee 5
0, 10621 Tallinn, Estonia gpsr.requests@easproject.com

Printed and bound by CPI Group (UK) Ltd, Croydon, CR0 4YY
16/04/2025
01846990-0001